Securing the City

Neoliberalism,
Space, and
Insecurity
in Postwar
Guatemala

Edited by
Kevin Lewis O'Neill
and
Kedron Thomas

Duke University Press
Durham and London
2011

© 2011 Duke University Press
All rights reserved

Printed in the
United States of America
on acid-free paper ∞

Typeset in Quadraat
and Magma Compact
by Tseng Information Systems, Inc.

Library of Congress
Cataloging-in-Publication Data appear
on the last printed page of this book.

Contents

Acknowledgments · vii

Securing the City
An Introduction · 1
   Kedron Thomas,
   Kevin Lewis O'Neill, and
   Thomas Offit

Part One: Urban History and Social Experience

Living Guatemala City, 1930s–2000s · 25
   Deborah T. Levenson

Primero de Julio
Urban Experiences of Class Decline and Violence · 49
   Manuela Camus

Cacique for a Neoliberal Age
A Maya Retail Empire on the Streets of Guatemala City · 67
   Thomas Offit

Privatization of Public Space
The Displacement of Street Vendors in Guatemala City · 83
   Rodrigo J. Véliz and
   Kevin Lewis O'Neill

Part Two: Guatemala City and Country

The Security Guard Industry in Guatemala
Rural Communities and Urban Violence · 103
   Avery Dickins de Girón

Guatemala's New Violence as Structural Violence
Notes from the Highlands · 127
   Peter Benson,
   Kedron Thomas, and
   Edward F. Fischer

Spaces of Structural Adjustment
in Guatemala's Apparel Industry · 147
   Kedron Thomas

Hands of Love
Christian Outreach and the Spatialization of Ethnicity · 165
   Kevin Lewis O'Neill

References · 193
Contributors · 213
Index · 215

Acknowledgments

This book began with a series of interrelated panel discussions on security and space in Guatemala City, including a double-panel at the 2006 American Anthropological Association Annual Meeting in San Jose, California. We are grateful to the participants in these sessions, especially Carol A. Smith and Timothy J. Smith, who both provided thoughtful and incisive comments in their roles as discussants in 2006. We are also grateful to our contributors for being responsive to our queries and for their patience during the review process. Many thanks to Indiana University, Bloomington, for supporting the translation of Manuela Camus's essay from Spanish into English by Michael Mosier. Thank you to James L. Watson for the direction he provided in the volume's initial stages and for his suggestions regarding the volume title. The anonymous reviewers at Duke University Press provided invaluable insights that greatly improved the quality of the final manuscript. In addition, we would like to thank Valerie Millholland, Miriam Angress, Amanda Sharp, and Mark Mastromarino for their support throughout the publication process. Shruti Krishnan of Indiana University also provided important assistance during the production process.

Portions of the essay "Guatemala's New Violence as Structural Violence," by Peter Benson, Kedron Thomas, and Edward F. Fischer were previously published as "Resocializing Suffering: Neoliberalism, Accusation, and the Sociopolitical Context of Guatemala's New Violence," *Latin American Perspectives* 35(5):38–58. An earlier version of the essay "Spaces of Structural Adjustment in Guatemala's Apparel Industry," by Kedron Thomas was published as "Structural Adjustment, Spatial Imaginaries, and 'Piracy' in Guatemala's Apparel Industry," *Anthropology of Work Review* 30(1):1–10. Kevin Lewis O'Neill's essay, "Hands of Love" was published by the University of California Press in *City of God: Christian Citizenship in Postwar Guatemala* (2010). The remaining essays have not appeared previously.

Securing the City

An Introduction

Kedron Thomas,
Kevin Lewis O'Neill, and
Thomas Offit

Neoliberalism, a term commonly used to describe the set of economic reforms that impels structural adjustment, is a practice. It is a kind of tool kit,
a set of institutions, logics, and rationalities that are used by people—sometimes sitting in government offices, sometimes vending crafts in crowded
streets—to understand inequalities and to respond to them. In the spirit of
Sherry Ortner (1984) and Eric Wolf (1980), who wrote of a different phase of
global capitalism, the essays collected here ask what neoliberalism looks like
on the ground and how it is practiced. How have Guatemalans come to inhabit
lives and spaces that are in large measure engineered according to neoliberal
logics? What do ordinary people make of these changing times, and what lessons are to be learned from their experiences? More specifically, what does
neoliberalism look like in Guatemala?

Guatemala's neoliberal moment is strikingly evident in practices and politics of security. Even after the close of Central America's longest and bloodi-
est civil war, which reached genocidal proportions in the late 1970s and early
1980s, Guatemala remains a violent country, though the political and cultural
coordinates of this violence have changed significantly (Nelson 2009). Guatemala has one of the highest homicide rates in all of the Americas averaging
about 17 murders per day, with much of the violent crime concentrated in the
capital city. The country also has one of the lowest rates of incarceration at
28 prisoners per 100,000 people (Canadian Red Cross 2006; Ungar 2003). The
average criminal trial lasts more than four years with less than 2 percent of
crimes resulting in a conviction (Wilson 2009). "It's sad to say, but Guatemala
is a good place to commit murder," one international observer remarked, "be-

cause you will almost certainly get away with it" (Painter 2007). More than ten years after the Peace Accords of 1996, postwar peace seems little more than a bloodied banner.

Postwar violence has coincided with a formal reconciliation process, an uneven transition from authoritarian regimes to democratic institutions, a shift from state-centered to free market economic policies, and a booming drug trade. About 90 percent of the cocaine shipped from the Andes to the United States flows through Central America, with 200 tons of the drug moving from Colombia through Guatemala into Mexico and finally to the United States each year (Seelke 2008). Guatemala City is now one of the most dangerous cities on the planet. Interestingly, the spike in violence in the postwar period has prompted not public debates about the structural conditions that permit violence to thrive in the first place, but rather a new set of practices and strategies that privatize what would otherwise be the state's responsibility to secure the city. These new efforts at security, evident as much in everyday lives as in social policies, constitute the practice of neoliberalism in Guatemala.

The question of security in Guatemala calls attention to three interrelated themes, which this volume investigates. First, there is the devolution of law enforcement to communities and private enterprises. Law enforcement measures now include the employment of private security forces, the formation of community associations, and, in the most extreme cases, vigilantism (including lynchings). Accompanying these strategies is a new common sense that involves blaming gangs and other unsavory segments of the population for danger and insecurity. While transnational criminal networks, such as Mara Salvatrucha and Barrio 18, bloat postwar Guatemala's tragic statistics, residents tend to embed the problem of violence with a moral vocabulary—with the language of delincuencia, or delinquency, as well as choice, character, and self-discipline. Each essay in the volume explores ethnographically how people experience the country's new violence and what they do to make the city or their communities safer, meaning less corrupt and crime ridden. For example, some Guatemalans employ private security services (Dickins, this volume), others give to charity and become deeply involved in organized religion (O'Neill, this volume), and still others invest in urban renewal projects (Véliz and O'Neill, this volume). What makes these practices neoliberal is not a simple logic of class interests, as David Harvey (2005) might have it, but rather the broad-scale transference of state functions to private citizens.

Second, our focus on security refers to the sense that life is much more dangerous in the postwar context than it has been in the past. This sense is evident in the mass media as well as in everyday conversations across Guatemala, where danger is most often experienced and represented as an urban phenomenon. With this dimension of security in mind, the essays explore the processes by which Guatemalans come to internalize and, in turn, respond to insecurity as a lived reality. Feelings of distress emerge from failed promises (Levenson, this volume; Camus, this volume), but they also reflect new entrepreneurial efforts in an uncertain economy (Offit, this volume; Thomas, this volume) and a more general discourse of terror in the postwar context (Benson, Thomas, and Fischer, this volume). This line of analysis treads carefully toward the phenomenological, suggesting that there is an experiential component to the practice of neoliberal security in postwar Guatemala.

Third, our concern with security draws on the fields of critical human geography and the anthropology of space, building on the observation that neoliberal responses to security alter how cities function. A collective sense of insecurity, for example, leads to the criminalization of poverty, a narrow focus on delinquency as the root cause of urban violence, and entrenched segregation (Low 2003). The essays collected here demonstrate, however, that it is not entirely accurate to understand Guatemala City as a "city of walls" (Caldeira 2001). In many mid-sized Latin American cities, such as Guatemala City, Managua, and San Salvador—which each have fewer than three million people and a relatively small number of wealthy residents—the strategies by which the very wealthy "disembed" (Rodgers 2004) themselves from society differ significantly from strategies observed in larger cities. While São Paulo's demographic contours, for example, allow the wealthy to all but retreat from public life, the practice of security in a mid-sized city, such as Guatemala City, leads to more porous relationships between those who can afford walls laced with glass shards and those who cannot. Segregation is more of an ideology than a lived reality in Guatemala City. At the same time, the essays collected here demonstrate that Guatemala City is inseparable from the rest of the country. A key strength of this volume is that each essay examines how discourses that locate danger in the capital city, together with neoliberal responses to danger, shape rural-urban dynamics. Urban crime and violence drive security guards to migrate from their rural homes to the capital (Dickins, this volume), rural entrepreneurs look to urban markets as sources of opportunity but also sites of danger (Thomas, this volume; Offit, this volume), and urban residents view the countryside as more innocent territory (O'Neill, this volume; Camus, this volume).

This volume, the first comparative ethnographic analysis of Guatemala

City, calls for greater attention to the ways that city and country are constituted in relation to one another in Guatemala. Though anthropologists have been writing about Guatemala for more than a century, very little is known ethnographically about the capital city. Most scholarship has focused on the rural Maya, drawing needed attention to a group that has faced broad-scale oppression and making lasting contributions to the social sciences. Research in the historically *ladino/a* (nonindigenous) capital city has often been viewed as uninteresting and even irrelevant, prompting many foreign researchers, like tourists, to leave Guatemala City only moments after their flights touch down. But social and structural dynamics evident in Guatemala City—the disparities in wealth, the intensity of crime, and the militaristic nature of much social response—are deeply entwined with changes happening throughout the country.

Guatemala City in Historical Perspective

Guatemala City was born from disaster. Multiple earthquakes led to the abandonment of earlier capitals (what are now Ciudad Vieja and Antigua), and the current site was chosen in 1773. The Plaza Mayor was the first public space available to the inhabitants of the new capital, and was home to the first street vendors, who have occupied the plaza continuously for more than 230 years (Gellert 1995). The liberal-period reforms by Justo Rufino Barrios—president of Guatemala from 1873 to 1885, whose landmark construction of the national railroad linked Guatemala City to the Pacific coast—transformed the sleepy capital into a major hub in the global coffee trade (Smith 1990). At the start of the twentieth century, the city expanded in size and population, booming from 55,000 inhabitants in 1880 to double that figure by the conclusion of the First World War. Jorge Ubico's regime, which tightly controlled internal migration to the capital in the 1930s through a series of forced residency and labor laws, helped establish the capital as a base of operations for the United Fruit Company, a United States–based corporation that soon became Guatemala's largest landholder (Schlesinger and Kinzer 1999).

When Ubico's regime was toppled in 1944 by a democratic and Left-leaning revolutionary movement, rural Guatemalans began migrating in huge numbers to the capital to work. By 1950, the population of the capital city had grown to nearly 300,000 people, and while Zone 1 remained the undisputed city center, the population sprawled out into the central valley. The "Ten Years of Spring" ended in 1954 as CIA-funded planes dropped leaflets onto the Plaza

Mayor, signaling to the crowds that a new regime was on its way to power. Framed by Cold War fears of communism, President Jacobo Árbenz's land redistribution policy was seen to threaten the interests of global capitalism, and in particular, the interests of the United Fruit Company.[1] Following the United States–backed coup that unseated Árbenz, Guatemala's government became increasingly militarized, while guerrilla forces began to mobilize in the capital city and the mostly ladino eastern region. In the 1960s, amidst active efforts by Maya people to demand cultural rights and recognition and to reclaim land, leftist ladino groups recruited highland communities through a narrative that emphasized a collective fight for freedom of organization, land rights, and democracy. The government's response to these groups was brutal, especially between 1978 and 1982. Large-scale massacres, scorched earth tactics, and widespread disappearances and displacements aimed at annihilating Guatemala's Maya population alongside leftist insurgents would later be understood as acts of genocide.[2] In the early years of the conflict, Guatemala City was a sometime battleground between revolutionaries and state-sponsored death squads. In later years, it became a refuge for those displaced from the western highlands by the military's genocidal campaigns.

Global awareness of the systematic human rights violations being carried out had forced the Guatemalan government by the mid-1980s to adjust its tactics in order to continue receiving international aid. Nonetheless, atrocities continued and went unpunished. The peace process began in 1986 with a series of talks that ultimately led to a United Nations–mediated peace agreement. The final accords were signed on December 29, 1996. According to the UN-sponsored truth commission report released in 1999, more than 200,000 people died or disappeared as a result of the armed conflict, of which more than 80 percent were Maya. The report also establishes that 93 percent of these human rights violations can be connected to the state (CEH 1999).

It was in the context of nascent civil war and the massive rural-to-urban migration set off by the conflict that anthropologists began to take notice of the capital. The first major anthropological work to deal with Guatemala City was Richard Adams's landmark *Crucifixion by Power* (1970).[3] The volume focuses on how the constitution and growth of the national elite, centered in Guatemala City, shaped power relations on a national scale and directly influenced life in the altiplano. As power became an important analytic for anthropologists, ethnographers of the Maya began to look to centers of political, economic, and social power for a greater understanding of the highland region. Adams's book includes a chapter by Bryan Roberts, who later produced a series of works (1968, 1970, 1973), most notably *Organizing Strangers*, which examined tenuous class relations in the capital and documented the lives of the urban poor. Roberts, whose more recent work has explored the political economy of urbanization in Latin America (Roberts 2005; Roberts and de Oliveira 1996; Roberts and Portes 2005) and the urban informal sector (Roberts 1991, 1994),[4] has had a tremendous influence on scholarship in Guatemala and the anthropology and sociology of Latin America.

Between 1973 and 1987, a period that includes the most intense years of the armed conflict, the population of Guatemala City nearly doubled from 890,000 to just over 1.6 million (CITGUA 1991). This dramatic growth reflects a steady stream of rural-to-urban migration linked to the conflict and the inequitable distribution of arable land. For many, life in villages and small towns became either too dangerous or economically untenable, and the imagined opportunities of the city beckoned. Another major factor in the city's growth during this period was the devastating 1976 earthquake. The catastrophic quake, measuring 7.5 on the Richter scale, left 23,000 dead and over 1.2 million people homeless. Guatemala City was hit hard. The earthquake wounded 16,549 and killed 3,370 urban inhabitants, and destroyed 99,712 homes, rendering nearly a half million residents homeless (Johnston and Low 1995; Thomas 2007). Water services shut down. Thousands were buried alive. People slept in the open air, considering it safer to be in the city streets than in their homes (Montenegro 1976).

Despite the level of destruction, many people migrated from outlying rural areas to the capital immediately after the quake, looking for work and refuge (Gellert and Pinto Soria 1990). When they found little of either, the newcomers began constructing shelters from whatever materials they could scavenge in whatever spaces were available. Squatting meant that Guatemala City would mushroom in a disorganized way—without infrastructure, without planning, without permits. Even today, approximately one-fourth of the nearly 2.5 million people residing in the metropolitan area live in what Guatemalan authorities define as "precarious settlements" (INE 2004; Morán Mérida 1997: 8),[5] a reference to "neighborhoods built with fragile materials such as cardboard, tin, or, in the best of cases, cement blocks" (Murphy 2004: 64). These settlements tend to exist beyond the reach of property rights regulation or the most basic of social services, such as water and electricity.

Migration patterns have dramatically shifted urban demographics in Guatemala. The indigenous population, once almost exclusively comprising rural agriculturalists, accounted for only 6 or 7 percent of the total urban population from 1880 to 1973 (Gellert 1995: 96). In recent decades, the Maya nearly tripled their representation in the metropolitan region to around 20 percent (CITGUA 1991). As a result, there has been more ethnographic work in the capital city and on the Mayas living there. Santiago Bastos and Manuela Camus produced a series of joint studies of Maya migrants to the capital (1995, 1997, 1998; see also Camus 2002) that document the complex intermingling of indigenous and urban identities. Other anthropologists have challenged and reshaped our understandings of Maya identity and ethnic relations in Guatemala through their work with the politicized class of urban indigenous leaders who form part of the pan-Maya movement that gained momentum during the peace process (see Fischer and Brown 1996; Nelson 1999; and Warren 1998).

Research on urban ladinos has increased as well. Notably, studies by Deborah Levenson (2005) and Camus (2005) build on the earlier work of scholars such as Laurel Bossen (1984) and Roberts to examine how working-class ladinos contend with rising levels of unemployment, diminishing opportunities for collective organization and fading senses of group affiliation, and the failures of state modernization programs. Investigations of crime and violence in Guatemala City by AVANCSO (1996), Ailsa Winton (2007), and Caroline Moser and Cathy McIlwaine (2004) add to the larger sociological and anthropological literatures on violence in urban Latin America. The essays in this volume contribute to the study of violence, including political and popular responses to security concerns, as well as urban indigeneity and shifting class relations, all central themes in current scholarship on Guatemala City.[6] The capital has become an especially productive site for ethnographic research, yet the theorization of the city remains woefully incomplete.

Neoliberal Guatemala

David Harvey defines neoliberalism as a set of economic policies guided by the ideological perspective that "human well-being can best be advanced by liberating individual entrepreneurial freedoms and skills" (Harvey 2005: 2). This definition affords a general sense of the ideological underpinnings and cultural assumptions of structural adjustment programs, first tested by United States economists in Chile in the 1970s. It says less, however, about the specific ways that neoliberal policies and ideologies come to be practiced and experienced in a place such as Guatemala, how they intersect with national predicaments and politics, and the frictions produced as neoliberal rationalities stream together with the various cultural logics of everyday life. Neoliberal economic and political reforms implemented in Guatemala beginning in the 1980s included the standard adjustments mandated in many countries via World Bank and International Monetary Fund loan programs—market liberalization, privatization of industry and state services, reductions in public expenditure, and opening to foreign trade. Right-wing dictators and, later, democratically elected leaders aligned with interests of the United States expanded these reforms, a process that recently resulted in the signing of the Central America Free Trade Agreement. Along the way, everyday life for many Guatemalans has changed in fundamental ways. Neoliberalism serves as a backdrop, if not a central analytic, for each of the essays in this volume. In addition to shaping state and popular responses to security concerns, the structural and social changes that neoliberal policies have effected in Guatemala underlie the widespread economic, political, and physical insecurities that many urban and rural residents face.

In Guatemala, neoliberal economics meet the historical and cultural contingencies of a nation shaped by a strong indigenous presence and a de facto unfinished peace process. As William Robinson (2003) explains, the system of subsistence agriculture that sustained highland communities for centuries and ensured a measure of economic and even political autonomy became increasingly untenable over the course of the twentieth century. Subsistence farming was initially restructured with the rise of coffee and fruit plantations in the nineteenth century. The agricultural export sector, which experienced a boom in the 1960s and 1970s, and the genocide that targeted highland communities in the late 1970s and 1980s further undermined the subsistence system. Neoliberal measures accelerated this trend by both flooding the domestic market with cheap imported food and encouraging the capitalization of landholdings. While a small percentage of Maya farmers have successfully entered the export market, the vast majority of rural Guatemalans have been greatly disadvantaged by these changes. They have undermined not only an economic system, but also an important set of cultural practices tied to cultivation (Fischer and Benson 2006; and Green 2003).

These changes in the rural highlands led to waves of migration to the capital city and surrounding towns, where the neoliberal strategy of export-led development brought some low-wage work in maquiladoras (factories where garments and other goods are assembled for export). Many urban migrants as well as rural residents, however, resort to informal economic activities such as petty trading to make ends meet, their life chances further diminished by the reduction in state services that is mandated as part of neoliberal reforms. On the whole, neoliberal policies have exacerbated longer-term historical processes including the proletarianization of rural populations, the semiurbanization of and increased class differentiation in rural peripheries, increased internal as well as transnational migration, and the concentration of impoverished Guatemalans in the capital city's metropolitan region (Robinson 2000; Smith 1990).

All of this looks quite different from the sweeping social, economic, and political promises made in the Peace Accords. Neither do these lived realities mesh with the promises of progress found in the master narratives that travel alongside structural adjustment policies. The peace negotiations were said to usher in a new era of democratic process and economic growth at once, since disparate groups were invited to the table to voice their concerns and contribute to a new vision of Guatemalan nationhood while also realizing new opportunities for employment, education, and entrepreneurship. The accords included important endorsements of human rights in general and indigenous cultural and political rights in particular, education reforms to enhance rural achievement, and participatory mechanisms to thicken civil society and diminish the political and economic "distortions" of race and culture, including requirements that women participate in rural and urban development planning (Jonas 2000). But neoconservative technocrats and international financial institutions were also actively involved in shaping the peace process, and their interests generally won out over demands for truly substantial democratic and social justice reforms (Robinson 2003: 113). As social scientists have repeatedly pointed out, the decade since the signing of the accords has seen increasing disparities—in education, health, housing, socioeconomic status, and access to capital—that actually diminish possibilities for the full democratic participation of all citizens (Chase-Dunn 2000; Jonas 2000; Robinson 2000).

One particularly bright spot in the postconflict period has been the vigorous indigenous rights movement that emerged in the early stages of the democratic transition and gained strength during the peace negotiations. The movement has sought full political membership and participation for indigenous Guatemalans, using the Peace Accords as a means to frame questions of political inclusion in the language of cultural citizenship.[7] Led by a determined cohort of Maya leaders involved in various grassroots organizations, the pan-Maya movement challenged the hegemonic denigration of

Mayan languages, dress, and culture by promoting the legitimacy of traditional practices, emphasizing the economic contributions of indigenous populations, and seeking political and legal reforms to protect civil liberties, punish discrimination, guarantee indigenous representation in government, and secure public support for bilingual education (the Peace Accords officially recognized twenty-one Mayan languages spoken in Guatemala) (Fischer and Brown 1996; Warren 1998). The movement has been a tremendous source of cultural resurgence for indigenous Guatemalans and a focal point of international NGO and human rights activism. Yet neoliberal policies and accompanying ideologies have often limited the efficacy and scope of these goals (Benson 2004; Nelson 1999). Charles Hale (2002, 2005) has developed the concept of "neoliberal multiculturalism" to describe how neoliberalism, as much a political moment as an economic one, embraces cultural rights claims made by disadvantaged groups, but only insofar as they do not cross over into "radical" demands for "control over resources necessary for those rights to be realized" (2005: 13). In the Guatemalan case, the state celebrates cultural difference and acknowledges the cultural rights that activists within the pan-Maya movement have worked to secure. The state has done little, however, to address the structural conditions that make the majority of indigenous (and nonindigenous) Guatemalans vulnerable to poverty and insecurity (Hale 2006). More than 80 percent of Maya men and women live in extreme poverty. Three-quarters of indigenous people do not own land. Diane Nelson's (1999) work on the semiotics of nationalist public culture complements Hale's focus on structural disparities: the language of multiculturalism permits the state (and corporations) to acknowledge the cultural value of the country's Maya majority while continuing to tacitly legitimize ethnic superiority through economic reforms that fail to attend to the disproportionate structural marginalization of indigenous populations.

This volume draws on the insights of previous studies of neoliberalism in Guatemala that address how these policies have further entrenched uneven structures of political, social, and economic power, while focusing on the ways neoliberalism is now practiced and experienced by ordinary Guatemalans. The authors are especially concerned with the role of urban space—its concrete materialization and its meaning in mass media and popular discourse—in configuring relations of power in the postwar moment. How does space inform competing social meanings of poverty and violence among rural and urban Guatemalans? How is space a key resource in official or informal projects that seek to clarify material and symbolic boundaries between differently positioned or valued groups of citizens? As the promises of postwar peace and stability fail to keep up with realities of deepening social inequality and new forms of violence, what spatial logics and practices are used to make sense of daily life?

Security and Insecurity

Guatemala's internal armed conflict may have ended more than a decade ago, but everyday life for many Guatemalans continues to be fraught with violence. Survival teeters on meager earnings in informal economic activities, and the state remains ill equipped to deal with social and health problems common across the developing world (McIlwaine and Moser 2001; Pérez 2004). Crime rates in Guatemala have soared in recent years. The number of homicides jumped 40 percent from 2001 to 2004 and continues to rise (USAID 2006). In 2005, the Inter-American Commission on Human Rights reported that Guatemala had the highest murder rate in Latin America.[8] Guatemala City's homicide rate—one of the highest in urban Latin America—is 109 murders per 100,000 inhabitants, nearly eleven times the rate labeled a "crisis" by the World Health Organization. A few comparisons help to put these numbers in perspective. The number of violent deaths in Guatemala over the past five years equals the death toll of the massive 1976 earthquake that leveled parts of the capital and nearby towns. Perhaps even more shocking is the fact that Guatemala's current homicide rate far exceeds the average number of Guatemalans killed each year as a result of political violence during the armed conflict (Canadian Red Cross 2006; Painter 2007).

The gendered dimensions of the violence are painfully apparent. More than 2,200 women were violently murdered in Guatemala between 2001 and 2006, often in ways that are themselves gendered, involving rape, sexual assault, and sexual mutilation. Amnesty International has reported that this number wildly outpaces the rate in Ciudad Juárez, Mexico, where activists and NGOs have long fought for international awareness of feminicide. Of more than six hundred cases of women reported murdered in 2005, only two convictions had been handed down a year later (Amnesty International 2006; cf. ASIES 2003). Even so, the numbers given above are likely lower than the country's actual crime rates. Informal conversations with police and rescue officials reveal that only certain violent deaths, such as those of laborers, and not others, such as those of gang members, tend to be included in official tallies. This is not to mention the climbing rates of assault, theft, robbery, and other violent and nonviolent crimes in the capital city, where mass transit and urban marketplaces are daily targets of criminal activity.[9]

Striking levels of crime and violence in Guatemala City represent a shift in the spatial coordinates of danger in Guatemala. The Peace Accords ended an armed conflict that had begun in Guatemala City and eastern departments but quickly moved to rural regions in the western highlands (Carmack 1988; Stoll 1993). Today, violence is concentrated in Guatemala City, though "talk of crime" (Caldeira 2001) is certainly not confined to the urban center. Gangs are an increasing problem in the capital but also in small towns and semiurban municipalities (Rodríguez and de León 2000; Winton 2005). Estimates put the number of gang members nationwide at anywhere from 14,000 to 165,000 (USAID 2006). Despite the lack of data this discrepancy reflects, gangs are commonly blamed for the nation's security problems and social ills by the mass media, in community-level responses to crime, and in everyday conversation. Lack of police protection and government programs to curb crime and violence, widespread distrust of authorities, and pronounced differences between state and local cultural understandings of justice and rights all explain the growing numbers of neighborhood watch groups as well as lynchings—of which there were more than four hundred cases in Guatemala between 1996 and 2002 (MINUGUA 2002; Sieder 2003).

Angelina Godoy's (2006) investigation of lynchings in the highland region gives a useful account of how the destruction of community institutions and social ties during the conflict continues as collectively experienced trauma today. Militarized and violent forms of authority instituted during the conflict "remain embedded in local practices," and "community life itself . . . ha[s] been deeply infused with violence," she argues (Godoy 2006: 84; Sanford 2004). She points to a fundamental rupture of social life during the conflict—the disappearance of thousands of people, the fragmentation of communities, and the often blurred lines between perpetrators and victims—as a phenomenological foundation on which distrust and fear have been established among those who experienced la violencia, either directly or indirectly (see also Green 1999). The legacies of the armed conflict are an important dimension of the social insecurities Guatemalans experience today, and ethnographic research is indispensable for gauging the social and psychological weight of the violence in terms of collective memories, testimonials, and social critique.

If the spatial organization of violence has shifted in the postconflict era, however, so has its sociopolitical context. Dennis Rodgers (2006) suggests

that Latin America as a whole has experienced a shift in the political economy of violence in the post–Cold War, postconflict era. Noting that "crime is
not a new phenomenon, and political violence is by no means extinct," he argues that violence has become "democratized." The state now controls neither
the means nor the direction of violence; rather, it increasingly appears "as an
option for a multitude of actors," for a multitude of reasons (268). Edward F.
Fischer and Peter Benson (2006) refer to this shift as the neoliberalization of
violence, meaning the outsourcing and privatization of violent acts, the per-
sonalization of victimhood, the rationalization of violence in terms of anticitizens (e.g., gangs), and the empowerment of dangerous forms of community response. The informalization and privatization of security is a significant
trend in Guatemala (Kincaid 2001: 52; Paley 2001). Approximately 7 percent
of Guatemalan households currently pay for their own personal security.
The number of private security guards working in homes and businesses is
estimated at 80,000, compared to 18,500 police officers nationwide (USAID
2006). Avery Dickins's essay takes an ethnographic look at the private security industry, illustrating how realities and rumors of urban violence, taken
together with patterns of rural dislocation brought on by structural adjustment policies, promote rural-to-urban migration among young men who see
private security as desirable work. The guards she depicts have come to see
urban violence as a potential vehicle for upward mobility in the face of declining rural economies, while their patrons see the private rather than public
consumption of security as a preferable response to crime.

This volume builds on the work of Godoy, Rodgers, and others by situat-
ing these changing forms of postconflict violence within a broader context of
fear and insecurity and attending to how neoliberal policies have exacerbated
these conditions and shape responses to them. The essay by Benson, Thomas,
and Fischer on "resocializing suffering," for example, makes a strong case
for understanding the origins and outcomes of Guatemala's "new violence"
in terms of structural and societal conditions related to rural and urban economic restructuring. In the absence of state services, a pervasive condition of
structural violence puts already disadvantaged groups in Guatemala at greater
risk of violent behavior and victimization. Official narratives about violence
that neglect this fact encourage citizens to understand the new violence as the
result of informal economic activities, not a part of the formal system, and as
the problem of marginalized social types, including gang members. This approach, which places promises of security and realities of insecurity, promises of formalized economic growth and realities of informal subsistence and

entrepreneurship, within a single conceptual framework, calls attention to the failures of societal responses to address root causes of violence. In Guatemala, these underlying structural conditions are dire. Neoliberal reforms have contributed to a situation in which nearly 60 percent of the population lives below the poverty line and one in five people live in extreme poverty (World Bank 2007). Guatemala, along with Brazil and South Africa, has the most unequal income distribution in the world (UNDAF 2000 quoted in Preti 2002: 110; UNDP 2000). The education system has left the country with the highest illiteracy rate in the Americas after Haiti (Preti 2002); 65 percent of indigenous women are illiterate. The efforts of international aid organizations and the innumerable NGOs that began working in Guatemala following the Peace Accords—another example of the privatization of what might otherwise be seen as the state's responsibilities—only go so far. Guatemalans experience pervasive food insecurity (Shriar 2002), unemployment, political instability linked to lack of participatory mechanisms and widespread corruption, and ubiquitous fear of police and military forces (Pérez 2004), all together with the widespread availability of arms in a postwar setting (Winton 2005).[10] Insecurities and personal hazards "conspire to create a condition of relentless vulnerability for poor urban residents" of the capital city in particular (Beall and Fox 2006: 6). Reliance on an unstable, monetized informal economy, lack of sufficient housing, limited access to water and sanitation services, vulnerability to environmental hazards (Beall and Fox 2006), and discrimination against indigenous people and women (Preti 2002: 110): all of these factors contribute to a social setting characterized by structural violence.

An important feature of the postconflict era is the popular call for *mano dura* (firm hand) solutions to violence, including military interventions, social cleansing campaigns, and lynchings (Godoy 2006; Sanford 2008; Thomas and Benson 2008). Many of this volume's essays highlight state-level and community-level responses to crime and violence, examining how a common view of criminals and other unsavory social types as the source of violence reflects the influence of cultural assumptions about individualism built into neoliberal theories about economic systems. Each essay in the volume contributes to the theorization of how "talk of crime" shapes the lives of Guatemalans who often imagine their relationship to the state and capital city through the lenses of urban violence and danger. Yet the specter of danger itself is something that has been preconfigured in terms of dominant representations of the delinquent, the youth, the criminal, the gang member, and the pirate—the anticitizens of a neoliberal social order.

City and Country

Arjun Appadurai has referred to contemporary cities in the Global South as "cracked and refracted" images of global processes (2000: 627). Uneven development, rampant inequality, and rising crime rates contribute to an overall sense of disjuncture and distortion. In this section, we take a closer look at the ways that neoliberalism, security, and related transnational processes shape the spatial and social configuration of Guatemala City and the dynamic relationship between city and countryside in Guatemala. One feature of many contemporary cities is the fortified enclave, a spatial configuration that contributes to the sense of disjuncture and fracture that Appadurai describes. Gated communities use private security guards, surveillance technology, and imposing walls to protect wealthy residents from actual and perceived threats. These enclaves can be found throughout Latin America (Low 2003) as well as in Africa (Ferguson 2006), Asia (Falzon 2004), and the United States (Cattelino 2004; Chesluk 2004). The most enduring critique of gated communities comes from the Brazilian context. Teresa Caldeira (2001) argues that fortified enclaves have transformed public space in São Paulo. Their proliferation has contributed to the association of poverty with crime while also emptying the public sphere of those who can afford private security. Fortified enclaves have left São Paulo broken and fractured; they have made the city feel more dangerous than it already is.

The spike in violence and insecurity in Guatemala over the last decade has similarly altered spatial organization in Guatemala City. As mentioned above, the retreat of state services has included limited spending on the country's police force and a spike in the amount of private security demanded by urban elites. Clusters of private condominiums cocooned by guns, dogs, and mercenaries now speckle Guatemala's highways, particularly between the capital and Antigua, one of Guatemala's storied tourist destinations. Fortified enclaves also segregate Guatemala City's more exclusive zones from the more popular ones. Zone 1, for example, is Guatemala City's oldest and most historic zone; it is the home of the national cathedral, high courts, and national palace. As Véliz and O'Neill recount in their essay, Zone 1 has become particularly dangerous in recent years, with a disproportionately high rate of violent murders taking place within its parameters. Once Guatemala's seat of power and wealth, Zone 1 has now been abandoned by Guatemala's urban elite for peripheral zones largely built up over the past two decades, complete with fortified homes, upscale shopping malls, and private security forces.[11]

Despite similarities with the Brazilian case, Guatemala City is not a mega-city. The capital's urban elite do not match in number or buying power those in São Paulo, Mexico City, or Mumbai. As Rodgers (2004: 120) argues, fortified enclaves in mid-sized cities such as Managua and Guatemala City are not so much self-sufficient islands of refuge and privilege as they are secure nodes in a network of protected spaces through which the urban elite travel in their daily routines. Véliz and O'Neill recount in their essay how wealthy Guatemalans are trying to reclaim Zone 1 of Guatemala City as one such secure, privatized node. Plans include ridding the historical city center of less desirable elements, including street vendors and the clients who depend on their cheap goods (Véliz 2006). Urban renewal programs such as that proposed for Zone 1 create retail and recreational spaces that are not only heavily secured but also characterized by forms of conspicuous consumption well beyond the reach of Guatemala City's poor and even middle-class residents.

Outside the sanctuaries lie urban spaces with limited security, limited resources, and mounting problems. Much of the city has simply fallen off the grid. Again, this reality is not particular to Guatemala City. The rate of worldwide urbanization and the desperate conditions in which many urban residents survive is striking. According to recent estimates, one billion of the three billion urban residents in the world today live in slums, "vulnerable to disease, violence, and social, political, and economic exclusion" (Beall and Fox 2006: 5). Conditions of structural violence and neoliberal market rationalities in places such as Guatemala City fuel the deterioration of living conditions for the urban poor and motivate against effective state responses (ibid.: 10).

Life in Guatemala City slums has been examined in the work of several scholars, whose contributions include analyses of youth involvement in gangs, family life and social organization, and perceptions of violence (Espinosa and Hidalgo 1994; Morán Mérida 1997; Moser and McIlwaine 2004; Roberts 1973; Winton 2003). This volume focuses on the everyday lives of those who have, by and large, managed to avoid the worst living conditions and are part of the city's working and middle classes. The essays provide an in-depth look at class stratifications in the capital city and changing senses of distinction and difference among groups whose social status has been thrown into flux in the neoliberal era. Manuela Camus's essay looks at citizens of Primero de Julio, a once decidedly middle-class neighborhood where people increasingly feel disenfranchised as well as disconnected from the visions of modernity and progress they previously held for the city. Thomas Offit supplies a more hopeful portrait of urban opportunity. His essay follows an indigenous entrepreneur who has achieved relative success in the informal sector by drawing upon rural ties, including kinship networks, to establish retail empires in the city streets. As noted above, Véliz and O'Neill show another side of the street vendor story, as wealthy interests threaten the city center's curbside markets.

Beyond a portrait of contemporary urban life in Guatemala, the essays in this volume highlight the circulations of people, goods, media, social and political movements, and crime across rural and urban space. Anthropologists have clearly demonstrated that urban space is often experienced as something completely other than the countryside. At the same time, urban studies that neglect the relational dynamics between city and country sidestep the historical and experiential processes through which urban and rural spaces are produced in physical terms and in the social imaginary. This volume confronts the tension between these two contradictory perspectives by advancing the argument that spaces are not inherently connected or disconnected. Rather, scholars as well as residents of Guatemala come to perceive space one way as opposed to another. Critical inquiry into how perceptions of space have been shaped over time and the social and political effects of these modes of perception is especially urgent in a country where the distinction between rural and urban space is historically charged with powerful meanings: the city associated with ladinos and modernity, the countryside associated with indigenous people and tradition. Essays by Avery Dickins de Girón and Kedron Thomas delve into how urban space is imagined from the countryside, including how urban violence and insecurity figure into representations of the city and into economic decisions made among merchants and migrants with ties to the capital city and its markets. Kevin Lewis O'Neill investigates the urban perspective on rural life. His essay explores the specific figures and fables that circulate about the rural poor within one of Guatemala City's booming neo-Pentecostal megachurches. This volume makes a strong case for understanding Guatemala City and country as inextricably linked and mutually constitutive. This is an especially effective approach, we argue, to understanding mid-sized cities around the world. Viewed as fluid and dispersed locations (Gupta and Ferguson 1997) and hubs of translocal political, economic, and social processes, it is untenable to define mid-sized cities as bounded entities (Frisby and Featherstone 1997; Graham and Marvin 2001; Soja 2000) set apart from surrounding rural and semiurban zones. This volume takes discourses of security, experiences of insecurity, and transnational processes linked to neoliberal agendas as fruitful grounds for exploring the ways city and country are presently bound together.

The Book

Securing the City is divided into two parts. The first part, "Urban History and Social Experience," provides a historical and ethnographic analysis of Guatemala City's rise as an urban center. The essays focus on processes that have transformed how urban space is organized and experienced in Guatemala as well as continuing struggles of group affiliation and exclusion that impact who has a right to the city. The volume's second part addresses how the country's urban and rural spaces interrelate, with particular attention to the work of the imagination (Appadurai 1996) in shaping not only perceptions of space and security, but also everyday practice in the realms of politics, religion, and work.

The first part opens with Deborah Levenson's essay entitled "Living Guatemala City: 1930s–2000s." Her subject of analysis could be framed with a seemingly uncomplicated question: How do people get by and make sense of their world in a place as precarious and dangerous as Guatemala City? Moving through the life histories of three generations of youth in one working-class urban family, she shows how youth have conceived of their selfhoods and made their ways through the specific modernities of which they were a constituent part. The essay conveys a powerful history of the political, economic, and cultural changes experienced in Guatemala City in the last century, leading to new perspectives on the rise of neoliberalism and how security is practiced by young people in the capital today.

The next essay, "Primero de Julio: Urban Experiences of Class Decline and Violence," authored by Manuela Camus, also places Guatemala City in historical context, looking at changes over four decades in one urban neighborhood. Camus, one of the foremost anthropologists of Guatemala City, couples her ethnographic findings on contemporary forms of class insecurity, social suffering, and violence in the capital city with a genealogical analysis of patterns of discrimination that inform how people respond to situations they find threatening. Residents of Primero de Julio interpret the loss of middle-class social standing they are experiencing in terms of the inability of indigenous migrants to successfully adapt to the urban environment, which they believe results in the delinquency and crime encroaching on their neighborhood. The essays by Camus and Levenson raise important questions that later essays continue to unravel: How do deeply rooted ideologies of race, class, and gender inform contemporary responses to rising inequalities? How is urban space materially and symbolically reconfigured alongside meanings of poverty and crime as institutions and ordinary citizens practice neoliberal rationalities?

The next two essays take up these questions in addressing the lived experiences of urban street vendors, participants in an informal economic sector that has proliferated in the wake of neoliberal reforms. Thomas Offit's essay, "Cacique for a Neoliberal Age: A Maya Retail Empire on the Streets of Guatemala City," looks at the ways that neoliberal ideologies of individual autonomy, economic rationality, and entrepreneurship seem convergent with the social and economic practices that have turned some indigenous street vendors into retail kings. "Privatization of Public Space: The Displacement of Street Vendors in Guatemala City," authored by Rodrigo J. Véliz and Kevin Lewis O'Neill, addresses the divergent meanings that urban space holds for vendors who make their living on the streets of Guatemala City's historic Zone 1 and the developers who promote "urban renewal" as a way to save the city's historic center from what they view as degradation, crime, and blight. These first four essays provide the reader with a historical backdrop against which the neoliberal period takes shape as a distinct political, economic, and social field, along with in-depth analyses of how economic changes, rising security concerns, and explosive urban growth are transforming the city's human and social geography.

The volume's second part begins with an essay by Avery Dickins de Girón entitled "The Security Guard Industry in Guatemala: Rural Communities and Urban Violence." Dickins addresses the multifarious effects that neoliberal reforms and rising crime rates have had in the department of Alta Verapaz, a rural region north of the capital city. Patterns of rural dislocation together with real and perceived conditions of violence in the capital, she argues, fuel the migration of indigenous men to Guatemala City, where the private security guard industry promises economic opportunity and encounters with urban modernity as it is imagined from the countryside.

The two essays that follow feature ethnographic glimpses from Tecpán, a large town located about an hour's drive west of Guatemala City. "Guatemala's New Violence as Structural Violence: Notes from the Highlands," by Peter Benson, Kedron Thomas, and Edward F. Fischer, takes up many of the themes addressed in Dickins's essay to examine how new forms of violence and social suffering in Guatemala reshape relations between the capital city and the highlands. The authors are especially concerned with liberal political and moral models that narrowly interpret violence in terms of individual suffering and culpability, models that converge with mano dura politics and privatized security. Enduring legacies of state violence and the social and economic insecurities brought about by neoliberal policies shape life in both Guatemala City and the countryside, even if the problem of violence is often portrayed as a distinctly urban one. Kedron Thomas's essay, "Spaces of Structural Adjustment in Guatemala's Apparel Industry," examines the economic life of Maya entrepreneurs from Tecpán who supply informal markets in the highlands and in Guatemala City with clothing, usually featuring pirated logos of popular brands. Thomas highlights how a social imaginary that links urban space, danger, and criminality affects their market decisions, at the same time as international trademark laws have turned these indigenous men and women into criminals themselves. Neoliberal reforms have made it increasingly difficult for apparel producers to earn a living, blaming them, as "pirates," for the nation's social and economic ills.

The volume's final essay returns to Guatemala City to consider how rural spaces are imagined by urban residents concerned about not only the safety but also the souls of Guatemala's indigenous population. In "Hands of Love: Christian Outreach and the Spatialization of Ethnicity," Kevin Lewis O'Neill focuses on Christian outreach programs instituted by some of the most prominent neo-Pentecostal megachurches in Guatemala City. In an ethnically diverse city where over a third of the population lives in extreme poverty, O'Neill's essay considers why urban residents need to leave the city to do charitable work. He examines the program participants' decisions to help people in the countryside rather than the city streets, tracing the church's moral construction of indigeneity and poverty alongside its conceptualization of urban versus rural space. The four essays of the volume's second part contribute to the theorization of how perceptions of urban and rural space—whether premised on notions of urban violence, urban opportunities, rural decline, or rural innocence and deservedness—shape institutional and individual practices in a neoliberal era.

Notes

1. See Stephen Schlesinger and Stephen Kinzer 1999.
2. The conclusion that periods of Guatemala's armed conflict are best understood as genocidal is not an uncontested argument. Diane Nelson (2001), for example, suggests that questions of intent complicate the charge of genocide, given that genocide's legal construction pivots on the intent of the powerful to eradicate the powerless.

3. While Adams's work was the first major *anthropological* work to deal with Guatemala City, this does not mean that there was no earlier academic research that addressed the capital with a social-science perspective. Theodora Caplow's (1949) pioneering work on the social ecology of Guatemala City and Michael Micklin's (1966, 1969) work on the psychological effect of urbanization on a sample of men in Guatemala City are notable. In addition, numerous historical studies have been published in Spanish on various aspects of the city's growth and development (see Gellert 1995; Gellert and Pinto Soria 1990; and Velásquez Carrera 2006 for recent exemplars).

4. The urban informal sector has drawn repeated interest from scholars of Guatemala City, including Juan Pablo Pérez Sáinz (1990, 1997); Pérez Sáinz and Menjivar Larin (1991); Gustavo Porras Castejón (1995); and Thomas Offit (2008; this volume).

5. Guatemala is considered a unique case in the region because the percentage of its population living in urban areas is relatively low (47 percent in 2006, compared to an average of 70 percent in Latin America and the Caribbean; World Bank 2006). As Carol Smith (1984) has pointed out, this statistic is offset by the fact that most of the nation's urban population resides in one overdeveloped metropolis, Guatemala City. Guatemala City is eight to ten times larger than the second most populous city of the nation, Quetzaltenango, a city in the western highlands that has itself recently attracted interest; see, e.g., the excellent historical studies by Greg Grandin (2000) and Irma Velásquez Nimatuj (2002).

6. See also recent work on Guatemala City by Kevin Lewis O'Neill (2010a) and Thomas Offit (2008).

7. See Fischer 2001; Fischer and Brown 1996; Hale 2002; and Warren 1998.

8. Inés Benítez, "Guatemala City: New Commission to Investigate Prisons, Police," Inter Press Service, August 2, 2007.

9. In 1996, 67 percent of urban Guatemalans surveyed said they or someone in their family had been the victim of a common crime (e.g., assault) that year (Pérez 2004). See also INE 2006.

10. See also Lara, Julio, Olga López, Leonardo Creser, and Coralia Orantes, "Sociedad armada, población violenta." *Prensa Libre*, August 19, 2007.

11. Zones 9, 10, 13, and 14 are considered the wealthiest and safest zones in Guatemala City today.

Part One

Urban History and
Social Experience

Living Guatemala City, 1930s–2000s

Deborah T. Levenson

Today Guatemala City is infamous as one of the poorest and most dangerous cities in Latin America.[1] Older residents remember lovely neighborhoods and better times under clear skies, but today few would deny that the city edges on uninhabitable. Infrastructure deteriorates, the city has deindustrialized, and crime is everywhere, every day.[2] The working poor are Guatemala City's majority, and the family wage economy that constitutes their time-honored strategy currently depends on the emigration of relatives who send money (now in rapidly decreasing amounts); the "informal economy" of goods and services; and the illegal economy of drugs and black-market clothing, cars, appliances, and other commodities. The last of these sources, however risky, appears to be the most reliable urban employer of youth, an age group that represents the city's future, the greater part of its population, and one half of those designated as poor (see Offit, this volume, for discussion of youth in the informal economy). Unlike Buenos Aires or Rio de Janeiro, there are few myths or colorful narratives about this capital city; it is a literary subject only in Guatemalan writer Miguel Ángel Asturias's chilling 1930s novel El señor Presidente, where it makes an appearance as the setting for a police state replete with beggars, night prowlers, dark alleys, traps, lies, cells, spies, and corrupt politicians. It is easy to envision Guatemala City as a complete disaster, another rapidly decaying slum on the "planet of slums" (Davis 2006).

My point of departure in this essay, however, is that the city is not dead. Popular culture and the intersections, relationships, and varied activities of the over 2.5 million people who live in the capital make Guatemala City more than a static embodiment of inequalities wherein the rich live in gated communities and the poor in shantytowns of misery. Politics and economics have informed the possibilities available to people as they have moved in and given shape to their surroundings; people are part of the city's infrastructure (Simone 2004). In the 1970s, a large urban movement gave qualities of democracy and popular power to neighborhoods, workplaces, schools, and the streets—despite, because of, and in the face of state terrorism. In the 2000s, however, "peace" time, neoliberalism, global financial disaster, unemployment, corruption, and violence frame how people live, with perhaps greater difficulties for viable national life than they have ever experienced.

This essay looks at city life from the late 1930s to the 2000s through the coming-of-age narratives of four people from three generations of the Cruz-López family: its founder, María Cruz, an indigenous woman who arrived in Guatemala City alone at age twelve in 1938; her daughter Isabel; and Isabel's two sons, René and Andrés. All four have been modern protagonists, making their lives in the manners they thought best while still being aware of other options. When they told me their stories, each drew on different yet overlapping aspects of the rich urban repertoire offered by, among other things, Mexican movies and "world" youth culture, progressive movements of workers and women, liberal discourses of success and failure, and Christianity.

This family and the city are both studies in diversity and connections. I once sat in María's small apartment with kin that included a college graduate who works in finance for a multinational company, an unemployed truck driver with a certificate in computer skills, an organizer for a peasant organization, an unschooled vendor whose son works in the Sudan for the United Nations, a domestic worker, and a former guerrilla struggling to start a motorcycle repair shop. Most are Catholics or Evangelicals and one is a nonbeliever. The family is presumably ladino (nonindigenous), as are the majority of the city's residents; however, María is of indigenous descent.[3] In kind with many others in the city, their zone, Zone 7, is heterogeneous. Most of its residents are poor (as are the majority in the López-Cruz family), but middle-class families also live there, and so do the absolutely impoverished who make their homes in and their living from an enormous garbage dump. Although the upper class resides in guarded compounds in Zones 10 and 14–16 of the city's twenty-two zones, there are few demarcated spaces that belong solely to the middle class, lower classes, or extremely poor. More often, they commingle throughout the rest of the city. Zone 12 offers an extreme case in which one of the city's wealthiest private schools borders one of its largest shantytowns. Hardly the result of planning, this variety, like that within the López-Cruz family, speaks to the broader histories of modern change and conflict in and beyond Guatemala City.

María

María's early years unfolded under a liberal dictatorship that maintained a low-wage rural export-oriented economy and used forced Maya labor to build national infrastructure. The Liberal Party dictator Manuel Estrada Cabrera (1898–1920) had brought his version of modern times to María's hometown of Salamá in Baja Verapaz by financing a bridge over the Río Salamá, a prison, and public schools. By the mid-1930s, under the liberal dictator Jorge Ubico (1931–44), Salamá had telegraph service; a middle class; a hospital; and, in 1934, a paved road connecting it to the capital (Conde Prera 1989). María's mother was of Maya descent, but she knows little else of her history. Her father's relatives, whom she has met here and there, were ladino. However, "mixed" people like María went unrecognized as such, and she learned to use the pejoratives *inditos/inditas* to refer to indigenous people, without claiming to be ladina or indigenous herself. María's family was poor, Catholic, and kept small by high infant morality rates; only María and her older sister survived her mother's many pregnancies. Her father worked breaking horses, and her mother made tamales to sell. From an early age, María helped her mother with this; she did not attend school, which was not available in any case. When María was six, someone—she suspects her father's ladina lover—murdered her mother. Deeply saddened, María recollects only that she sold the bread that her sister baked in order to support both of them over the next six years.

Her memories of leaving Salamá are vivid. When María turned twelve, her sister sent her to work in a middle-class household. Soon after she arrived, she was blamed when the child she tended was injured in a fall. María recalls:[4]

The mother beat me, the father beat me, and then my sister beat me until I was black and blue . . . I ran to the cemetery. I screamed to my mother, "Why did you abandon me!?" and wept and wept; . . . the bus owner saw me all black and blue and asked what happened. I explained. I said I wanted to run away to the capital. He said he would pass at three in the morning driving the Salamá-Guate bus and honk three times and I should run out [and] get on and he would take me. I put on my dress, shawl, and slip but I had no shoes. I watched the clock. I was proud that I knew how to read the clock: 1 — 2 — 3! He honked! I went out barefoot with my hair so long and the *ayudante* [driver's assistant] swooped me up and off I went into the night.[5]

A new road, bus, and friend—not ethnic, religious, or kin community—offered a way for María to move on, and she eagerly took it. Fortunately the driver took good care of young María while the bus wound down the road. He bought her refreshments, and when the bus arrived in Guatemala City, she recollects: "He took me to his aunt who ran a *comedor* [small restaurant or lunch counter], 'look, this is a good girl, she can work.' So I went to work for her; . . . she gave me a place to sleep in the back with some boarders and the bus driver; . . . she brushed my hair. She was affectionate; . . . she loved me, she brought me sandals and an apron. The family took me out on Sundays, we went everywhere, La Sexta, Cerro de Carmen."[6] Thus, twelve-year-old María stepped off a bus into a city of 166,456 people in order to immediately become a servant. Never to be homeless, she recalled the street people, "*los indios* and other poor people," rounded up to do forced labor. Controlled by laws that prohibited whatever threatened Ubico's rule, the city was subdued, and for María, safe. She had no knowledge of the clandestine activities of those who would overthrow the liberal dictatorship, and they said nothing about the plight of domestic servants. A major event in Guatemalan history, the revolution of 1944 is not part of her memory.[7]

The city delighted María. El Centro housed nearly half of the city's population—wealthy, middle class, and poor, including thousands of domestics. For years she never went into the barrios where the other half lived in constructions of adobe, leaves, and, as she puts it, *cualquiera* (whatever) without water or sewage (Gellert 1995; A. Solow 1950). With a lovely acoustic shell in the gardened Parque Central, electricity, trolleys, traffic lights, paved streets and new government buildings, El Centro was the city at its most citified.[8] The city's glamour, the "sparkling modernity" noted by period writers and by María, was located on several blocks of El Centro, where María walked with her employers on Sundays (Caplow 1949; see Véliz and O'Neill, this volume). There were pharmacies; well-to-do dress, shoe, and paper goods stores; banks; restaurants; the Hotel Palace; and the electric company. Guatemala's new department stores, such as La Perla on Sexta Avenida, known as the "Tiffany's of Guatemala City," offered stunning imports such as cashmere sweaters and Max Factor cosmetics. Nearby on La Sexta stood the Art Deco *palacio del cine*,

Teatro Lux, which advertised parquet floors and the era's famed Hollywood and Mexican movies.[9]

In kind with many domestics, María lived in El Centro with different employers. The streets were safer than some of their households. After the aunt died, María explains:

> Her son sold the restaurant and a compa [coworker] told me about a family on the street that needed a servant; . . . turned out they were from Salamá and godparents of one of my father's children . . . My father turns up one day with a woman and children. "¡Mi hija! What are you doing here?" He offered to take me to Tiquisate, where he was going to work. I got mad. I knew he only wanted me to watch his kids. I was very rebellious. Listen, one house where I was had boarders, military men and one was the owner's son and one night he slipped nude into the corner where I slept . . . I had never seen a nude man and he threw himself on top of me and I grabbed a stick . . . and hit him hard and screamed for help, loudly! His parents came and grabbed him and there was a lot of yelling . . . and I left. I went around the corner to the Jefe de Policía's house. I knocked. I explained. They took me in and I stayed there for a while.

Barely an adolescent, María defended herself alone. Savvy about her father's notion of incorporating her into the family, she refused to go with him. Later, she fled to the streets in order to escape rape and found comfort from the chief of police, who sent her to work as a domestic for a German couple. After they left the city, she made her way to a Chinese restaurant, where she worked for its owners, the Lee family, and there she met Miguel, a sixteen-year-old tailor. María remembers: "That's where [at the Lees'] I bought my first possessions . . . shoes and a Victrola. We [she and other young female employees] had our room and we'd practice dance steps! I was always happy listening to the radio in the kitchen. I liked Guatemalan music, no Mexican music, only marimba—12 Calle, Los Altos! I loved marimba! That's where I met my first boyfriend, Miguel. We'd go dancing at the Porvenir de los Obreros.[10] I sent to get a dress made. I bought a matching handbag, shoes and a pair of imported stockings."

Although the terms of her occupation separated her somewhat from the cash nexus, she cheerfully used her small earnings for the material culture of the middle-class "New Look" female style—matching clothes and accessories—and a Victrola record player. María also loved the king of urban culture: radio. Aired were English, German, and hygiene lessons; BBC news; and the music of swing, opera, and *marimba doble*, the national favorite.[11] *Marimbistas* played at the Teatro Lux, at state events, and at places such as El Porvenir, where María and Miguel danced to smart, lively waltzes (Taracena 1983). Despite her problems, the city became her anchor and pleasure, a place where she generally felt loved until Miguel betrayed her:

> Miguel and I were in love, he took me to Lake Amatitlán, to his mother's, but one day I saw him kissing another girl . . . I told him if he wanted respect, he had to respect me. I grabbed the other girl . . . by the hair and pulled; . . . I pushed her to the floor . . . that's how mad I was . . . It was *terrible*; . . . . his mother had already told me it was all right to marry Miguel even if I didn't have family because she loved me and would make me my wedding dress, a white dress not with very expensive cloth, a nice white cotton cloth. I couldn't love him so I went to Coatepeque with a lawyer's family that moved there.

By the 1940s, success had fattened Coatepeque, a southern coastal town. Mechanized export agriculture made it a prosperous ladino commercial center of three thousand inhabitants. Coatepeque had a hotel named La Europa, a movie theater, restaurants, schools, an electric company, and the Boy Scouts. There, however, María had more problems with sexual harassment, and she finally left domestic work and found another job and a social life with young Salvadoran women workers, whom she found "lively and independent." It was in their company that she met her future husband. She explains:

> The lawyer wanted to, you know, have . . . sex with me and I said *no*; I fled the house in the night. I ran to the Hotel Europa! I told the doorman Mingo what happened and asked to sleep in the doorway; . . . [The next day] he got me work there. Everyone [in Coatepeque] knew I was a good worker and a cook. One day the wife of Teófilo says, "I need a cook." So I went with her; . . . she liked me, but I got a better job cooking at the electric company. That was when I met Tono [Antonio López, who became her common law husband]. We [she and the Salvadorans] went to the movies on Sundays. I loved, love, Pedro Infante [Mexico's beloved twentieth-century movie idol]. We saw *all* his movies. He was the man of my dreams . . . handsome, sweet-blooded. One day I saw this man there, a cop, but good looking. He looked exactly like Pedro. To look at

my husband was to look at Pedro. He wanted to talk to me; . . . he had fallen in love with me . . . He swore I had to be his; he sent flowers and one Sunday he caught up with me. I was walking . . . as always accompanied by friends.

Tono walked up to María and introduced himself. She replied: "Policemen have a bad reputation, just like soldiers they make fun of women, abuse them and leave them. I don't want to hurt you or be hurt, so I am not interested in you. Don't bother me . . . I don't want to be unhappy. I just want to work in peace, so don't cross my path." He persisted, of course, and María concluded the story of her youth, the end of which she judged to be her unity with Tono and the start of "troubles."

Young María epitomized much about Guatemala City—child labor, sexual abuse of servants, lineages of mixed indigenous and ladino descent—but nowhere in the urban cultural and social configuration were she and her counterparts represented or legitimized. Girls labored without recognition as members of the urban working class and without acknowledgment as child workers or as children. The only modern culture that reflected her life was in Mexican cinema. She especially recalls *Nosotros, los pobres*, the tale of a humble carpenter, played by the handsome Pedro Infante, who honors and defends poor mestizos by challenging wealth, power, and the sexual abuse of women.[12] In the movie, justice is served in an urban space defined by rural-to-urban migration, the poor are noble and resourceful individuals, poverty is dignified, and the rich are predators. She embraced this world on film. It is not hard to see María's shifting and sexually dangerous adolescent life in a film in which disorder is given form by modest people who resembled her physically. Like them, she could escape catastrophe and persist. The movie version was superb: a girl finds romance with a handsome, caring Infante, the sort of man María would have loved to marry.

From the time that María came to the city, unfamiliar people became the friends and allies who composed her world. A resilient and daring child with a gift for being found and finding, she met the bus driver, his aunt, the Lee family, Miguel, the police chief, and Mingo, among others. María turned strangers into friends who helped her achieve a kind of personal autonomy. María surely kept her strength and independence within certain bounds of customary female behavior and deferred to males, but only if that met her needs. Feathers might have stuck to her, but she lived a modern life in a modern city, the capital, and a modern town, Coatepeque. Instead of staying put, she fought for joy for herself and safety from male abuse, without certainty about the results.

María and Tono lived together for several unhappy years. They had a boy who died in infancy and two girls, Isabel and Blanca. Tono drank and proved unreliable in the normative male role of economic provider. To earn money, María opened a comedor inside their place in Coatepeque. After Tono's transfer to the town of Puerto Barrios, María again started a comedor in their quarters. María blamed the death of her first child on home birth, and thereafter sought hospital care. Pregnant with Isabel in Puerto Barrios, she traveled to see a private doctor in Guatemala City. When the time came she went to Guatemala City alone, and unable to locate her own doctor, found a sympathetic cabdriver who took her to the hospital and even kept an eye on her after the baby's arrival. Two years later, she gave birth to Blanca in a private clinic. With this growing family, María pushed Tono to improve his status in the department, but he did not. Fed up with his aimlessness, drinking, and flings, María moved back to Guatemala City at the beginning of the 1960s with her mother-in-law, Isabel, and Blanca. Without money and with only pots and pans as tools, María supported her caravan of females by vending food in the markets and streets. She went into business the day after she arrived by selling her chuchitos and atol at a construction site, where, she had noted on the day of her arrival, the workers had nowhere to eat. Tono drifted in and out of their lives until María and he parted company forever after an incident that left María and her daughters in prison. By the time of their brief incarceration, Tono's mother was dead, which left María alone with two small daughters in one room that she rented in Zone 7.

Isabel

Isabel's first memory is of Tono leaving: "I woke in the middle of the night, he was covering us—we had two brown ponchos—with one he covered us and he took the other and left." Her second memory is of his absolute abandonment of her.

> My father was mujeriego. He had relations with another woman. My father worked in Cobán then [still in La Policía Nacional], and he went there by airplane. My mother took us to the airport to see him off. She [the other woman] was there! My mother made a big scandal—she hit my father, beat up the woman, hit the policeman. We were taken pris-

oners—me, Blanca, my mother, and the woman. They took us to the women's prison, and Blanca and I were put in the prison nursery. I was four maybe. Blanca was a baby! We cried like crazies when they separated us from our mother; . . . they woke us up early to feed and wash us. We spent time there until a neighbor came. My father didn't take us out. He got the other woman out.

The family finally left jail when María asked a departing prisoner to contact a neighbor who shared their surname; they were released under his cognizance as a relative. This nightmare became the proof behind María's warnings against men. The encounter in the airport would be Isabel's last with her father, and her first with state institutions and officials. It was an encounter strikingly different from María's experience with the Jefe de Policía some thirty years before.

Isabel grew up in a city that had been turned upside down twice since her mother's youth. It had experienced a renaissance in political economy and culture between 1944 and 1954 when the reformists attempted democratic "First World" modernization through innovative education, civil rights, land reform, and industrial development. In 1954, however, the military coup violently dismantled these rural and urban programs. Yet this second turning of the city on its head did not cause a return to the conditions of 1943. The desire for democracy and reform remained, and economic development continued, albeit on different terms. Isabel learned as a child that "some honest politicians had tried to end poverty and the U.S. overthrew them because the Frutera [the United Fruit Company] did not want land reform." That "good" politics could end inequality was part of the commonsense culture of her times.

Urban protests in 1962, when Isabel was four, and the actions of guerrilla groups in eastern Guatemala started the process whereby the countryside and city became polarized between leftists whose ideas harked back to the 1944–54 period, on the one hand; and right-wingers who were inspired by Opus Dei, had state power, and used new forms of terrorism to control the population, on the other. Protest, death squads, and mangled bodies composed an abnormal everyday life. Isabel remembers the "disappeared," and rumors of their fate. But her memories of the 1960s and early 1970s center on a more tangible situation: her family's unrelenting poverty was the constant "major event" as she and the city grew.

De facto dictatorship and death squads in the name of anticommunism oversaw the most intense capitalist modernization Guatemala had ever known.

Two dramatic developments spanned Isabel's youth. One was the extension of large-scale export agriculture, which swelled unemployment and rural-to-urban migration (Orellana 1978). The second was Guatemala's first significant industrialization, which centered in the capital and allowed Isabel a part in the development of an industrial working class.[13] Foreign and Guatemalan capitalists opened textile factories such as Nylontex—where Isabel would work as an adolescent—and ACRICASA, where she subsequently worked. Greater productivity in the city and the countryside yielded new prosperity for the wealthy and new poverty and political terror for the lower classes.

Isabel grew up "alone" with her sister and mother, and poverty made meals unpredictable. María's strengths and vulnerabilities in the face of desperation and solitude frame Isabel's childhood memories:

> My mother was the fighter who sustained us. We were so poor. My mother made tortillas in the day and worked in El Zócalo in Calle 18 at night. Sometimes we did not eat, or only half ate. Once Blanca was crying from hunger and we had only one egg, and I cooked it to feed her. My mother never disappointed us. On Christmas Eve we had a crèche always. She was tireless. She started work at five at night. When she left at night, she locked us in. After we started school, a neighbor opened the door so we could leave in the morning. We got dressed alone, we ate, although most times we didn't—we just went to school. We walked alone and scared. We learned early to take care of ourselves. We thought we were impeccable. Imagine how we looked! We lived in a room. One room was everything. We were alone, absolutely, there was *no one* but us.

María insisted that her daughters attend school to avoid the illiteracy that affected her urban life. Being Catholic did not stop María from sending them to an Evangelical school—it was close, cheap, and without the political conflicts of public schools.[14] By Isabel's own account, she was a smart and dutiful student who won her teachers' affection and pretended that she "accepted Christ," despite her disinterest in Evangelical salvation.

The three of them lived in a *colonia* in Zone 7. By then the poor and middle classes had become segregated from the rich, and there were now two Centros in the city. The first was the old one, which was deserted by the elite and rapidly deteriorated into Zone 1 (see Véliz and O'Neill, this volume). The Parque Central became a venue for poor people who socialized, demonstrated, and preached. By the early 1970s, La Sexta, the elegant avenue of María's first years in the city, was crowded with stores that sold cheap cosmetics and outdated imported appliances, and with police who fought with vendors for control of its sidewalks. Fumes poisoned the air, and the once visible volcano started to disappear behind smog.

The updated southern Zona Viva (Zone 10), where the elite now lived and the poor rarely ventured, became the "real" Centro. Here were banks, boutiques, beautiful walled residential areas, expensive *colegios* (private schools), hotels, restaurants, office buildings, and embassies. The majority of the city's 700,000 residents lived in the old and new *barrios populares* in Zones 2 to 7, 12, and 18 to 21. Little infrastructure existed in these zones, and few Catholic priests worked in them. Internationally affiliated and funded Evangelical churches provided the poor with a cheap version of what the Catholic Church gave the rich: private religious schools and moral comfort (Garrard-Burnett 1998). Except for the years when Manuel Colom served as mayor (1974–79), attempts at city planning had ended in 1954.[15] In the 1940s, the government of Juan José Arévalo had established Isabel's childhood colonia (a designated area within Zone 7) to provide affordable housing for government employees. After the 1954 coup, however, it lost state services and its status as a domicile for state workers. Marked by empty lots, it attracted rural migrants and residents who could not afford other parts of the city. By the time Isabel was eight, its cornfields and cows were starting to disappear. It had no garbage collection, no sewage, six public faucets for its 3,000 people, and high infant mortality rates. In common with many other children, Isabel lived with her female-headed family in a cement-floored room without electricity.

Isabel remembers her young self as "obedient, never rebellious." She and Blanca "never went out." They were confined to the colonia and enclosed within a room. She never journeyed to Zone 1, and her limited journeys to Zona Viva left her deeply humiliated and dejected. Poverty set the terms and emotions of her internal and external life. She recounts:

> Once my mother lost her work and she sought work in a house, in a restaurant, wherever; . . . since she didn't know how to read or write. This was very sad, very, very hard for me; . . . when she looked for an address from an ad or a sign or word of mouth she asked me to write it down, and she took me to find the address. I was about seven. I walked with her in Zones 10 and 9, sometimes when we found it, they said they had already found someone, or something. We kept going out like that for days, without finding work. Blanca stayed home alone, and I went looking for work with her. I felt tense, but I had to accompany her because

she couldn't read. Sometimes we would come back at four or five without finding anything. I remember the streets in Zone 10, so long, walking and walking. I felt the sadness of the situation. I cried and cried.
She felt bad taking me, but I was all she had . . . She had no one, just us.

María eventually found work cooking in a Zone 1 restaurant, but in 1966
she was injured in an accident. Isabel remembers that María had no savings:
"We owed rent and when she came from the hospital, how would she pay the
back rent? And the restaurant shut down. She didn't have work, or money.
I don't know from where she had a Victrola; she gave it as rent. We had no
clothes! I had a friend from secondary school, Wilma—we're still friends—
she had a better standard of living. She saw how I was and gave me clothes.
I gave most of them to Blanca." Months later María found work in a Zone 4
restaurant where she stayed for years. By the late 1960s the family had electricity at home. Isabel was enthralled by the new popular culture she heard
on a secondhand radio that her mother purchased and in the few movies she
watched. She loved the Beatles, the Venezuelan-Mexican Enrique Guzmán,
and the Spanish singer, Rafael, whose fan club—Guatemala's first—Isabel
yearned to join. These stars brought new youth imagery to Guatemala.

A pioneer of Mexican rock-and-roll, Guzmán started in a Mexican group
called Los Teen Tops and appeared in films such as *Twist locura de juventud*,
which Isabel saw. He was on the cutting edge of a teen culture that crossed
borders to project a moderately priced youth style and represented a new per-
sona—the essential teen who bumped and twisted past class and ethnicity.
Unlike the relationship between the milieus of Infante's films and María's
struggles, Guzmán's world was distant from Isabel's, which had little freedom from parent or poverty. Rafael's poetic songs arrived a bit later; he was a
delicate loner on a bittersweet quest, not a party guy. But the messages of his
music affirmed that "being young" existed as one singularity or another. De-
tached from Central American realities, this music contained a critical speci-
ficity: adolescent agency, feelings, and sexuality. A turning point in the history
of city youth, this music gave them a "youth" that existed beyond filial, work,
and school responsibilities.

This is not to say music freed Isabel. When Isabel reached twelve, she fell
in love with twenty-year-old César. As with her mother, an image attached
to a dream mediated her choices. She explains: "He was my first boyfriend—
having him was an illusion, an escape from the house—a kiss, a dream, your
first dream . . . What I liked, I laugh about this with my kids: . . . in those days

there was the *cantante* Rafael. I thought he looked like him! I saw the likeness; I said he was Rafael." The following year, Isabel started secondary school and won academic awards. But after she turned fourteen, César impregnated her. She recalls: "I was a good student, I could have gone on . . . and I was the first to get pregnant . . . because I fell in love with a man who didn't respect my youth. I knew nothing about sex—my mother told me nothing. I didn't know anything about pregnancy. When they said I needed a cesarean I thought that was great. It made me so happy. I didn't know it was worse." Faced with a crisis of legitimacy, an enraged María threatened César with a rape charge unless he married Isabel. Isabel was "numb" at then learning that César had already been forced to marry another impregnated minor. But no options existed in María's mind, and Isabel married César after his divorce.

Wishing for a sweet teen romance with Rafael's double, Isabel ended up a mother and wife at fifteen, and a few months later, a member of the new industrial working class and the family wage economy. Because César was not going to support their son, Andrés, Isabel reluctantly left school to find work. Moreover, because María worked, young Blanca had to leave school to care for Andrés. Literate and quick to learn machine skills, Isabel found a job at Nylontex, a new plant employing hundreds of young women. In kind with her mother's early experiences, Isabel's entrance into the workforce brought the threat of sexual violation, among other problems. The sexual abuse of the young female workers at Nylontex was the industrial version of that of female servants: employer rape was "normal," Isabel says, and backed up by a repressive atmosphere:

> The girls were young at Nylontex. The boss and his son liked young women, they took advantage of them . . . sexually; . . . the son and his cousins took off with the workers, wealthy young men, and no one said anything—it was normal. It was a nylon factory, with machines. I worked packaging stockings. I liked the work OK, but not the repression. They got you out of the bathroom fast, "Hey, Isabel, you've been in there 10 seconds already," and so forth. We were young and liked to fool around so when the boss was not there we chatted; we had snacks secretly under the table; . . . a compa and I were sharing an apple one day . . . and a supervisor watching from behind suspended me for one day. Maybe if the wages had been decent and the managers not sexually abusive that would not have made me so mad, but it did; it was the whole package.

Low-wage, repressive industrial growth, as well as an existential chasm between the working-class self and national growth, led Isabel and others to listen to the clear, constant messages of the guerilla groups, which by the 1970s advocated revolutionary change instead of a return to the 1944–54 reformism. In 1973, when Isabel was sixteen and her son Andrés one, rising world oil prices triggered the beginning of an economic crisis. Angered by sudden inflation and encouraged by the regional social imaginary of revolutionary change, by the mid-1970s workers; professionals; and university, high school, and even primary school students were organizing in Guatemala City. The state and elites increased terrorism against unions, strikes, occupations, and demonstrations that by then shared one name: *el movimiento popular y revolucionario* (the people's revolutionary movement). The 1976 earthquake aggravated conflict with its classed consequences: well-built homes survived, but the majority fell; 22,000 primarily poor citizens (or some other noun) lost their lives; and companies such as Nylontex actually docked workers for their absence in the days following the quake. Isabel feels that her "youth ended with the earthquake," because, she says, "I was beginning to understand what was what," and she joined the fast-paced visionary urban labor movement (Levenson-Estrada 1994). A new consciousness of reality, and not, as in María's mind, uniting with a man, ended a youth that Isabel thought was "stupid" after she became an advocate for herself and others.

Inside a new subculture, Isabel joined others to fight injustice and "materialistic values in favor of the moral, the people." Withstanding sexism in the labor movement, this "well-behaved" daughter of a strong mother self-consciously took the identity of a strong activist. As Isabel explains, the movement: "gave me a true significance, something to *really* do for the first time. My mother totally opposed this. She said, 'they will get you; they will pull out your tongue, cut off your feet,' which was possible, but I could not leave the union. I liked it—it was my life, my only formation." Isabel worked twelve hours a day, six days a week at Nylontex until 1978, when she got a job at the new, Japanese-owned ACRICASA textile plant, where she helped organize a union composed primarily of young women. In 1979, these workers occupied and threatened to blow up the factory unless the company signed a union contract, which it quickly did. However, the state tried to destroy this union and others in the city. In June 1980, three young female ACRICASA union leaders, one of whom was pregnant, were kidnapped, never to reappear; in the months that followed almost all the unions in the city disappeared, along with hundreds of activists. Isabel chose to replace one of the missing women on the union executive committee. She said she was "that mad." She did not retreat from her identity or her friends when civil war engulfed Guatemala. In 1984, the Coca-Cola Workers Union broke the silence of repression in the city by seizing the plant to stop it from closing, and Isabel joined in. When a handful of workers formed a new labor federation in 1985, Isabel was present. When women formed a women's group, Isabel was involved, and she remained active at ACRICASA, despite the union's fragility.

After both Andrés and Isabel's second son, René, moved out of the apartment that she and María still share, Isabel moved into one room of it, painted the walls orange and the ceiling sky blue because she had long wanted a room, "not for a boyfriend, just a place for me, just that." In 2000, ACRICASA laid off workers and Isabel lost her job. She used her severance pay to take secretarial classes. Unable to find any subsequent secretarial employment, she started selling cosmetics door to door, but she wanted to be with "interesting, involved" people, and she found her way to a new peasant organization wherein she gave leadership training to women throughout the country. However, the European funding that maintained the organization and her paid job within it dried up in 2008. She has applied for work in nongovernmental projects, though a sharp turn for the worse in María's health has obliged Isabel to remain home tending to her mother and receiving financial support from her sons. Frustrated by being turned into a stay-at-home woman, she recently commented: "Thank God my mother is getting better, but I am getting crazier by the day!"

Andrés and René

The first memories of Isabel's sons, Andrés and René, are angry ones of her departures, either to go work or to go to political meetings. Their grandmother drove them "crazy," but both sons remembered María, not Isabel, as a protective figure. Andrés said that "Abuela [María] was dominating, authoritarian, and fought with my mother about attending political meetings, but she did a good job raising us." What that meant was keeping René and Andrés fed, clothed, off the streets, and in school.

Andrés and René grew up in an even more dangerous world than had Isabel—one without optimism, protest, or dreams of a better Guatemala. For most of the boys' childhoods, city residents lived in fear and horrific suspense. In 1980, when René was five and Andrés eight, the three young women from Isabel's union were among twenty-seven trade unionists kidnapped on one day alone in the city; such was the nerve-shattering state of affairs. Andrés recalls worrying, "Why wouldn't my mother be next, or next after next?" By 1982, it was common in the city for soldiers and tanks to rush to blow up "safe-houses," and news of military massacres in the countryside began to arrive. When René was nine and Andrés twelve, their mother was busy taking risks in order to support the Coca-Cola workers' yearlong plant occupation, which the boys visited. Two years later, traveling by bus with María on their first trip outside the city, they saw soldiers beat and remove passengers at a roadblock. A year or so after that, the military had all but defeated the guerrillas in the countryside after destroying hundreds of villages and tens of thousands of lives, and it returned the country to civilian rule after slicing civilians and civilian institutions to pieces.

The Guatemalan military did not destroy the urban public schools, and within the schools they attended, the boys found a sense of structure during the 1980s. With the destruction of left-wing teacher and student organizations, school became the single "stable," "normal" location for city youth. Furthermore, interest in education increased.[16] The familiar tune that education was the way to get ahead had new meaning to those whose aspirations to end poverty had been blown to bits; now the only way out of poverty seemed to be individual mobility. The ideology of neoliberalism held that achievement meant moving up the ladder within the status quo of inequality. Blood had overwhelmed the discourse of el pueblo as powerful and of capitalism as unnatural, evil, and changeable. Reality was reality; nothing would change.

Isabel was adamant that her sons graduate high school, and in 1985 she increased her overtime to ensure that her sons would not waste homework time with part-time jobs. School was important to the brothers, who thought it the key to employment and security. After finishing his secondary school education, Andrés continued at El Instituto Nacional en Computación because, he explains: "Computers are everything, everywhere—that's the skill to have! . . . I wanted to get a good professional job. I didn't want my mother supporting me." Andrés had not been inspired intellectually by any of his public school teachers and sought out the educational route that he felt was most practical. René, on the other hand, had an older teacher in primary school whose pedagogical style drew on Liberation Theology and Ivan Illich. She was committed to teaching empowerment through meaningful skills, and René responded strongly to her style. He recalls:

I liked school, schooling is very important. The school was ordinary, but I had a wonderful teacher; she demanded a lot. She was interested in me. I was a very good student. She did projects, like a painting contest and starting a class newspaper. It had only three pages, but we wrote the articles. I had her from the time I was seven until eleven. We started the paper when I was seven; . . . we kept it going. We sold it for a little more than cost—we were a cooperative. We started parties to replay national politics. She had a lot of ideas like a savings account; the students lent money to the parents. This was very important for me; . . . it held my life together and gave me direction . . . I see her sometimes. I almost invited her to the wedding, but I definitely will invite her to my university graduation. I was an achiever in school: on my own. I won a scholarship to the Colegio Americano [considered the city's best]. I didn't go. I was stupid not to, but all the other students there had money and what would I have? Also they had no accounting degree; there was no useful degree for me. It is all college preparatory . . . My mother never knew. I didn't think it was such a big deal then. I don't know what she would have thought. And I thought maybe they did it just for publicity. Scholarships for the poor!

At age fifteen René felt trapped between class "realism" and striving for a university degree. He needed to play it safe and get an accounting degree—which he did—and not go into a college preparatory track; on the other hand, he was "obsessed with getting a university education." He decided not to accept a private school scholarship because of the challenges he would face as a working-class kid from Zone 7 in a school of wealthy kids; he says he had "pride, and hated the paternalism of a scholarship."

The brothers led conservative lives. They went to *quinceañeras* (girls' fifteenth-birthday parties, similar to "sweet sixteen" celebrations in the United States) and family birthdays, but rarely to movies or clubs. Their visits to prostitutes were a convention of which María and Isabel approved because "better a prostitute than someone's daughter."[17] Although Andrés played soccer as a child in the 1970s, by the 1980s the brothers stayed inside because the street brought "problems." Television became ubiquitous in that decade. Isabel acquired one, and, starting at the ages of eight and eleven respectively, René and Andrés watched it every day. Their memories of TV lack devotion to any show or star. They watched TV, period: reruns from the United States, Mexican soap opera, news sponsored by the Guatemalan Army, static. They watched from boredom, the new youth disease.

In contrast to street youth, René and Andrés emphasize, they were "tranquil," distant from involvements. Andrés says he was "pretty old fashioned . . . I didn't drink. My friends were schoolmates; . . . the kids on the block were thieves—mareros, the breks[18]—who said I was an anti-brek and bourgeois. That was all about clothes. They dressed in fancy jeans, name-brand tennis shoes, colors. I dressed neatly, simply. I wasn't an anti-brek, because the anti-brek are bourgeois who have cars and belong to the upper class. Mareros were poor. I didn't have money, but they picked fights with me. They fought dirty . . . I didn't like the streets." The mareros or breks had style writ large. Informed by the global youth look (and taking their name from break dancing), youth who joined the new maras rejected the clothes of the poor in favor of expensive, name-brand styles. Resentment toward a new street pride from the "lowly poor" and the appropriation of brands like Reebok and Levi led upper-middle-class youth to form the anti-breks to which Andrés refers. Andrés and René defined themselves against all that "other," whether brek or anti-brek. The brothers were barrio youth who took the "high road" on their way to being men with jobs, resisting alcohol, fashion, drugs, and extra women. Encouraged by the values of hard work and family that María had tried to inspire in her grandchildren, Andrés and René chose responsibility and respectability, even if these were dull and difficult. Exploring the city—or being really of the city instead of being of their home, family, and schools—did not appear desirable.

The city had become a very scary place. Buses were not only rundown; in addition, teenage thieves preyed upon passengers and drivers. By the time the boys were in their teens, Zone 7 had over 128,000 residents, slightly fewer than the city's population when María first arrived there. By the late 1980s, Zone 7 had unisex salons, CD and video stores, a Wendy's, acupuncturist and therapist offices, Evangelical churches, pharmacies, maquiladoras, bars, cheap restaurants, pizza and ice-cream parlors, furniture and auto supply stores, gas stations, and even two malls. Modern commerce went on everywhere, but without the glamour and sparkle of the late 1930s and 1940s. Over one-half of Zone 7 residents lived below the United Nations poverty line. Zone 7 had a bad reputation and few centers of sociability; Zone 1 had become the poor people's hangout. The noise and smoke of Isabel's youth were epidemic by the 1980s, and this old Centro was now the center of headaches and colds. It was a strain to talk in a cafe over the sound of vehicles. The sky was invisible and everything opaque: the corner restaurant might be a front; counterfeit dollars could be bought in the movie theater's bathrooms. La Sexta, where María loved to promenade as a girl, was itself invisible behind the neon signs jutting out over it.

Few spaces existed in the city outside of home and school for "good" youth from poor families. Boredom, confinement, fear of the unknown, the silenced past, new politics without definition, the demise of the movimiento popular y revolucionario and of a language of class—all of this conspired to leave René and Andrés in a difficult situation, one which they could only counter with their own individual initiatives and connections. Many teenagers joined Evangelical churches precisely to protect themselves from the pitfalls of working-class life, including drinking, sexual abuse, and drugs. Some entered the gangs, where all of these violations flourished in collective forms. Many others, like Andrés and René, focused on achieving dreams such as marriage with a virgin, a church wedding, home ownership, professional work, and intellectual achievement. At nineteen Andrés married a young woman. He could not find work in computers, so Isabel found him a job at Coca-Cola before the birth of his first child through her old union ties. It was a relationship, not education, that landed him his job. Coca-Cola was one of the few workplaces to have a union, and therefore offered reasonable pay and benefits. Andrés supported the union and attended its meetings, but in kind with the few unions that survived and with most Guatemalans in the 1990s, Andrés was not political. By the time he was twenty, his aims included buying one house for Isabel and María, and another, "my own house, for my family, to have a decent life." His job was difficult. He delivered Coca-Cola in an area in Zone 7 that was (and is) controlled by maras that had by then become dangerous, and every day he had to negotiate to protect himself, his helper, and the armed guard on the back of the truck by paying a "war tax" and even hiring mareros on occasion to help load empty bottles and unload full ones. After he worked there almost a decade, the company laid him off to avoid paying certain benefits. He now plans to emigrate temporarily in order to work, and return home with enough savings to buy a used truck and haul sand to construction sites, having witnessed the current explosion in home and apartment building funded by drug and arms money. The global economy and the national lack of workers' rights define his paths to securing a livelihood.

His brother's situation is similar, but it is framed by what René describes as his "new class status." René and his wife, a bilingual secretary, lived for years in a modest apartment near Isabel and María. With his diploma in accounting, René worked over fifty hours a week as an accountant for a well-known multinational company and studied four evenings a week to graduate from the prestigious Jesuit Universidad Rafael Landívar. After graduation, he landed a well-paying job in another multinational company and moved to another neighborhood and into another lifestyle in which he could afford to send his only child to Colegio Monte María, the city's best private school for girls. René became a supporter of a centrist political party, whose candidate in 1999 was in René's words "smart, a Landivarista." Self-identified as part of the professional class, René reads the paper regularly, stays informed about national politics, and opposes right-wing politicians, who are "criminals and assassins." René supports unions, but he feels that his mother made a mistake. He explains that when he was young he thought that "she was doing the right thing—helping the poor. Later I realized staying poor is one's own fault. No one is going to improve oneself except oneself. Who gains most works the hardest. She could have done other things. She could have studied, had a career, she could have earned more with a career . . . Maybe my abuela couldn't, but my mother could have become more."

René's view that his mother could have been "more" represents an important transformation in some males' attitudes toward females, because he means more than a housewife as well as more than a militant. But René's sense of more is also a retreat from the more that Isabel became. In her late teens Isabel fought for social justice in Guatemala, when the possibility to do so existed. No doubt predisposed to activism by her mother's steady example of marching forward against all odds, Isabel was among an urban minority that took history into its hands. Isabel became the "most" and the "best" a working-class woman could be—a labor activist. The ideas René has adopted inhibit him from seeing how large Isabel became in the city's and in her personal, gendered history. On the other hand, following in his mother's determined footsteps, René tirelessly takes advantage of historical possibilities through the power of education and money.

Being More

Modern twentieth-century achievements—decreases in child labor and infant mortality and quantitative increases in education—are visible inside the Cruz-López family history. Amidst these modern advancements, wealthy Guatemalans increasingly travel abroad to study, play, and work in elite environments. Children of the city's working poor, however, have lost spaces—places to shop and stroll (see Véliz and O'Neill, this volume), even cheap dance halls. The majority of youth are confined to the home, school, and the church unless they take to the streets, or as more and more do, travel across borders without documents.

In their different searches for more emancipated existences, María, Isabel, René, and Andrés have always thought that life is up to them. Their urban *desde abajo* (from below) modernity has taken shape as a renovating spirit and creative drive, as each has tried to avoid the terrible stagnant predicaments of the city. No constant, warm-hued landscapes or wide communities nurtured them. Even the blessings of school, the third generation's steadiest institution, for René revolved around just one teacher. This family's protagonists are modern individualists, who do not climb over people or hurt themselves to survive. María made decisions to leave situations that wounded her. "Reality" did not make these decisions obligatory. She kept on "keeping on" with a life that belonged to her and not to her birth family, ethnicity, or men. In her youth, "all that was solid melted into air" and there she was, alone (Berman 1988). She is conventional—she wanted a wedding, a white dress, a husband—but not at any price. María sought freedom and autonomy in the life-or-death way.

Isabel's youth was defined by her mother. But there came a point when she took her life into her own hands to join a union, which amounted to putting her life in jeopardy given the political situation at the time. Trade unionism in Guatemala City was not sponsored by the state or by a political party; it was not that type of modernity. It was a modernity desde abajo. Inspired by Liberation Theology, common sense, and Marxism, it was a "cognitive praxis" in which self and society were imagined anew (Eyerman and Jamison 1991). She found an identity that she has maintained despite the fact that spaces for organizing are today small and almost apolitical. Influenced by the example of her mother's strength in solitude, Isabel has nourished her female activist identity.

Gender, rectitude, and anger are important elements in these stories. Sexual assault and gender-specific humiliations and tasks did not oblige María and Isabel to become fighters; rather, such experiences created painful emotional conflicts that they felt they had to resolve. They made the city safe for themselves, and they have enjoyed their lives. Discovering one's own transformative power has been harder for Andrés and René, and their options have narrowed in "peacetime." However, they have not slipped into a sense of masculinity defined by the power of violence, as many others have, and they try hard to secure safety for themselves and their families in the city. With subjectivities informed by warm relationships and modernist hopes, the Cruz-

López family is more than what surrounds them. That this is so at least makes imaginable a different Guatemala City.

Notes

1. In the late 1990s, the homicide rate in Guatemala City was the third highest in Latin America, after Medellín and Bogotá, Colombia. See, e.g., "La tercera ciudad más peligrosa de Latinoamérica," *Siglo 21*, July 24, 1999. In 2004, at least one person in 42 percent of the city's households reported being a victim of crime, and by 2007 a full 56 percent of all Guatemalans lived below the United Nations designated poverty line (Torres 2008:1–11).

2. Those who live in wealthy gated areas in the city do not escape crime. They are kidnapped for ransom, their homes are robbed, and their cars are stolen from even well-guarded parking areas.

3. In contrast to many towns in Guatemala, in Guatemala City, ladinos are not empowered as a group.

4. All quotations from the Cruz-López family are from taped oral histories that I conducted between 1998 and 2005.

5. The bus did not stop. The driver's helper pulled passengers aboard as the bus slowed down.

6. Cerro del Carmen still is a park on a hill with a church on top. Once a popular Sunday spot for picnics and family portraits taken by ambulant photographers against elaborate painted backdrops of Paris or Lima, it is currently dangerous.

7. For different reasons, a few elite families, members of the middle class, schoolteachers, and artisans plotted against Ubico in the early 1940s. A coalition overthrew Ubico in 1944. The left-wing artisans and the feminists who formed the Alianza Feminista and advocated day care centers and communal kitchens for women in factories did not address the problems of domestics.

8. Ubico had constructed a new National Congress, Supreme Court, and National Police buildings, among others.

9. Charlie Chaplin's *Modern Times* played in Teatro Lux. Few conservatives would have taken offense at Chaplin's critique of industrial production lines.

10. This was an artisans' mutual aid society formed in the late 1800s. By the 1930s, it provided insurance, night classes, and a social center that was considered respectable.

11. *Diario de Centro América*, October 12, 1938. The English programs had extraordinary English texts for students to memorize. One ran, "If it should attack, kill it. It would be better to kill it. What should you do if he should disappear? I should find him." *Diario de Centro América*, November 20, 1935.

12. *Nosotros, los pobres* (1948) was the most famous film in a trilogy directed by Ismael Rodríguez, and it was probably the most viewed movie in twentieth-century Mexico.

13. Because Guatemala lacked a sufficient internal market, and this due to the sort

of modernization it had already experienced, industrial development happened under the auspices of the Central American Common Market. This accord gave Guatemala access to the regional middle-class and upper-class consumer market to which industrial development was geared.

14. This was both María's and Isabel's explanation of why the daughters attended an Evangelical school.

15. Colom was assassinated in 1979.

16. The first civilian president after the war, the Christian Democrat Marco Vinicio Cerezo placed emphasis on education rather than social reform as the number one solution to poverty. Most nongovernmental groups and international agencies such as the Inter-American Development Bank have done this as well.

17. Mothers often gave sons money to visit prostitutes. The idea that prostitutes were not "daughters," i.e., did not come from good homes, was common; moreover, not being a "daughter" indicated that the prostitute's family was unknown and therefore not a threat in the case of pregnancy. Needless to say, even though the male right to go to prostitutes was respected, prostitutes were not.

18. *Mareros* and *breks* were terms used interchangeably in the 1980s to refer to the new gangs of that period whose members danced brek (United States break dancing) among other activities. The sole purpose of the "anti-breks" was to beat up or try to beat up the breks.

Primero de Julio

Urban Experiences of
Class Decline and Violence

Manuela Camus

Amid unprecedented postwar violence, the people of Primero de Julio, an urban neighborhood on the outskirts of Guatemala City, have experienced *desclasamiento* (loss of class distinction), a social phenomenon resulting from the failure of the authoritarian state's postwar structural adjustment policies and plans for development. Once considered the site of Guatemala City's emerging middle class in the 1960s and 1970s, Primero de Julio is now a space of institutional neglect, a locale where the men and women of this neighborhood have become the objects and agents of violence. As their neighborhood becomes just one more dangerous place in the capital city, older generations lament the loss of class status. Forms of social solidarity based on nationalism, class standing, and ideologies of progress and change that were previously meaningful for them have fragmented in recent decades. Youth in the neighborhood, who see few viable employment options and a growing organized crime and gang presence, often search for social and economic resources at the very border between legal and illegal activities. Loss of class standing in Primero de Julio mixes all too well with new forms of physical and symbolic violence.

For neighborhood residents, neoliberal reforms—which have contributed to the process of desclasamiento—and postwar violence—which is partly a response to forms of institutional neglect and socioeconomic insecurities—are interrelated at the level of social experience. Everyday experience, however, is often interpreted by residents in light of long-standing discriminatory attitudes toward the country's indigenous population and the poor. Residents of Primero de Julio blame their neighborhood's youth—more specifically, its indigenous, poor, and marginalized youth—for the problems that now render their everyday lives precarious. This essay examines how neighborhood residents understand and come to terms with desclasamiento. It also explores how residents' responses to increasing violence and insecurity in the neighborhood are influenced by Guatemala's extensive history of discrimination and social inequality, and how these responses are shaped in relation to the state's failure to address current conditions.[1]

The Diverse Generations of Primero de Julio

Primero de Julio began as a public housing project for lower-class Guatemalans and is now one of the most densely populated neighborhoods in the metropolitan area of Guatemala City. Inspired by a United States–fueled economic boom, 5,000 housing units were constructed in the neighborhood in 1966 with financing from the Inter-American Development Bank. It was a star project—the largest of its kind in Central America—and would include health and educational services and green areas.

Compared to the urban disorder of adjacent neighborhoods, Primero de Julio was to be a refuge of hygiene and social sanitation. The project, however, had its limitations and contradictions. For example, the neighborhood was sixteen kilometers from the city center yet lacked parking areas for cars, the symbol of middle-class success par excellence. The speed of construction was also rushed. Guatemala's president laid the first stone on August 9, 1966. Only eleven months later, he inaugurated 2,187 houses that had been built in 120 business days. The pace of the construction—an average of eighteen houses per day—suggests the quality of construction. Primero de Julio also bordered lower-class neighborhoods, all of which had different histories and an "inferior" status as a result of their social composition. These were (and continue to be) poor areas of marked ethnic and racial hybridity. By all accounts, Primero de Julio was from the very beginning an uneven effort at modernity.

Even before the massive construction project began, the area was inhabited by various ladino (nonindigenous) Guatemalans and immigrants from other Central American countries. Yet despite the diversity of origins, those who called Primero de Julio home in the 1950s and early 1960s fit a common profile. They were mostly young families whose heads of household were roughly thirty years old. They were "hardworking, healthy people," as those from the neighborhood like to say about previous generations. The majority of them worked for the state, but there were also salaried businessmen and workers in industrial plants such as Coca-Cola or Cervecería Centroamericana (the Central American Brewing Company). Above all, Primero de Julio consisted of people who aspired to be middle class. They were professionals who worked hard for a living while also cultivating a sense of belonging and identity that facilitated social networks and communication within the neighborhood setting.[2] They were a social sector that participated in what many social scientists would call the illusion of modernity and believed themselves to be the beneficiaries of social change, progress, and development.

This first generation in Primero de Julio did not assume that theirs would be an easy future. Rather, they tended to conceive of their lives in terms of struggle and sacrifice, viewing the world as a highly competitive place with an unsteady economy. In this sense, entry into Primero de Julio became an opportunity to participate in upward social mobility, to become part of an "emerging middle class" (Camus 2005). They grew up under the dictatorial regime of Jorge Ubico (1931–44) and came of age in the decade of "The Revolution" (1944–54). In many ways, it was during this era that Guatemalans began to urbanize as well as understand themselves for the first time as social actors. They developed an elemental sense of citizenship, a shared ideology of advancement through education — as manifested in the doctrine of "humanist socialism" espoused by President Juan José Arévalo. And they embraced the sense of social distinction that came with being "lettered" and "educated," which for them also meant "civilized." The urban modernity that these residents sought was imagined in contrast to their own origins as lower or middle-class mestizos or campesinos. Correspondingly, they associated "being modern" with being middle class and expressed themselves in a nationalist yet distinctly Catholic discourse of equality. This meant, somewhat predictably, that Primero de Julio's first generation extolled the virtues of work, honesty, and family unity.

A "second generation" of residents came of age after the counterrevolution of 1954. The members of this generation saw themselves as urban and educated. They were products of the 1960s and 1970s, which meant that they endured the authoritarian modernization brought about by state militarization and economic dependence on the United States. The military, backed by the United States, justified its own rise to power in terms of a staunch anticommunist position. The heavy hand of the military led many citizens to embrace revolutionary change and declare war on the Guatemalan state. As students, the members of this and the following generation became politicized with a demanding sense of citizenship that was more radical than that of their pre-decessors.

The "third generation," those who reached adulthood at the end of the 1970s and during the 1980s, comprised children of Primero de Julio's first generation. This group was supposed to enjoy the privileges of modernity that their parents had worked hard to secure. Their worlds, however, would be turned upside down by the internal armed conflict and the difficult period of structural adjustment that would characterize the postwar period. Today, during interviews, the majority of residents no longer subscribe to an idea of progress or change—not by way of education, migration to the United States, reform, or revolution. This third generation came of age in an environment in which one worked to lift oneself out of poverty, without looking to state institutions or grand narratives of social advancement for assistance or in-spiration. They identify more with the politics and policies of the postwar era than with any ideals of modernization or revolutionary ideas that might have defined earlier decades.

In all, the first generation had received a very formalist and mass-based education, one which nonetheless allowed for the production of solidarity and friendship, as residents saw themselves as a cohort of equally educated citizens. Those who continued on to higher education attended the public uni-versity, where students worked while they studied. Following a near-idyllic childhood in the neighborhood and its educational institutions, as adults they faced revolutionary outbursts in Central America and a cruel polariza-tion: either fall in line with the official regime or face repression, violence, and bloodshed along with the other insurgents. Primero de Julio, in turn, produced both leftist militants and members of the national security forces. During the 1970s and 1980s, the neighborhood saw attempts against the lives of *judiciales* and high-ranking police officers,[3] as well as abductions of local union members. As guerrilla factions established safe homes in the commu-nity, trucks carried young people away to the Adolfo V. Hall Military Academy.

After the signing of the Peace Accords in 1996, the ideological struggles that had marked previous decades diminished; however, the violence did not. A new form of "internal" violence began, one that originated from within the neighborhood and surrounding areas. Residents viewed the postwar state as unequivocally corrupt and disinterested in their social sector. The implemen-tation of structural adjustment policies, which included the privatization of state services, radically modified Primero de Julio and its living conditions. The principles of the entire economy shifted, creating a situation of widespread unemployment and limited social mobility and prompting international migration (Pérez Sáinz and Mora Salas 2007: 46). Low pay and lack of opportunities, social services, and security have typified the last two decades. The effects of these developments on poor youth in the neighborhood and surrounding areas have included the formation of youth gangs and the rebellious and rather public donning of gang-related tattoos. In the postwar period, Primero de Julio quickly entered a state of precariousness.

Javier Auyero's comparative exploration of neoliberalism in the French *banlieue* and the *villas* of Buenos Aires is helpful for understanding urban spaces such as Primero de Julio. In these spaces, one finds the "diminishing of social networks, a decrease in the working-class and organizational capacities along with an increase in the informalization of the local economy, and lastly, an increase in day-to-day violence, the illegal drug trade, and repressive state measures against the poor" (2001: 24–25). Auyero emphasizes that this process causes new (or reconfigured) expressions of violence and fear, and, as Manfred Liebel explains, "The increase in violence is not only a consequence of poverty, but has its origins in the growing social inequality that leads many people to feel that they are being treated unjustly. Moreover, it creates desperation and anger" (2004: 99). These authors provide a fitting description of how everyday life has changed for the residents of Primero de Julio. The public schools that had once been the pride of the neighborhood are now filled with children who arrive from surrounding areas. These children are usually of a lower economic class, and many are indigenous. Viewing the schools within the community as having lost their status as quality institutions, many residents now send their children to private schools. Those who go on to study at Guatemala's public university feel disillusioned because of the university's loss of prestige,[4] by the devaluation of their degrees, and by high levels of unemployment. Most university students (from Primero de Julio but from other places as well) do not finish their degrees due to family commitments, economic difficulties, or disappointment with the lack of employment opportunities (Camus 2005: 252). While many men and women from Primero de Julio continue to pride themselves on producing university-trained professionals, the community no longer does so.[5]

As social mobility has declined, the lines between legal and illegal work have become blurred.[6] Now, illegal dealings in contraband, drug trafficking, forging documents, selling stolen goods, kidnapping, robbery, and prostitution have become commonplace in the neighborhood. Youth live under the disapproving gaze of adults who feel that the young people have broken away from the model lives of hard work and education set forth by previous generations. Those of the older generations, who see themselves as "healthy, hardworking, and honorable people," are confused by the lifestyles and seeming lack of values among the new generation. At the same time, youth in Primero de Julio have little in common with those who lived through the ideological struggles and state violence of the war years. They are much more interested in consumption and global trends and much more preoccupied with the new forms of violence in the neighborhood linked to the processes of exclusion described above. In turn, youth are blamed by the older generations as well as politicians and the media for Guatemala's current social problems (see Benson, Thomas, and Fischer, this volume).

Members of the community describe the neighborhood today as "decadent." They see signs of degradation, impoverishment, and violence all around them. There has been an observable decline in the community's status and in the sources of its previous distinction, including the privileges of a valued education and professionalization, salaried positions, and ideals of citizenship such as equality and respect. The general feeling is that the neighborhood has changed, and not for the better. According to a woman born and raised in Primero de Julio, "My father used to say that we belonged to the middle class, but now we don't." What was formerly "a family neighborhood" is no more. Many of the neighborhood's original families have now left, renting homes elsewhere. As a result, "the neighborhood isn't what it used to be. It was very united before, but now you don't know what kind of people are living next door," said a schoolteacher and member of Primero de Julio's first generation.

The Language of Violence

The idea of delinquency—which refers to youth, especially young men, out of control—is a common explanation for Guatemala City's new violence.[7] This general trend finds particular expression in Primero de Julio. The neighborhood's young men have gone from being their community's hope (e.g., in the 1950s) to being understood as a threat and a danger. In the 1990s, men and women understood those who disrupted Primero de Julio's tranquility as "intruders from the outside," yet it is now evident to residents that the neighborhood has created its own criminals. More people can identify the muggers, drug dealers, vagrants, and those deported from the United States to Guatemala on felony charges as having come from Primero de Julio. Guatemala's recent surge in violence related to transnational gang circuits and drug trafficking is difficult for people to come to terms with and to understand. Searching for an explanation, they resort to the term *delinquency*, casting the violence in moral terms. A retired teacher commented, "We were a group that arrived with other principles. The children grow up now and they have a different upbringing and they have broken away from a sense of mutual respect and community." Another middle-aged woman added:

> Those of us who live here in Primero de Julio had the opportunity to study more and to overcome more economic obstacles, if you will. The people who lived in La Florida [a nearby neighborhood] were a little more humble, like people from a small town. The bad thing is that the children of these people who at first weren't bad ended up in gangs because of the bad people that influenced them, and now those people are coming over here. Now, the kids from here and the kids from other places have been corrupted. There is no longer much differentiation between economic levels.

This particular woman, as one reads in her comments, has internalized this loss of class standing. She does not blame outside forces entirely but rather suggests that today's youth, a lost generation in her view, have caused the violence and economic insecurity that she experiences.

Young people in Primero de Julio refer more frequently to *la mara* (the gang) than to "Guatemala" or "Guatemalans," whereas terms that expressed a sense of nationalistic solidarity were common among preceding generations. Now, phrases such as *la mara de pisto* (the rich gang), *la mara honrada* (the "honorable" gang), *la mara grande* (the big gang), *la mara normal* (the everyday gang), Mara 18 (the Eighteenth Street Gang), *mara de chingadera* (the gang that fucks with you), or *el círculo de la mara* (the gang's inner circle) are ready at hand for neighborhood youth. These terms have become ways to identify oneself and to identify with others from the same generation. One of the characteristics that anthropologists and sociologists highlight when referring to contemporary urban youth culture is the fragmentation of a sense of community given the deterioration of social and family bonds. Young people today have invented new forms of collectivity and draw on new (or recycled) social categories, often based on aggressive forms of social distinction; they use classifiers that are often insulting or demeaning, casting other youth as inferior. In her analysis of how Guatemalan youths perceive society, María Cecilia Garcés de Mancilla (2003) evidences this social fragmentation and the ways that class and ethnic background shape how young people view those around them. Garcés identifies a number of terms that youth use to classify other people: *choleros, shumos, mucos, roqueros, trasheros, burgueses, fresas, caqueros, hippies, moteros, narcos, cholos.*[8] These terms connote various shades of class and ethnic distinction and are often drawn from the realms of music, politics, soccer, and religion. Among youth, these terms are used to discriminate, disqualify, racialize, demean, and classify the other.

Young people from Primero de Julio now interact more with the lower classes. As social distinctions between the neighborhood's inhabitants and those from surrounding areas dissolve, residents frequently become identified as *choleros, mucos,* or *shumos,* labels that connote lower class or social standing and ethnic difference. Many youths have close friends from poor families, some of whom are indigenous. They study and play together in the same classrooms and soccer fields. Many young people note that they have a vibrant social life within the Primero de Julio neighborhood: they share with their neighbors, visit one another, and go out together to dance, play soccer, or practice karate. At the same time, the increasing perception that those from the neighborhood are now on equal social footing with people from surrounding areas, with the poor, or with "Indians," creates tension in Primero de Julio. This new sense of equality intensifies feelings of lost class standing for the neighborhood's middle-class ladinos.

Drugs, Gangs, and the Indigenous

What had been an age of authoritarian modernization, professional aspirations, education, citizenship, and patriotic nationalism has given way to the rule of the marketplace. For those with sufficient means, consumption has become an important expression of class position, an opportunity to distinguish oneself socially even as opportunities for gainful employment are becoming scarce. Unemployment in Primero de Julio, which was almost nonexistent in the recent past, has become the norm. Underemployment and socioeconomic polarization are also on the rise. Young people in the neighborhood have much lower expectations for achieving work, sustaining a career, or achieving a comfortable middle-class existence than previous generations. Primero de Julio's present generation sits somewhere between the formal and informal economies as well as between modernity and a sense of failed expectations. And amidst this economic and existential instability, the men and women of Primero de Julio tend to rely on racist and classist ideologies to make sense of their changing world.

Although it is common to hear the term *delinquent* used as a broad label for youth in Guatemala, this category covers a wide range of lifestyles available to urban youth. In Primero de Julio, young people identify (and identify others) as *traideros* (flirts), *futboleros* (soccer players), *religiosos* (churchgoers), and *formales* (squares), among others. At the same time, there is an entire lexicon that can be applied to those who create problems in the neighborhood, including delinquents, drug dealers, gang members, and thieves. As one resident, a thirty-eight-year-old man and owner of a small business, noted: "Normally they don't steal in the neighborhood, but go elsewhere. They steal, con, or hold people up, which are three different things. Most of the gang members are kids. For example, those who con are guys my age or a little older. Those who hold people up are much younger than I am, maybe under twenty years old, thieves, pickpockets. And those who steal, maybe there you have all ages. Stealing is like going to an office and robbing it."

At a basic level, two relatively new and threatening models of delinquency have emerged from the neighborhood streets: *narcos* and *mareros* (drug dealers and gang members). Although these two groups have different aspirations, status, social origins, and "occupations," they communicate and intermingle in complex ways. Drug dealers and gang members are mutually antagonistic, yet interdependent. Drug-related activity tends to displace the gang members and thieves, but the thieves are useful for the sale and consumption of drugs or as *sicarios*, or hired killers. Primero de Julio is now a drug-distribution hub, which causes a great deal of violence: there are more than ten murders every year in the neighborhood due to internal disputes over territory or drug deals that have gone wrong. Maco, a young inhabitant of La Isla—a particularly impoverished part of Primero de Julio built on the edge of a ravine, from which many gang members originate—talks about the violence that characterizes gang activity in the neighborhood. "Today, there's a different type of problem here," he begins. "Now it's gang members that have their own businesses. Before, there was one here, El Chato, who killed a lot of gang members, but they got him back for it. El Chato was in the newspapers. He was the one they killed in the red blazer; they killed him with his mother or his grandmother for some dispute between drug dealers. He was leaving his house and they came by and shot him."

Another resident of Primero de Julio, Otoniel, discussed changes in the neighbors: "Suddenly they show up with jewelry, and you think, what's up with this guy? Where did he get it if before he was just as poor as we are? They look for their place and they get it." Otoniel is talking about drug dealers, who are sometimes socially integrated into the community as a certain kind of "businessman." The drug dealers are known by, are even friends of, other residents. Their cultural symbols are signs of middle-class status: cars, cellphones, sunglasses, nice clothing, and good taste in food and drink. Many drug dealers earn a certain degree of social status and respect from other residents of Primero de Julio, in part because of their participation in middle-class forms of consumption. In contrast, the mareros, or gang members, live in "marginal" areas. Still, gang graffiti is visible throughout the neighborhood. All of the interviewees could recognize those individuals belonging to Mara 18 or Mara de la Calle 20. The former, from La Isla, is large and marks its territory. The latter, as one resident said, "isn't as gang related" but rather "more involved in drugs." They are better dressed and more associated with the settling of accounts and their own self-protection.

The current context of violence and delinquency within and around Primero de Julio has led people to associate the ills of society with gang members. Moreover, a local common sense built on centuries of discrimination assumes that the young people who are causing the problems are indigenous. The fact that the indigenous population has long been cast as ignorant and uneducated by nonindigenous Guatemalans contributes to this sense, and in the areas in and around Guatemala City, the category "gang member" or "delinquent" generally assumes a poor, indigenous young person. As noted above, residents of Primero de Julio would have conceived of themselves historically as somewhat isolated from the surrounding lower-class neighborhoods with higher indigenous populations. The loss of both social and racial distinction that residents feel today converges with the popular idea that a racialized, poor, and uneducated population is the source of the problems that have entered the neighborhood.

People talk about gang members and drug dealers in the neighborhood as young people who have been "contaminated" and "damaged." These social types are assumed to have emigrated from rural areas, where the indigenous population is higher, and are said to have become accustomed to the easy life of "vagrancy" in the city. According to Remigio, a community resident:

There are a lot of murderers around the market in La Florida and Santa María. It's very dangerous there. Most of them are gang members. They don't work and they go out and assault people. Those people are no longer useful to society because they cause a lot of damage to humanity. The majority of those who come across the ravine are of indigenous origin. The people who work the land over there live well, but then they come over here and they get lost; here, others corrupt them and force them to take drugs. They contaminate them mentally and ruin them. You can tell they're indigenous people by their surnames and skin color.

Such statements reflect the powerful ways that historical divisions along class, race, and geographical lines shape the way that Guatemala's new violence is perceived in urban areas such as Primero de Julio.

Delinquency, then, is not simply a problem of youth getting "out of control," though this is a common expression. It is more precisely conceived of in terms of long-standing discriminatory attitudes toward indigenous people and a spatial logic that sees indigenous people as belonging to rural areas and nonindigenous (and therefore, so the logic goes, more educated, civilized, and cosmopolitan) people as rightfully belonging to the city. Luisa, a woman in her forties, put it this way:

Indigenous people are ruined when they come to the capital and they forget about where they came from, as if their eyes pop out of their heads with what they see here. I feel they don't go about things the way they ought to; rather, they go about them a different way. Indigenous people that come here are abusive. I'm not racist because I worked with the army. Imagine, 90 percent of the troops here in Guatemala are indigenous, but I've realized in the different places I've been to that the indigenous people are very different from those that live here in the capital. They come here and then open their minds and eyes to other things. At least, there are a lot of indigenous people in the gangs.

This argument corresponds to a classic dichotomy between city and country and between ladinos and indigenous people in Guatemala, with the indigenous imagined as coming from and belonging to rural Guatemala and ladinos understood as possessing a more urban culture (see O'Neill, this volume; Thomas, this volume). Luisa's comments participate in the mapping of urban violence onto indigenous men and women who are "out of place" in the capital city.

The Failure of the State

While most of the blame for Primero de Julio's problems falls on the backs of the city's poor, marginalized, and indigenous population, residents also feel that the state has not fulfilled its role as a protector and guarantor of rights, including public safety. According to the inhabitants of Primero de Julio, the state and its institutions are responsible for resolving conflicts and preventing violence. They expect the police, judges, and prisons to carry out these functions. Many residents have worked in state institutions such as schools and government agencies or at nongovernmental organizations, positions in which they saw themselves in part as agents of law, of "civilization," and of development. Yet the model of a liberal, democratic state promoted in these agencies and organizations is not working for them, and residents commonly feel a sense of abandonment as potential solutions seem harder and harder to come by. While many residents maintain a strong sense of communal identity within the neighborhood, there are no institutions in place to convert these feelings of solidarity into policies that address current problems.

Focused on the need for public safety, residents demand a heavy-handed government response. In spite of their generally leftist political views, the people of Primero de Julio want authoritarianism, the death penalty, and the militarization of security forces. One woman, for example, explained:

> I'm not going to have someone locked up. What for? So that in three days when that person is free they come looking for payback? I wouldn't be afraid, but I have children. Our society should be taking care of these problems, but unfortunately in Guatemala there is no justice. If I had finished my law degree, I think I would have been a judge in charge of executions: those who are sentenced to death should be executed. I'm in favor of the death penalty, first of all because they don't have mercy for anyone. And if you murder someone, you should die the same way, as in the law of "eye for an eye, tooth for a tooth"; it's just that easy. Actually, and may God forgive me for thinking this way, but this crime affects us so much, that if I could I would take all of these gang members and give them lethal injections, incinerate them, and put them in little boxes, because that way crime would go down a little in Guatemala.

Residents do not see any viable collective alternatives for controlling the rampant crime and violence in their neighborhood. Indeed, there are various obstacles to their collective organization. The sheer number of residents makes coordination difficult. Also, economic insecurities including unemployment and class decline contribute to a situation of transience in Primero de Julio. Every day, more and more houses are up for sale. And because it is a working-class neighborhood, people find it difficult to donate their time, and they cannot afford private security guards. The Neighborhood Association never provided an efficient organizational structure, and the existing local government (an auxiliary mayor) does not have the capacity to serve the needs of 18,000 people. There was an attempt by some residents to form a neighborhood watch with security patrols, but this did not gain widespread momentum, and the participants themselves became objects of suspicion. As one resident stated, "It was people who showed up to offer their services who said, 'look, we're going to protect the streets, we're going to circulate all night and blow our security whistles.' Some of them were from the neighborhood and some weren't. So they earned twenty quetzals or so a month [an exaggeration that implies "very little"], and they made the rounds. But people ended up saying that they were thieves and that they were going around controlling the neighborhood, not protecting it."

Owning a weapon has become a popular way to defend oneself and one's family, in much the same way as gun ownership exists as an ethic and ideology of personal and household protection in North America (O'Neill 2007). In fact, there are shopkeepers who have "liquidated" people who tried to rob them. One resident said, "A friend of mine says that he must have gotten the thief. He says that he heard some noises one night, but he had his gun and—" Another person explained, "I know a man who's an engineer, and to scare off thieves and prevent them from breaking into his house, every night he fires his gun—bang, bang, bang!—as if to say, 'here we are safe, we are protected.' In the streets of the neighborhood I've seen people with guns. There are definitely weapons out there." And an older storekeeper made a similar comment: "You hear gunshots all night long. I'm telling you, they shoot off a round— pow, pow, pow!—over here, later up there, then over there, and if you don't hear twenty shots in one night, you haven't heard anything."

Business owners and some private citizens also defend themselves by making deals with kids in the streets. These deals often create a vicious cycle in which criminal activities and violence are condoned and those who carry them out protected. For example, one youth who is a drug dealer in the neighborhood described how some neighbors protect him and his friends:

> They take care of us, I mean, I think if someone sees us hiding something and a policeman asks them about it they say, "No, sir. I didn't see anything." There's a certain amount of protection. One day, there was a big uproar in the street because some kids were selling drugs, and the police showed up and then about twenty women arrived and took the

kids back [he laughs] to their houses. So, yes, there is a certain amount of protection. For example, here in the Golfo Pérsico [they call part of the neighborhood "Persian Gulf" because of all the "chemicals"] they give us food. It's not a question of obligation nor is it very organized, but someone will say, "Shh, come here, come here." They might give you beans or chicken soup or anything. There's one woman there who keeps track of everything, and if you ask her she can tell you how many have died there.

Similarly, many shopkeepers prefer to pay a "tax" to neighborhood youth rather than risk attack or robbery. They give a small amount of money to gang members or offer them something from the store in exchange for promises that they will not be harassed, robbed, or assaulted.

Lynchings, which are most commonly associated with rural areas in Guatemala, have also been carried out in reaction to the violence. The following quote comes from a fifty-year-old shop owner:

There have been some nasty situations. There was one in the news a few days ago, where they beat a kid up. Some carjackers went over to La Isla thinking that they could get away, but the people that were around there grabbed them and beat them up. About six months ago, I was involved in a similar situation where some guys got beat up. There was such a commotion that people were getting out of their cars to see what was happening. I'd say there were 300 people there. The police and the firemen arrived, but they wouldn't have been able to do anything because 10 policemen against 300 is nothing. What happened was they had stolen a girl's watch, and she ran to tell her brother. The brother ran after the guys and as he ran, people asked him, "What's going on?" and he'd say, "There's a thief." More and more people joined him. It was on the outskirts of the neighborhood and the buses couldn't even get through because there were so many people. We're tired of having people steal in the neighborhood.

During my fieldwork, I came across many cases like this one that are not reported in the media. These cases normally involve beatings, but some end with the death of the supposed criminal. Lynching has been publicized and studied as an effect of the internal armed conflict—as part of Guatemala's postwar culture of violence and the state's actions against the indigenous population (Godoy 2006). Most of these studies focus on rural lynchings and do not at-

tend to the frequency with which lynchings take place in and around the capital city—those that have targeted pickpockets, gang members, rapists, and
carjackers.[9]

Residents of Primero de Julio see the state and its institutions of justice
and security as inadequate and even uninterested in the problems they face.
Corruption within the justice system, police force, and other official institutions is a serious problem, and one that makes addressing crime and violence
even more difficult. The police are accused, for example, of systematically participating in extrajudicial executions and being involved in criminal groups,
a situation that continues unresolved in spite of its thorough documentation
(Samayoa 2007; Solano 2007). There is total distrust of the police in Primero
de Julio as in other parts of the city and countryside. As one resident com-
plained: "I would throw out those lazy bums who are in the barracks and
police stations, getting fat, not doing anything to clean up areas overrun by
gangs. 'All right, whoever brings me the most heads of gang members will
receive a reward. Go out and kill them.' That would be one solution. Another
would be to clean up the police force. Change the budgets, for example. Take
away half of the budget from institutions that are worthless, that don't produce results." This person's comments question the competence of the police,
but do not question the authority of the institution or its role in "cleaning up"
the streets. Similarly, they do not question the causes of the crime and violence
that have overrun Primero de Julio; rather, they express a vague hope that one
day the state will do something to eradicate those who carry it out.

To whom do the members of the community and city dwellers in general
turn in order to address the problems of insecurity and violence that they
face? The adult population that came of age under the welfare state and military governments generally embraces institutional measures, yet such efforts
often end in frustration and desperation. Another segment of the population takes matters into its own hands, using personal firearms as protection
or forming alliances with gang members and drug dealers, tacitly accepting
their "authority." In other urban spaces, people form their own watch patrols.
These approaches are not mutually exclusive, and many of them contribute
to the establishment of "parallel legal systems" that attempt to fill the gap
left by the state's failures. The state, in turn, condones citizens' paralegal attempts at protecting themselves, in effect delegating to citizens the responsibility for their own safety. The fact that none of these responses is adequate
for addressing Guatemala's contemporary problems leads many to call for
a heavy-handed response. Politicians and government institutions play into

this desire for public safety by substituting old threats of guerilla combatants with new threats of drug trafficking, gangs, migration, and terrorism, in an attempt to justify a return to authoritarianism. This kind of response would most certainly target Guatemala's poor and indigenous populations, those who commonly, however unfairly, bear the blame for the country's (and especially Guatemala City's) problems. If Guatemala's past serves as an example, a militarized, authoritarian solution would not serve to improve the lives of Guatemala's citizenry. Although it may be difficult to imagine alternative solutions given the disrepute of state institutions and the absence of collective responsibility in contemporary Guatemala, new possibilities might emerge through the recuperation of shared life experiences and the formation of novel social pacts in communities such as Primero de Julio.

Guatemala City is one of the most violent spaces in one of the most violent countries in the world. Based on extensive fieldwork, this essay has attempted to approximate the concrete and historical experience of such instability and insecurity in Primero de Julio—a neighborhood that has experienced the loss of class status over several generations. The neighborhood ultimately serves as an example of what happens when urban violence meets uncertain economies and when the promise of modernity fades away alongside the retreat of state services. The result is a kind of insecurity that makes multiple generations question their place in the world as well as their immediate futures.

Notes

1. The basis of this investigation comes from Camus (2005) and was financed by the Norwegian Agency for Development and Cooperation (NORAD). The fieldwork was done in 2003 and 2004 and focused on documenting the everyday lives of Primero de Julio residents. The research consisted of formal and informal conversations, observations, and archival work with each of the generations detailed in this essay. I have continued communication with people from Primero de Julio through the present time. Additionally, I wish to thank the Center for Research on Inequality, Human Security, and Ethnicity (CRISE) of Oxford University for their support.

2. La Asociación de Vecinos (the Neighborhood Association) could have been a viable representative body, but the opportunity was lost. It came into being after the *Banco Nacional de la Vivienda* (National Housing Bank) received all of the payments for the houses. Although the community members received jurisdiction over the association, it became a mafia that controlled a significant part of the collective resources such as private parking lots and tax income from the markets. Attempts over the years by some of the neighbors to resuscitate it have proven unsuccessful. Recently, the municipality of Mixco has taken over administration of the neighborhood.

3. The judiciales were members of the police unit responsible for political repression.

4. La Universidad de San Carlos (USAC) has long been a vehicle of social mobility. In the 1970s, it became more common for students to work and study at the same time, especially as more affluent students began to attend the country's private universities. A division began to emerge between those who attended USAC—those who had to work and study—and those who attended private universities as full-time students. Those at USAC took much more time to finish their degrees than those at private universities and often did not finish at all. This process has led to USAC's loss of prestige within the Guatemalan context.

5. According to a survey conducted in the neighborhood, the majority of jobs (89 percent) held by those between the ages of thirty and forty-five (those who supposedly benefited from the state's modernization programs) are in the areas of manual labor and office work (see Camus 2005: 174–75).

6. Kessler (2004) proposes a similar idea when he describes the reality of Argentinean youths who, as a survival strategy, combine the logic of the workplace with robbery.

7. One could carry out a gender-focused reading of such explanatory models because they are generally focused on men and hide transformations in the world of women. However, in general across Guatemala, public and private spheres previously inhabited solely by men have been opening up to women. More specifically related to the present discussion, women have been taking jobs in paralegal spaces such as security forces and mafias in recent years. Women are now exposed to risks that used to be exclusively masculine. The fact that women are entering previously forbidden, masculine spaces can produce extreme reactions on the part of men, which may in part explain the rise in murders of women in Guatemala, a trend that some now label feminicide (Sanford 2008).

8. *Cholero*: used to designate lower-class, poor, or dark-skinned individuals as well as people without "taste." *Muco*: another insulting term similar to cholero, also associated with gang members. *Shumo*: a word with disrespectful connotations that may refer to the poor *chusma*, or riffraff, but also carries a clear ethnic content when applied to those with indigenous features. *Cholo*: closely associated with youth culture in Latino barrios in the United States, it refers to a gang member with a particular style of dress (baggy pants, chains, cap worn to one side) who is a fan of rap music. *Fufa, fufurufa, fresa, caquero, burguesit*: used by the lower classes to designate someone who is *de pisto*, or who puts on airs. The rest of the terms are self-explanatory as cognates.

9. Even though the data available from the Policía Nacional Civil are not reliable, according to Commission 16, which includes the police substation in Primero de Julio, there were 11 lynchings in 2007. According to a report by the Guatemalan Human Rights Ombudsman's Office, there were 17 people lynched, 60 attempted lynchings, and 113 people threatened with lynching nationwide in 2008. The department of Guatemala reported the most lynchings, with 53 percent of attacks occurring in urban areas.

Cacique for a Neoliberal Age

A Maya Retail Empire
on the Streets of Guatemala City

Thomas Offit

Don Napo took me to the best restaurant I have ever been to in Guatemala. He invited me to lunch, so we left his shoe kiosk on the corner of 18 Calle and Sexta Avenida in Zone 1, got into his van, and drove into Zone 10 of the capital. We parked on a small side street and proceeded on foot to the restaurant. We were both wearing T-shirts and jeans, looking like we belonged more to the sidewalks of El Centro than the cafes of Zona Viva. We were accompanied by his wife and eight young men, his relatives who were also his employees, varying in age from eleven to twenty-three. We walked in a small glass door and proceeded down a mirrored hallway until we were greeted by a maître d' and a coterie of formally clad waiters. As they escorted us to our table, many of the other diners looked up from their meals at us, this strange underdressed group entering their lunchtime lair of starched tablecloths and shining silverware. Don Napo did not act uneasy and seemed to know some of the staff members; he was in a well-traveled space—for him, if not for me. We settled into our table, and Don Napo ordered lunch for the entire group. The waiter brought us our drinks and, soon after, an elaborate salad with spinach leaves, bacon bits, and a silver decanter of dressing. We dressed our salads, and I picked up my knife and fork to dig in. Don Napo grasped three or four of the broad spinach leaves in his hand, then folded them in half; he scooped up some dressing, bacon bits and a tomato, and ate them. It was an extraordinary beginning to an extraordinary meal with an extraordinary man.[1]

Don Napo eats salad the way he eats tortillas and beans, and he does so in some of the best restaurants in Guatemala City. He owns and runs a very successful retail shoe business based in the streets of the capital, a job that requires that he be comfortable in Zone 10 eateries and the sidewalks of 18 Calle in Zone 1. He comes from a space traditionally assigned to the Maya— the rural western highlands of terraced fields and steep gorges—but he has become a man of the space available to a new generation of working-class Maya in neoliberal Guatemala—namely, Guatemala City. He is a man of the business world and a man of the streets, so to succeed he must eat salad, and he likes to eat it like tortillas and beans. He is a shrewd (some would say ruth- less) businessman, yet he is also a common man, at ease speaking K'iche' to a young woman while fitting her shoes on the sidewalk. He says that he behaves as the situation dictates, or, in the words of Edward F. Fischer, he behaves as those who "have strategically co-opted aspects of the discourse and philoso- phy of the new, neoliberal world order and integrated them into a program consistent not only with external conditions but also with the internal logics of Maya Culture" (2001: 246). Fischer's work focuses on political activists and export agriculturalists, but Don Napo is not interested in questions of politics or identity, and he farms only as a hobby. Don Napo's world is founded upon success in the streets and the cafes of Guatemala City, and his story points to a new path that some Maya have taken in response to this new world order, a path that fuses their core values and beliefs with those necessary to succeed as an entrepreneur in the streets of an increasingly neoliberal capital.

There is excellent research available on how Maya working in domains such as export-oriented agriculture, maquiladoras, and típica (handicraft) vending have reacted to economic globalization and neoliberal restructuring.[2] Yet Guatemala City has been largely ignored, in spite of the fact that roughly 25 percent of its inhabitants are Maya, not to mention the thousands of Maya who work in the city and still are identified as living in their rural commu- nity of origin. This is an especially egregious shortcoming since according to the 2002 census, Guatemala is 46 percent urban—nearly 15 percentage points more than twenty years ago—and almost one-third of all Maya live in urban areas. Guatemala City dominates urban life in Guatemala, and as indicated by David Harvey (2005), neoliberalism, in both theory and practice, often begins in dominant urban centers.

Most anthropological research on neoliberalism to this point has focused on the hegemonic aspects of the political economic program and group ac- quiescence, or more frequently, group resistance, to this project.[3] Following research by James Ellison (2006), this essay explores how neoliberal ideology has been utilized by individuals within "traditional" cultures. In the case of the Maya, I am interested in how culture is used to rationalize individualistic economic practices—a cornerstone of neoliberalism—while maintaining a strong cultural connection to one's ethnic group and community of origin. Neoliberalism can be, and largely has been, imposed from above (Harvey 2005). Yet it can also be employed from below to forge a hybridity that allows economic success and ideological/cultural continuity in a neoliberal age. This essay is a reflection on this hybridity as exemplified by Don Napo, a K'iche' Maya from the western highlands, who over the course of twenty years went from being a sickly child of subsistence farmers and migrant farm workers in the altiplano to the head of an informal empire on the streets of Guatemala City.

In Guatemala, as throughout Latin America, informality is the rule rather than the exception (Portes, Dore-Cabral, and Patricia Landolt 1997; Portes and Roberts 2004). According to the Guatemalan National Survey of Employment and Income of 2004 (CIEN 2006: 7), three-quarters of all Guatemalans work in the informal sector, including nearly 90 percent of all rural workers and more than 60 percent of all urban workers. Informality is closely linked with the related domains of education (fewer than 20 percent of high school graduates and more than 90 percent of those without formal education work in the informal sector) and ethnicity, with Maya far outnumbering ladinos (nonindigenous) in the percentage employed in the informal sector.

The same survey also estimates that the informal sector produces only one-third of all the gross national product, and that the average productivity of an informal worker is less than one-fifth that of a formal worker (CIEN 2006: 7–8). While these figures make informal activity seem insignificant in comparison to formal economic activity, the same survey indicates that average income for informal workers is more than sixty quetzals (about eight dollars) per day, far surpassing the legal minimum wage and pointing to the viability of informal labor for workers, if not for the national coffers. Nevertheless, with more than half of all Guatemalans and nearly three-quarters of all indigenous Guatemalans living below the poverty line (INE 2006), informal work has not meant substantial economic progress for the typical worker.

Don Napo is in many ways typical for informal sector participants and street vendors—in particular, he is indigenous and male, has no formal education, has marginal literacy, is almost exclusively a comerciante (vendor, in the sense that more than 95 percent of all the goods he sells are purchased from others and not manufactured by him), and relies on family labor to staff his enterprise. Yet he is also unusually successful—for example, he owns some of the property where he sells, a characteristic of only 5 percent of informal sector workers (CIEN 2006: 11). Moreover, his income likely surpasses the average informal worker's earnings by a factor of twelve or more, based on my estimates. As this essay shows, despite the precariousness common to the informal sector and especially evident in street work, Don Napo and his workers have a great deal more security than most others in the informal sector. While Don Napo's economic triumph may be exceptional in neoliberal Guatemala, his particular success has much to do with his ability to adapt his traditional Maya beliefs to the urban informal economic milieu and forge a truly neoliberal Maya path to success.

Don Napo's economic origins, his growth as a successful entrepreneur, and the way he runs his empire all can be traced to his belief system as a Maya Indian, a long-established tradition of "penny capitalism" among indigenous Guatemalans, and an internalization of various aspects of neoliberal ideology, specifically the ideologies of entrepreneurialism, "free" markets (and the accompanying withdrawal or reconfiguration of the state), and, perhaps most importantly, the need for labor flexibility (see Solow 1998). Don Napo has used this complex combination to take advantage of the opportunities available on the streets of Guatemala City and provide for himself and his relatives. His massive success is exceptional, but his utilization of traditional beliefs and economic practices do point to a path, an *otro otro sendero*[4] that some Maya have and will utilize to advance economically in today's Guatemala.

Don Napo's Origins

Don Napo was sick as a child. In the early 1970s at the age of eight, before the worst violence of the civil war had come to his region, he left his pueblo in the western highlands and went with his family to the south coast of Guatemala to pick cotton. There, he became ill. Upon the family's return home, he could no longer eat meat; nor could he run and play with the other children, and his father could no longer take him to the milpa or send him to the town center, a seven-mile walk, loaded with wood or *limones* on his back. At first he was just very tired, then he began vomiting at least once a day, and then he took to his bed. His hair fell out. His mother became very concerned, as she had always believed that he was a special child, destined for great things. Don Napo attributes her belief to the fact that he was born on a Wajxaqiib' B'aatz', the day when Maya day keepers (calendrical diviners) are initiated. His mother took him to a local Maya curer, and she bought remedies for his illness at the local market, but nothing seemed to work. Finally, his mother told him that he was going to die. A few days later, he had a dream in which he was told that to be cured he must return to the place where he got sick, and then go to a new place. The next day, nearly two years after first contracting his illness, with money he was given by his mother, he went back to the south coast in search of a cure. He went to a medical clinic, was diagnosed with anemia, was given a series of shots by a local doctor, and recovered soon after. Upon his return home, he packed his bags and set out for Guatemala City's famed Mercado La Terminal.[5]

This is Don Napo's origin story, and he has repeated it to me many times over the course of our ten-year friendship. Through the story, he establishes himself as a "child of destiny," struck down by a dire illness, yet preordained to overcome it through hard work and spiritual fortune. It is a common story for those from his pueblo. He came from a hardworking and poor family where child labor was the norm and education was not a viable option. He and his family shared a strong belief in the power of dreams and the importance of one's birth date. They believed that destiny saved him from an early end and directed him to the path of his future. It is a story with strong cultural resonance among Guatemalan Maya: one faces illness and through dreams finds a vocation. It is a story similar to those of shamans in Momostenango as recorded by Barbara Tedlock and Dennis Tedlock (B. Tedlock 1992; D. Tedlock 1997).[6] It is also a story of radical individualism: a small boy with a strong work ethic leaves his family and goes it alone in search of his destiny. It is a story similar to the Horatio Alger narratives that form the mythic backbone of today's neoliberal dream. Don Napo's origin story is then typical—typical of a pueblo-born K'iche' Maya, and typical of a dynamic entrepreneur in a neoliberal age. It tells us that he will overcome any obstacle to achieve success, without anyone's assistance.

La Ascensión

Don Napo came to La Terminal alone, carrying a small bag of clothes, some money his mother had given him, and nothing else. He was robbed by an older boy upon his arrival, and slept in the street for two nights, scavenging for food and hiding from both police and predators. His third day, a vegetable vendor who spoke K'iche' took pity on him and offered him a place to sleep in exchange for some odd jobs. With a roof over his head, Don Napo then found a job as a *cargador*, carrying large bundles of produce and dry goods for shoppers, a task he performed for two years. He then moved up to selling matches, garlic, and cinnamon as an *ambulante*, or peddler, all the time saving money.

At thirteen, he began to sell an older ladino vendor's stock of shoes, and when the man retired only two years later, Don Napo bought out his stock and set up his first fixed kiosk in La Terminal, a small table two meters wide and one meter deep, selling soccer cleats at about two dollars a pair.

This too is not an exceptional story. Don Napo was a child entrepreneur, with a keen business sense and a strong work ethic. As Sol Tax said of another group of highland Maya more than fifty years ago: "I find it hard to imagine a people more endowed with the spirit of business enterprise than the Indians . . . that I know best. There is probably no Panajachel Indian over the age of ten who has not calculated a way to make money with his available resources . . . I know of boys 8 and 10 years of age who have set themselves up in business, selling independently of their parents. Boys of 12 and 14 are apt to be pretty sophisticated traders" (1953: 18). Much like Tax's informants, Don Napo was a "penny capitalist," moving from a cargador of other people's merchandise to an ambulante vending foodstuffs to selling shoes from a fixed market *puesto*. His entrepreneurial skills, showcased from a young age, are historically common within his culture, but his rapid rise as a vendor reflects the changing neoliberal context in which, for many Maya youth, rural production and trade have given way to urban distribution and consumption as a means for economic and social advancement.

Success for Don Napo was the result of individual effort and finding the right product to sell at the right time, of being ever ready to change direction as the market dictated. While he was given opportunities to apprentice and learn about urban vending from the *paisanos* who came to his aid, Don Napo credits his own drive, his own intelligence, his own work ethic, and his particular destiny for his massive success, while others have merely survived. He is a truly flexible vendor. And as anyone familiar with the lives and labors of street workers throughout the modern era can attest, flexibility to exploit the right economic niche at the right time in the right way is a shared characteristic of nineteenth-century "street urchins" such as Oliver Twist as well as the young boys who work for Don Napo today.

The young Don Napo used this type of flexibility to accrue capital during the late 1970s and early 1980s as an established vendor in Guatemala City. At the time, migrants were pouring into the city in order to escape the Guatemalan Army's scorched earth campaigns in the highlands. He gained economic capital, of course, but also cultural capital from his work in the streets and markets, and not in state-funded schools or through the aid of social welfare programs. Ironically, his major worry at this time was theft, as the state could not meet its most basic neoliberal goal of providing a safe haven for market transactions, a point I will address further in the section "Two-Way Streets." Don Napo's success at this point was both the result of a cultural logic that emphasized penny capitalism and a neoliberal logic based upon fierce individualism, risk-taking behavior, self-reliance, and the flexibility to take advantage of economic opportunity unhindered by state interference or regulation.

Dominio

In late July of 2005, Don Napo asked me to come to a shoe fair at the industrial park in Zone 9 of the capital. By this time, Expocalzado—La Exposición Internacional de Calzado, Materias Primas y Maquinaria (International Footwear, Raw Materials, and Machinery Exposition)—had become a typical trade show. In a generic hall, a variety of manufacturers displayed their new lines, in this case shoes, plying their potential customers with food and beverage, all in hopes of booking large orders for the upcoming season. Customers, predominantly middle-aged men, wore badges around their necks and dressed in sport coats or shirtsleeves. Vendors were dressed smartly in suits and usually accompanied by one or two young attractive women to entice their clientele. In stark contrast, Don Napo entered the great hall in a leather jacket and soccer shirt accompanied by his wife, two of their small children, and as before, seven of his employees, boys between the ages of twelve and twenty-one. All were wearing the T-shirts and pants they had worn to work earlier that day. They were immediately inundated with greetings from all parts of the room, and vendors stood in line to greet Don Napo and the young boys, all by name, while his wife and children stayed in the periphery.

The boys were quickly ushered to the kiosks by the vendors, and proceeded to go over the merchandise, communicating with each other in K'iche' while the obsequious manufacturers showed off their wares. Needless to say, the sight of middle-aged ladino men fawning over Maya boys seemed out of place in this setting, but the ability that the boys had to place vast orders and their knowledge of the pricing, discounts, and payment options they could negotiate from the vendors belied where the power lay in the room. At the Expocalzado, the working class, young, and Maya entered the boardroom, and in a situation where commerce made the rules, Don Napo was king and his princely retainers called the shots.

Don Napo is truly a retail king. His empire comprises three storefronts on 18 Calle, four street kiosks, two bodegas, a three-story concrete building and storefront located ten feet from the cathedral in his hometown, and a shoe distributorship and warehouse that caters to small vendors on the south coast. Yet he is also something of a cacique in that of the twenty people who are in his employ full time, seventeen are members of his extended family and the other three, though unrelated, come from the *aldea* (hamlet) where he was born.[7] While he seeks to expand his empire throughout Guatemala and ultimately to the United States, his is a family enterprise. He strongly believes that one can only trust family members and, on occasion, those from one's own pueblo. This belief has deep resonance within his culture, as one community member's success should be shared, especially within the family, a noted practice among highland Maya households (see, e.g., Annis 1987; Ehlers 1990; Little 2004).

This communal ethos also benefits Don Napo and fits with the spirit and practical requirements of an entrepreneur in the neoliberal mold. By employing his younger kinsmen, he is guaranteed a loyal labor force over which he has a good deal of control both on the job and away from work. He himself can utilize his existing relationships with their families, all of whom are located in his pueblo, to guarantee their obedience and reliability. He can pay them less since he is in close communication with their families and makes steady contributions to the family coffers, giving his workers only small amounts for themselves in addition to room and board. He also can appeal to the youths' family ethos to ensure loyalty as he represents his interests as theirs, though they have no formal ownership stake in his operations, much as a more traditional cacique head of family represents the family in his prosperity. By employing family members he also guarantees a very flexible labor force, as there are more kinsmen available for work in peak seasons, and workers can be quickly sent back home in case of illness or slow business. Keeping labor costs low and his labor force obedient and flexible allows Don Napo to keep his prices low, a tremendous advantage in a street retail market that is in fierce competition for customers. Much as Greg Grandin (2000) shows in his study of the Maya entrepreneurial class in Quetzaltenango that success depended on the combination of Hispanic strategies of accumulation and patriarchal caste power, Don Napo's success is due in large part to his ability to combine cultural traditions and neoliberal strategies.

Cacique en La Ciudad

Don Napo's melding of neoliberal individualism with a Maya cultural-economic logic has brought him great success. As Tax's research demonstrates, this logic is not new to the Maya; he wrote: "The Indian is perhaps above all else an entrepreneur, a business man, always looking for new means of turning a penny" (1953: 12). Yet few if any *panajacheleño* penny capitalists managed to develop into full-blown dollar capitalists at the time of his writing. Tax explained this seeming anomaly, anticipating the modernization theory and world systems critiques that came fifteen years later, as follows: "Although I purpose to describe the economy of Panajachel, and at very least by inference to show why the material level of life is so low, no solution is offered. A very good reason for this is that while the problem has its consequences locally, its cure involves the whole region, the whole of the larger society, and, indeed, much of the world" (Tax 1953: 9). Carol Smith's (1975, 1978) research detailed what kept Tax's penny capitalists so poor: namely, a regional market system that disenfranchised rural Maya, whose products (and profits) moved from local Indian markets to ladino-dominated urban markets. In neoliberal Guatemala, Edward F. Fischer (2001) has documented how the growth of nontraditional export agricultural production has allowed some highland farmers to bypass this system and advance economically. Don Napo, I argue, has similarly bypassed these constraints by participating in a new Maya-dominated market, itself urban, that now covers city streets and plazas and affords different opportunities to its participants than did the rural markets of Panajachel some fifty years ago.

Recent estimates indicate that more than 75 percent of Guatemalans work in the informal sector, more than in any other Central American nation (CIEN 2006). While this figure encompasses a wide variety of economic activities and locales, urban street and market vending are one place where Maya are thriving. Whereas they were once limited to selling products they themselves made, their experiences as rural penny capitalist traders has led them to great success as retailers of the modern consumer goods Guatemalans crave, particularly clothing. The continued expansion of street vending in Zone 1 of the capital since the earthquake of 1976 (see Porras Castejón 1995), despite numerous state attempts to limit or eradicate it (Véliz and O'Neill, this volume), has made the streets the preferred outlet for the urban poor and working class to purchase dry goods. In the years following the Guatemalan Peace Accords, the Guatemalan state has implemented structural adjustment policies, and the accompanying reconfiguration of the state, now even less involved in market regulation, has opened the spaces of the streets to informal vending. It is in this space, where taxes and worker benefits are unknown, that retailers can sell the low-profit but high-volume goods that the citizenry demand.

It is in the city streets that Don Napo has succeeded, and this makes him different from both Tax's penny capitalists and the petty bourgeois of Quetzaltenango profiled in depth by Grandin (2000) and Irma Velásquez Nimatuj (2002), as well as from the Maya women who dominated highland market sales from the late nineteenth century (Carey 2008). Unlike Tax's vendors, he has an enormous and diverse potential client base, access to credit from manufacturers, and no middlemen to drain off his profits. Unlike the Maya middle class of Quetzaltenango, neither was he born with the good fortune of land wealth, nor does his wealth come by his acting as an intermediary between the local Maya and the ladino elite. Don Napo has made his money selling to popular or working-class urban residents, and the continued expansion of his domain raises him to a level far above penny capitalist or petit bourgeois. In this way, Don Napo has managed to traverse the spatial divide that traditionally separated (urban) ladinos from the (rural) Maya majority (see Thomas, in this book), a divide that was originally bridged due to the emergency needs of the rural populace following the earthquake of 1976 and the scorched earth campaigns of the early 1980s, but that has since broken down entirely. The aforementioned reconfiguration of the Guatemalan state, once notorious for restricting rural–urban migration and the movements of rural Maya during the nineteenth century and early twentieth, made the urban streets the ideal marketplace for Maya comerciantes. Following Miles Richardson's (1980, 2003) analysis of the central plaza of Cartago, Costa Rica, and the work of Setha Low (2000; Low and Smith 2005) among others, the plaza and streets of the downtown, once the domain of the ladino elite, were opened up to all who sought to earn from them. Yet, as Véliz and O'Neill (in this book) point out, the streets of El Centro are now being reorganized in the name of "urban renewal," a euphemism for the displacement of the popular classes and their puestos in favor of upscale, private businesses meant to serve the needs of the elite and tourists. While waves of internal migration and the widespread informality that characterizes neoliberal Guatemala City have permitted Maya such as Don Napo to carve out a productive niche, there are still frequent attempts to eject them in favor of the commercial dreams of the traditional ladino elite.

Two-Way Streets

Don Napo's use of rural–urban migration patterns and his reliance on his own kin network have certainly benefited him, but this flexibility also has advantages for the young kinsmen he employs. Critics of the neoliberal approach to labor market flexibility argue that such policies lead to worker disenfranchisement, a polarization of the distribution of wealth, a labor force being controlled by brute force or fear, and ultimately a global race to the bottom.[8] Judging from the results of several decades of neoliberal economic policies throughout the globe, these criticisms seem on target. Yet this type of flexibility has long been an attribute of the smallest and least-capitalized firms in Guatemala—namely, street vendors who participate in the urban informal sector—with less of the strife that has accompanied flexibility in larger economic domains. Much like neoliberalism, flexibility need not exclusively be treated as imposed from above, and as the stories of two of Don Napo's nephews illustrate, flexibility is a strategy that can be employed from below to allay the precariousness of everyday life for Guatemala City's urban poor.

For Ramón, Chistoso, and the other fifteen kinsmen who work for Don Napo, the aforementioned aspects of Maya traditional culture provide much justification for their compliance with Don Napo's demands, but ultimately the factors that keep them working hard despite low pay and mandated labor flexibility are to be found on the city streets themselves. Since all of Don Napo's workers are from his rural town of origin and all have worked in subsistence agriculture, they are all well aware of the tremendous hard work and monotony involved in farming and the lack of economic opportunity in their hometown. Don Napo in contrast offers them the city streets, full of action and diversion, a chance to participate in "modern" life. The bright lights of the city are part of the opportunity he offers them, and as he houses and feeds them, they get to experience the tumult of the city surrounded by kinsmen and with some degree of security.

The security Don Napo offers is reassuring to new migrants, but in the streets of Guatemala City, seemingly random violence, while never historically a stranger, has now become an everyday acquaintance. Robbery, extortion, carjacking, gang violence, and feminicide are regular events. Reports from the United Nations, Amnesty International, and a variety of international watchdog groups have all pointed to the real possibility that organized crime and violence are threatening the very stability of the nation. Chistoso himself was shot in the back in February of 2007, the bullet puncturing a kidney and coming dangerously close to severing his spine. It happened at ten o'clock in broad daylight while he was working at one of Don Napo's street kiosks. Chistoso was not the shooter's intended target, as robberies of street vendors are rare due to the effective vigilante responses of other vendors when they are attacked. In case of a robbery, for example, Chistoso has twelve other coworkers and kinsmen within earshot willing to come to his aid. But kinsmen cannot protect one from a stray bullet. Chistoso received medical care quickly because Don Napo was there to assist him. During his recovery he was nursed in Don Napo's house, by Don Napo's wife, until he was well enough to be sent back to his rural home to fully recuperate before returning to work in the city. While he was not paid during his recovery, his family did receive compensation from Don Napo for Chistoso's lost contribution to the family coffers, which is as close to worker's compensation as most Guatemalans, working in the formal or informal sector, are likely to receive.

Working for Don Napo does afford both exposure to and some protection from street life in Guatemala City, but the streets themselves have important lessons to teach young rural-born Maya, lessons they are eager to learn. While working for Don Napo, small-town boys such as Chistoso and Ramón become relatively sophisticated urbanites, building social and cultural capital by extending their social networks and knowledge base, resources they will employ in their struggles to get ahead. Ramón, who had never been to the city before coming to work with Don Napo, met friends on the streets who worked for a nearby vendor and together they hatched a plan to migrate illegally to the United States without the aid of a coyote. He set off with his new friends in August 2004 against the wishes of Don Napo and made it as far as Mexico City, when one of his friends died while trying to jump onto a moving train headed north. Ramón high-tailed it back to Guatemala and after some chiding from Don Napo and his mother, returned to work days later. Ramón did not make it anywhere near his goal, but his experience working for Don Napo gave him the skills, money, and connections he needed to make the attempt, and a safe place to land and work upon his return. The job security Ramón and Chistoso earn is perhaps the primary benefit of being one of Don Napo's boys and is their claim of equity for being such flexible workers (see Solow 1998). Ramón, for example, vows that he and his surviving friend will make the journey again soon, and until then he is happy to work for his uncle, continue to aid his family, and build his own monetary and cultural capital.

For Ramón and Chistoso, flexibility means having a chance to work on the city streets, begin their own vending operations, learn urban culture, and make connections both inside and outside of their kin networks that provide them chances at migration and other means of advancement. All the while, they are guaranteed some degree of economic security should the precariousness of the streets knock them off balance. They are good neoliberal workers: hard laborers, flexible in their skill sets, flexible in the terms and location of their work, learning to survive in an ever-changing economic context, and adventuresome in their pursuit of opportunities. They are also good Maya, deferential to their senior kinsmen, accepting of less for themselves in order to aid their families, contributors to a family-based economic endeavor.

Conclusion

What makes this family business work for both the owner and his workers? It is the combination of neoliberal flexibility, Maya cultural practice, and the opportunities available on the streets of Guatemala City. For Don Napo, flexibility allows him to maintain tight control of his labor force, reduce his labor costs, expand and contract his business as demand dictates, and employ his workers in locations and tasks that optimize his ability to maximize profits. He is a good neoliberal entrepreneur, as reward seeking as the multinational firms who dominate the global economy; yet he is also a good Maya, utilizing a Maya cultural logic to promote his cause and expand his kinsmen's opportunities. Using their cultural background to contort their way to success in a precarious time and environment, Don Napo and his workers are surviving in a globalizing neoliberal economy.

Don Napo's success is a typical Maya success, though his success is in no way typical.[9] His good fortune has much to do with the calendrical destiny of his birth and the power of his dreams. He practices a type of entrepreneurship that has been common to the highland Maya for generations. He has a tremendous work ethic that has been documented repeatedly by ethnographers of the highland Maya.[10] He maintains strong connections to his pueblo of origin and integrates his kinsmen into his business efforts. Don Napo's success is also a typical neoliberal success in that he has behaved as a brave entrepreneur, self-reliant and independent of the state or social welfare system for aid. He has found a way to maintain tight disciplinary control of his workers and limit labor costs, utilizing these savings to offer low prices and gain market share. He is a modern-day cacique, a noble on horseback (actually in a 2005 Toyota microbus) representing his culture, his aldea, and his lineage. He is also a profit-seeking entrepreneur, using every possible economic advantage to extend his domain as he rides through the streets of Guatemala City.

Notes

1. I have known Don Napo for twelve years, and over this time he has become my trusted friend. Research for this essay is based on hundreds of hours observing Don Napo's business, working with him and his employees, and holding multiple in-depth conversations with his staff and family. Funding for this research was provided at various times by the Fulbright-Hays Dissertation Research Fellowship, the Tinker Foundation, the Foundation for Mesoamerican Studies Inc. (FAMSI), and Baylor University.

2. On export-oriented agriculture see, e.g., Liliana Goldín 1996, Sarah Hamilton and Fischer 2005, Fischer and Peter Benson 2006. On maquiladoras see Petersen 1992, Goldín 2001, 2005; on típica vending, see Walter Little 2004, 2005; and on international migration, see James Loucky and Marilyn Moors 2000, and Jennifer Burrell 2005.

3. The anthropological literature on neoliberalism and exceptional critiques of this economic program can be found in work by Aihwa Ong (2006), James Ferguson (2006), and Pierre Bourdieu (1999).

4. Hernando de Soto's landmark volume El Otro Sendero (1987) was one of the first books to posit that the informal sector (the "other path" of his title) was the hope for economic development in his native Peru as opposed to state-backed oligarchs and their formal business enterprises or the Maoist philosophy of the Shining Path guerilla movement. I here posit that another path has been utilized by Don Napo for his rise, namely the combination of a Maya cultural logic and a neoliberal economic one.

5. Mercado La Terminal is the largest market in Guatemala City, home to a variety of retail and wholesale vendors who cater to urban clientele. It is also the final destination point for most buses that arrive to Guatemala City from the western highlands, as well as the departure point for buses traveling throughout Guatemala, El Salvador, Honduras, and Mexico. See Santiago Bastos and Manuela Camus 1995, and Camus 2002 for a detailed description of La Terminal and some Maya vendors who work there.

6. Barbara and Dennis Tedlock both wrote innovative and highly respected ethnographic accounts of their work with Maya diviners in the western highlands town of Momostenango. Both apprenticed with the renowned day keeper Andrés Xiloj (D. Tedlock 1997), and wrote about how their struggles with childhood polio were seen by Xiloj as proof that they were meant for an extraordinary destiny. Barbara Tedlock's (1992) work details many similar stories.

7. Caciques were descendants of the preconquest Maya aristocracy who were given special rights from the Spanish conquistadors, such as the right to ride horses and bear swords. Most importantly, they controlled land and wealth in the form of *parcialidades*, or the landed estates that were the primary form of agrarian production for the Maya

of the western highlands. They persisted through the twentieth century, though the term came more to mean a wealthy and powerful Maya, regardless of lineage (Carmack 1995).

8. General critiques of globalization along these lines are numerous, with Joseph Stiglitz 2003, Amy Chua 2004, and Brookings Institution 2007 being exemplars.

9. Since the years of Don Napo's greatest economic success in the late 1990s and early 2000s, informal sector vending in Guatemala City has become fiercely competitive, and it would be misleading to assert that anyone with Don Napo's particular ambition, work ethic, and family network would be guaranteed to prosper as he has in the same environment. He has succeeded where many have failed or only managed to tread water. After a visit with him in the fall of 2008, as the full repercussions of the economic crisis in the United States were only beginning to be felt, he said that the streets were not providing as they once had. In an irony appropriate to a neoliberal Maya entrepreneur, he was beginning to use his wealth accrued in the city streets to buy up farmland in the highlands, commenting that as land prices in his region are so low, and as so many of his kinsmen are available to work, farming for profit looks to him like a very viable enterprise in the near future.

10. See Sheldon Annis 1987, Fischer 2001, and Kay Warren 1998 for a few examples.

Privatization of Public Space

The Displacement of Street Vendors in Guatemala City

Rodrigo J. Véliz and
Kevin Lewis O'Neill

This essay details the politics of urban renewal in postwar Guatemala City and the neoliberal logic through which such renewal efforts become expressed. At the center of this essay is a struggle between Guatemala City street vendors, who have sold their wares in the Centro Histórico's Portal del Comercio for some thirty years, and a team of public and private actors who are working to develop the Centro Histórico for both public and private ends. This development team's effort at urban renewal braids together questions of public space, security, and economic development to make the argument that renewing the Portal del Comercio (a historic but perceived insecure area) is not just good for business but also good for residents of Guatemala City. A developed Portal del Comercio will bring increased levels of private security and, thus, more public space for Guatemalans to visit. This vision, however, is not without cost. The proposed urban renewal effort involves the forced removal of the Portal del Comercio's street vendors through what this essay understands as a neoliberal vision of space: a vision that reads public space as a raw material available for development. This is a vision that contrasts with the vision of Guatemala City street vendors, who largely understand public space as both a right and a resource. They believe that as citizens, they are at liberty to use their streets to make a living. This essay explores this tension in order to note that the formation of space in postwar Guatemala City through the language of economic development results in the exclusion of certain people and goods from supposedly public spaces—the privatization of public space.

The Politics of Business Improvement Districts

Contentious processes of urban renewal divide postwar Guatemala City. The capital city is carved into twenty-two zones that coil outward, like a snake, from the city's center, Zone 1. Urban sprawl and suburban developments hug the outer zones, making the capital's metropolitan area slightly uneven and, at times, obviously unplanned (Murphy 2004). As is the case with other Latin American cities, wealthy urban elites tend to live in more exclusive zones while working-class and poor residents live in more depressed areas. Economic segregation is nothing new to Guatemala City (AVANCSO 2003; Bastos and Camus 1998; Bossen 1984; Roberts 1973). However, postwar urban violence and efforts at economic restructuring are changing Guatemala City's spatial characteristics. A network of public and private actors rearticulates public places into semiprivate spaces through the practice of urban renewal.

The best examples of this process can be seen in Guatemala City's Zona Viva (Zone 10), 4° Norte (Zone 4), and the Centro Histórico (Zone 1). These urban renewal projects are akin to what North American developers call Business Improvement Districts, or BIDs for short (Houston 1997; Mitchell 2001). Business Improvement Districts are urban development zones where a blend of government programs and private investors create public spaces replete with upscale restaurants, shops, and apartment complexes. In Guatemala City, BIDs also feature private security forces, usually in the form of hired armed guards (see Dickins de Girón, this volume). Part of the theory behind BIDs is that urban revitalization and public safety can be better and more efficiently delivered by the private sector than by wasteful and often corrupt public officials. The ultimate goal of BIDs is to stimulate the economy, which is accomplished by providing secure, well-lit streets with wide avenues designed to inspire conspicuous consumption.

The Centro Histórico, as a BID, is a restoration effort driven by Guatemala City's municipal government, other state institutions, and the private sector. The general objective, detailed later in this essay, is to provide the city with a social catalyst, an opportunity for economic and cultural development that employs the charm of colonial architecture and a deep sense of history to make the Centro Histórico a viable place for consumption. The general plan is to generate small communities, shopping centers, and cultural venues, spaces that will attract Guatemalans of a certain socioeconomic class as well as international tourists. Yet, in order to make the Centro Histórico into an attractive web of consumption and leisure, the entire Centro Histórico needs to be reorganized—razed, in some places, and revised in others. The bus routes, for example, that bring people to and from the Centro Histórico have been (and continue to be) remapped to allow for ample sidewalks and walking paths. The Centro Histórico has also had to reclaim streets that have for quite some time been used by street vendors working in the informal economy. The struggle of these vendors to maintain their place of work in spite of the production of the Centro Histórico provides this essay's central case study.

Business Improvement Districts are public spaces in which all Guatemalans can embody (even if only for an afternoon) the flâneur of Walter Benjamin's Arcades Project (1998). The reality, however, is that not all Guatemalans are free to visit these spaces. Paradoxically, these efforts at urban renewal yield places that are not all that public—places that look inviting but that nevertheless restrict the flow of certain people and certain goods (see Hackworth 2006). The production of these supposedly public spaces excludes a range of men, women, and children, and in turn generates a whole new set of social relationships and spatial dynamics. Acts of exclusion happen explicitly (in the formal restriction of certain people from particular locations, such as bars and nightclubs, and in the forced removal of street vendors), as well as implicitly (with prohibitively expensive merchandise and the promotion of elite styles of speech and dress). These new public spaces, simply put, are public only for particular classes and for certain ethnicities. In a multiethnic, multilingual capital city, with a yawning gap between the rich and the poor and with stunning levels of insecurity, public spaces such as these have become surprisingly private.

These urban renewal projects in Guatemala City have also been met with resistance, making relevant Pierre Bourdieu's pithy insight that "aesthetic intolerance can be terribly violent" (1984: 56). In Zone 1, for example, Guatemala City's municipal government continues its renewal of the Centro Histórico with the support of private investors. Together they attempt to convert the area from a troubled city center wrought with gang violence and crime to a "dignified" space, one that people might visit on Sunday afternoons with their families in tow. The rub, however, is that the Centro Histórico has long constituted a major site for Guatemala's informal economy; it is where street vendors have sold their wares—from pirated DVDs to eyeglasses to kitchen supplies—for more than thirty years. The Centro Histórico provides street vendors with a relatively steady income and the working class with affordable places to shop.

This tension between urban renewal and the informal economy came to a

head in 2006, when the municipal government forcibly displaced street vendors from the Centro Histórico's Portal del Comercio in the name of urban
renewal and progress. A network of governmental and corporate actors employed market techniques, the language of economic development, and the
discourse of *delincuencia* (delinquency) to redefine the Centro Histórico as a
place set aside for certain classes of people as opposed to others—as a site for
formal consumption rather than informal haggling.

The government's efforts at urban renewal in the Centro Histórico make
sense when put into critical conversation with today's social scientific literature on private enclaves (Davis 1990; López and Rodríguez 2005; Low 2003;
Rodgers 2004) as well as a growing critique of North American BIDs (Hochleutner 2003; Hoyt 2004; Loukaitou-Sideris, Blumenberg, and Ehrenfeucht
2004).[1] The emerging consensus is that BIDs as modes of fortified enclaves
have come to substitute for and even define what has otherwise been known
as open and public space, while also threatening the promise of democratic
accountability (Pack 1992). Contrary to liberal notions of "free" urban space
and the governance that accompanies such spaces (Jacobs 1961; Joyce 2003),
BIDs now divide cities with walls—both actual (with concrete and razor wire)
and imagined (through discourses of fear and delincuencia) (Caldeira 2001).
As the literature notes, these divisions most often separate the rich from the
rest (Falzon 2004; Kuppinger 2004; Waldrop 2004).

Guatemala City provides a dramatic example of this widespread phenomenon. The privatization of public space in Guatemala City intends a world in
which poverty and crime (let alone class conflict and ethnic tensions) are
properly managed, which here largely means hidden or displaced. The goal is
a kind of semipublic space where an idyllic homogeneity exists across members of private communities. The reality is that efforts at urban renewal in the
capital city reproduce stereotypes, unjust social relations, and the violence of
segregation.

The problem with these new private spaces is that the world "beyond the
walls" continues to exist and that the construction and preservation of these
new spaces depends upon processes of criminalization. The displacement of
the Portal del Comercio's street vendors, detailed below, is just one example.
The criminalization of their livelihood permits state intervention while also
justifying the private security that now controls the Centro Histórico. There
is, in fact, a true struggle over the contours of public space in Guatemala City.
Yet, the struggle is not only between the rich and the poor or between the
state and its informal economy; rather, it involves the whole of Guatemalan

society. An array of actors reconstitutes Guatemala City's public spaces into private islands without any democratic process for those who have historically used public space for their livelihoods. Private interests often have very public effects.

Centro Histórico

The Centro Histórico is both a place and an effort at urban renewal in postwar Guatemala City. As a place, it includes the area that surrounds the capital city's central plaza. The oldest part of Guatemala City, the Centro Histórico is home to the national palace and national cathedral as well as some of the country's most historic public parks and private buildings. Moreover, when Guatemala City was founded in 1776, the ground on which the Centro Histórico now sits became the construction site for the residences of Guatemala's most elite families (Centro Histórico 2006). The area's geographical and cultural centrality to Guatemalan life produced a historical imagination that understands the Centro Histórico as the seat of Guatemalan power and privilege, a place of commerce. Some of this began to change in 1871 with efforts at liberalization, which initiated increased degrees of urbanization in Guatemala City through the construction of public buildings. These buildings intended to strike an architectural balance with the capital's many Roman Catholic churches, creating a cityscape equally committed to both church and state. The Centro Histórico, in turn, has long served as a place of power, where church and state officials lived alongside urban elites (Gellert and Pinto Soria 1990), while those areas mushrooming beyond the Centro Histórico became increasingly marginalized, both socially and economically.

Even today, a popular narrative largely scripted by urban elites strikes a rather nostalgic chord, remembering the Centro Histórico as a "glamorous" place where people would stroll through the streets to chat with friends and family (Acevedo 2006: 11) and where people could buy luxurious and expensive products from around the world (Roldán 2006). Urban elites largely remember the Centro Histórico as "the most elegant and comfortable place to shop" (ibid.). Even María Cruz-López, the subject of Deborah Levenson's essay in this volume, remembers the Centro along these lines. Levenson writes: "The city delighted María. El Centro housed nearly half of the city's population — wealthy, middle class, or poor, including thousands of domestics. For years she never went into the barrios where the other half lived in constructions of adobe, leaves, and, as she puts it, 'cualquiera' [whatever] without water or sewage (Gellert 1995; Solow 1950). With a lovely acoustic shell in the gardened Parque Central, electricity, trolleys, traffic lights, paved streets and new government buildings, El Centro was the city at its most citified." Levenson continues: "The city's glamour, the 'sparkling modernity' noted by period writers and by María, was located on several blocks of El Centro, where María walked with her employers on Sundays (Caplow 1949). There were pharmacies; well-to-do dress, shoe, and paper goods stores; banks; restaurants; the Hotel Palace; and the electric company. Guatemala's new department stores, such as La Perla on Sexta Avenida, known as the 'Tiffany's of Guatemala City,' offered stunning imports such as cashmere sweaters and Max Factor cosmetics." El Centro is remembered as the center of Guatemala's high society.

These descriptions, as both Levenson and María might admit, approximate the experiences of the elite but are otherwise historically incorrect. As historians now note, Guatemala City has always been (and continues to be) a place of extremes, a site of opposing forces—poverty and wealth, for example (Gellert and Pinto Soria 1990). The men and women who built the Centro Histórico with their own hands, who lived in labor camps, working for the lowest of wages, oftentimes become flattened by such nostalgia, their labor erased from the historical record. The fact of the matter is that the Centro Histórico never truly fit these nostalgic descriptions. Following the Guatemalan Revolution in 1944 and its famed decade of democracy, construction continued throughout the capital as a more robust middle class emerged. Elites who once called the Centro Histórico their barrio now moved to zones 9, 10, 14, and 15 to avoid this emerging middle class. This demographic shift changed the Centro Histórico dramatically. Moreover, Guatemala's 1976 earthquake, which leveled most of the capital city, left Zone 1's historic center in disrepair. Those who tend to propagate the above nostalgia, for example, are quick to add that Zone 1 is now "decadent and disordered" (Acevedo 2006: 11), noting that the Centro Histórico is crowded with indigenous "street sweepers and street vendors [who sell] objects that are not of interest" to the urban elite (Roldán 2006). Although it is protected (in name) as a heritage site, *capitalinos* (capital city residents) largely understand the Centro Histórico as unstable, dangerous, and wrought with both petty thieves and violent criminals. Some of this popular characterization has to do with aesthetics. The buildings themselves never recovered fully from the 1976 earthquake, with many of the structures standing low to the ground today and in need of cleaning and a fresh coat of paint.

The real problem, however, is that the Centro Histórico now serves as a major site for the city's informal markets. There, anyone can buy merchandise at low prices from street vendors; it is an economy that attracts unglamorous products such as dish towels and bootlegged heartburn medicine. Compounded with substantial security issues, there exists a very real contrast between today's spatial imagination, which places violence and crime in Zone 1, and the country's historical imagination, which recognizes the Centro Histórico as a place of honor. This contrast is what has turned today's Centro Histórico into an object of urban renewal. Today, the Centro Histórico exists not only as a place, but also as a network of state and nonstate actors, both private and public, who work to remake Guatemala City's historic center in the nostalgic image that they propagate. As with many BIDs, the city's municipal government ideally serves as a referee for a smattering of private investors—including bars, restaurants, and retail stores—and civil society organizations—including NGOs and cultural centers—that all contribute both time and money to the renewal project. Driving the project with the force of past glory, these organizations work to renew the Centro Histórico "so that all Guatemalans will have the symbolic value of a Plaza Mayor and a patrimonial spirit. This is an effort to construct a Historic Center in the very heart of the city, where one can live [in or around] a dignified downtown . . . [It will be a place] in which one can live, work, shop, and (of course) visit" (Centro Histórico 2006: 4).

These renewal plans include refurbishing historical landmarks, such as buildings, monuments, and parks; lighting and securing public streets so that tourists and citizens can safely negotiate the Centro Histórico both day and night; and developing the area by erecting upscale restaurants, shops, and apartment buildings. The ultimate vision is a historic center that is "restored, conserved, and valorized" (Centro Histórico 2006). The effort aims to create "spaces of expression and participation" for "residents, sales people, students, transport workers, office workers, and businessmen and businesswomen—for all those human beings who bring [the Centro Histórico's] streets to life" (ibid.). Those involved with the Centro Histórico struggle to secure and manage the area as a "place of recreation and a tourist destination" (ibid.). Tourism is in fact a strong motivator for this renewal program. Given postwar Guatemala's continued foray into the global free market, tourism is one of the country's potential lines for economic development. The country's incredible cultural and ecological diversity—replete with lush landscapes, jungles, and volcanoes—has prompted state and nonstate actors alike to place an increasing amount of hope in Guatemalan tourism as a nontraditional export. Much effort has gone into selling Guatemala as a place to visit (Little 2004, 2005; Nelson 1999).

Questions of security, however, continue to muddy these hopeful waters. A rather persistent U.S. State Department travel advisory, for example, warns tourists (North American and otherwise) of "murder, rape, and armed assaults against foreigners," asserting that "the police force is inexperienced and under-funded, and the judicial system is weak, overworked, and inefficient. Well-armed criminals know there is little chance they will be caught or punished." The travel advisory, in a cruel twist, even makes Guatemala's potential busy season for tourism the most dangerous: "Traditionally, Guatemala experiences increases in crime before and during the Christmas and Easter holiday seasons" (U.S. State Department 2008). The advisory also locates much of this chaos squarely in and around the Centro Histórico: "Pickpockets and purse-snatchers are active in all major cities and tourist sites, especially the central market and other parts of Zone 1 in Guatemala City." The warning continues, giving strong advice to tourists and business travelers alike: "For security reasons, the Embassy does not allow U.S. government employees to stay in hotels in Zone 1 in Guatemala City and urges private travelers to avoid staying in this area." With the travel advisory raising other haunting themes such as "child stealing" and "organ harvesting," as well as the "lynching" of suspected baby thieves by angry mobs (ibid.), Guatemala is not on any shortlists for travel to Latin America, and Zone 1 remains a place to avoid. The Centro Histórico as a renewal project swims upstream against postwar violence and insecurity.

The Centro Histórico, however, promises to make Guatemala City a safe and attractive place to visit: "The founding of the Centro Histórico's Citizenship Security Program is for the recuperation of public space and for a city that is much safer" (Centro Histórico 2006). This plan shifts the responsibility for public safety from the Policía Nacional Civil to private security forces. Together, so the plan goes, private and public actors will develop Guatemala City into a safe and attractive space to visit through this urban renewal project. Situated at the very center of this effort is the Centro Histórico's Portal del Comercio—a specific site for development within the larger development project. As the Centro Histórico literature states clearly, the Portal del Comercio has been an integral part of the national economy. Marqués Juan Fermín de Aycinena y Piñol constructed the Portal del Comercio in 1781 as a place for citizens to visit in peace, "without fear of being assaulted," and in the spirit of grand European plazas—Paris's Hotel de Ville, London's Trafalgar Square, and Madrid's Plaza de Santa Ana (ibid.). The Portal del Comercio, historically speaking, was a gesture to European sensibilities and upscale tastes. It was the area in which elites would stroll.

The promotional literature on the Centro Histórico, however, states that the Portal del Comercio has since been used for quite different purposes. Following the 1976 earthquake, the Portal del Comercio has been a place where street vendors squat, hawk their goods, and turn a profit (CIEN 2006). It was a transformation that took place alongside a number of other postearthquake adjustments. As Virginia Garrard-Burnett notes, the earthquake brought into clearer relief many of Guatemala's societal problems: "unemployment and gross inequities in income distribution; the vast chasm that separated the nation's poor, largely indigenous majority from the wealthy and cosmopolitan elite; and the societal stresses of increased urban migration by the poor" (1998: 127). Today, the Portal del Comercio reflects much of the nation's transformation: from the center of urban elitism to a commercial hub for the working poor. To develop the Portal del Comercio as well as Guatemala City, the Centro Histórico struggles to reclaim an imagined past for an even more imagined future. This effort at development stakes its claim on a history largely of its making by using a vision of public space mostly of its choosing.

The Problem of the Displaced

According to street vendors who work in Zone 1's bustling informal economy, the municipal government has continually threatened to remove them forcibly from the Portal del Comercio and to replace them with registered and managed street vendors who sell regulated goods (Chajón 2007). Their relationship with the government has forever been constituted by waves of struggle. Between periods of conflict with the municipal government, however, there have also been periods of relative calm. Street vendors remember when former president Óscar Berger served as mayor of the capital city and brokered an agreement between the municipal government and the street vendors' formal organization about such issues as trash and petty theft. This successful negotiation ushered in a relatively long moment of peace, even reprise, for both parties involved. Yet, the creation of the Centro Histórico and its plan to redevelop Guatemala City's Zone 1, especially the Portal del Comercio, reignited some of older battles between vendors and the government.

Street vendors as a unionized group have had great difficulties negotiating their place in the Centro Histórico urban renewal process.[2] At the start of the project in the early months of 2006, the municipal government offered them what seemed to be a reasonable proposal, explaining that the vendors would need to leave the Portal del Comercio during the renewal efforts but could ultimately return after some construction was complete. Street vendors reported in interviews that the municipal government justified this request with a need for more freedom to develop the area. The vendors acquiesced to this request since the renewal efforts promised an increased level of foot traffic, and possibly even more tourists, who might become active consumers. Long-term gain outweighed short-term inconvenience.

The municipal government, however, did not offer the street vendors anything concrete in return—a contract, a timeline, a business plan. One of the vendors recounted that the municipal government did not even provide them with a simple sheet of paper that might detail where they would be relocated. There was no clear sense as to how long the street vendors would be displaced, where they could go during their displacement, or when they would return, if they could return. There was also a lack of clarity about the street vendors' actual negotiating partners. The municipal government appeared to be the face of the operation, but a continual change of leadership and individual negotiators suggested a much more diffuse force. One street vendor even suggested that the Centro Histórico received secret funds from the European Union, or maybe the Cooperación Española, illustrating the perception that a host of outside forces were at play in the proposed development project. This comment also suggests a relationship between fragile markets and fragile nerves, both strained by a lack of transparency. The retelling of the initial negotiations phase brings to light the productivity of ambiguity that provided the Centro Histórico's backers and proponents with constant room to remaneuver. From the street vendors' own perspective, the municipal government's lack of transparency translated into a lack of respect; many believed that the government did not take them seriously and did not allow them to engage in real negotiations about their right to the streets—as both citizens and businesspeople.

In the months that followed, some specifics came into focus. The municipal government offered the street vendors alternative places where they might be able to work, all without guarantees. One of the suggestions was that street vendors could relocate to Seventh Avenue in another part of Zone 1. While the location itself was workable, the cost to rent a space to sell goods at this location was 600 quetzals (seventy-five U.S. dollars) a month, dramatically more than the seven and a half quetzals (one U.S. dollar) a month that the street vendors paid on Sixth Avenue and in the Portal del Comercio. Other proposals included relocating the vendors to a park close to Guatemala's Institute for Social Security in Zone 1, but the vendors insisted that this area, with its limited foot traffic, would be poor for business. Nothing seemed appropriate, let alone ideal. The municipal government suggested a cluster of temporary spaces that the street vendors could rotate through, but the vendors insisted on a fixed place throughout the year, noting that the informal economy's own irregularity could not be compounded by the irregularity of the space itself. Cycling through different locations would only confuse clientele. A final suggestion was the Parque Enrique Gómez Carrillo in Zone 1. This is ultimately where the street vendors agreed to relocate temporarily.

After months of back and forth without a clear sense of who was in charge and still not a word on how long the relocation would be in effect, the vendors decided to file proceedings with Guatemala's Constitutional Court to declare the procedures of the Centro Histórico as illegitimate. The vendors had received a favorable decision from the Constitutional Court in the past that addressed a similar confrontation between the vendors and the municipal government. However, the Constitutional Court is notoriously unpredictable in terms of the length of time it takes to come to a final decision. One vendor said that it could be "three days, three months, or three years." This time, the vendors waited a little less than two months. During the first half of September, the Constitutional Court denied the charges brought by the vendors against the municipal government, and with this, gave the municipal government the legal authority to complete the urban renewal they had planned. The overall tension around the case led to further negotiations about where the street vendors could sell and where they could not; however, these negotiations did not involve the entire group of street vendors at once. The Centro Histórico's new strategy was to deal with clusters of vendors at a time, dividing their voices to take advantage of a manufactured lack of consensus.

In an effort to garner support and goodwill with the municipal government, offshoots of the street vendors' formal negotiating group attended further negotiations with the municipal government without the support of the official leadership. Finally, in late September 2006, many (but not all) of the street vendors signed a document agreeing to leave the Portal del Comercio for a limited time. After the urban renewal was complete, they would return to their fixed places of work. While the vendors understood the agreement as temporary, it is clear now that municipal government officials perceived the document to ban vendors permanently from the Centro Histórico, making only temporary provisions about where the vendors could sell their goods next (in Parque Gómez Carrillo of Zone 1). Divided and conquered, several street vendors were not in agreement with the proposal, but regardless of the confusion, the municipal government physically removed the street vendors from the Portal del Comercio in September 2006 in order to begin construction projects.

Conflicting Conceptions of the Public

The conflict between the municipal government and the street vendors emerges in part from unequal power relationships, a history of institutional violence, and Guatemala's unstable economy. Above all, however, it stems from two very different conceptions of public space. The street vendors see public space as both a right and a resource. They consider their position to be rather straightforward: they want to work. If they had alternatives to working in the informal economy, they would be employed elsewhere, but they do not, so they make their living as street vendors (Véliz 2007). The municipal government, however, reads the politics of public space through an economic model: public space is a raw material available for development, and its value must be maximized, utilized to its fullest capacity. These two visions of the public clashed throughout the Centro Histórico negotiations, and exist in constant tension in postwar Guatemala City, as more areas undergo urban renewal in the name of development and progress, with little regard for those who work in the streets. The case study above ultimately offers glimpses into how the municipal government forced its vision of public space onto the street vendors' vision, despite small acts of resistance along the way.

The street vendors' conception of public space emerges out of a distinctly liberal history. Liberal notions of progress and utility guided Guatemala City's development in the nineteenth century (Webre 1989), culminating in President José María Reyna Barrios's beautification efforts in the century's last decade. With grand avenues and public parks, Barrios sought to transform Guatemala City into a "tropical Athens" or "Little Paris" (Peláez Almengor 1994). Central to Reyna Barrios's Parisian dreams was a liberal vision of public space. Avenues, parks, and monuments reflected an ideology; they were understood as open meeting grounds and venues for socialization. The construction of public space was a self-conscious construction of regulated freedoms—of spaces to walk and to seek pleasure. In its most idealized state, the construction of public space under Barrios's watchful eye actively trained people to "discover beauty as well as a democratic version of gentility" (Joyce 2003: 221). Public space aimed to foster the activities of persuading, debating, listening, compromising, and seeking common ground. These were the ideas of modern liberalism that accompanied dreams of industrialization and democratization; public spaces fostered freedom and individualism. And while this freedom came with its own regimes of governance, such as codes of conduct and police surveillance, the overall intent of liberal public space was the cultivation of a modern sensibility.

Guatemala City's street vendors, in many ways, still hold on to this liberal notion of public space, in the sense that they have a right to the city and that the city itself is a kind of sociality. From interviews and observations, it is clear that the Centro Histórico is not just a place to purchase merchandise at competitive prices (although this is one of its greatest functions); it is also an avenue through which Guatemalans of all ethnicities and classes generate social relationships. Zone 1 is, in fact, a place where Guatemalans meet family, bump into old friends, and exchange stories. While today's use of the Portal del Comercio conflicts with its original and rather elite intentions, the area nonetheless serves as a meeting place. Even in spite of growing security concerns, which are both constant and fierce, Guatemala City's informal economy can still be read from the perspective of Jane Jacobs (1961), who argues that city streets are where urban dwellers meet each other and where trade and commercial activities take place.[3]

Alongside the notion that public space is a right and, in turn, the very seat of sociality, there exists the complementary notion that public space is a resource. Work itself is a central issue for the street vendors. Selling goods in Guatemala's informal economy is the street vendors' way of providing for their families. During interviews, street vendors explained that their livelihoods were the reason for negotiating so relentlessly with the municipal government. As one street vendor explained: "What [the Centro Histórico] doesn't understand is that we are not merely forty-eight street vendors who will be dislocated. We are forty-eight families." The street vendors circled back to their lost earnings and often asked how they were supposed to support their families without the streets. How were they supposed to pay for their children's education without their stalls? And how were they to provide food and clothing for their loved ones without access to Guatemala's informal economy? Apart from these immediate concerns, those interviewed also wondered about how the renewal project would impact the informal economy at large. Urban renewal might introduce competitive merchandise and new price-points that further threatened their livelihood. As the street vendors recognized, urban renewal would not just change Zone 1's facades but also its economic landscape.

Those interviewed also explained with a certain degree of dejectedness that "the people in the municipal government now have the money. Do you think they care what happens to us?" One vendor commented, "They have education, they have manners, they are blond; we are never going to be like them." By "never going to be like them," this street vendor alluded to Guatemala's ethnic and social division, but he largely meant that he and his colleagues would not be "able to compete against them [the elite developers]" for the use of Zone 1—for the use of public space. These comments suggest that the street vendors do not just feel threatened by the municipal government but also marginalized in society. The street vendors, however, were not the only ones affected by the Centro Histórico renewal project. Many area shop owners, for example, insisted that the street vendors had never created problems for the area and that they, in fact, drove Zone 1's economy—both formal and informal. One owner of a garment shop explained that the street vendors brought traffic to the area, brought consumers, and that business without them would be painfully slow.

The Centro Histórico renewal program is driven by a vision of public space that is not so much liberal as neoliberal. The distinction is worth highlighting. A liberal vision of public space, echoing the work of Jane Jacobs (1961), announces that the free use of public space is a right and a resource, an idea that has legitimated Guatemala City's informal economy since the 1976 earthquake. And, as Jacobs notes, a liberal vision of public space makes clear that the more people use city streets, the safer those city streets become (Brantingham and Brantingham 1984; Felson and Cohen 1980). Encouraging the use of public spaces increases the number of people in the streets themselves, which bolsters both economic vitality and public safety. As people fill the streets to shop and to socialize, individuals fall under the safety of the crowd's watchful eye. Liberal constructions of public space assure that there is safety in numbers.

Guatemala City's street vendors, knowingly or unknowingly, draw on this liberal assumption to understand their presence in the streets and their business as good for both the economy and for public safety. By contrast, the Centro Histórico renewal project understands public space from a neoliberal perspective—as neither a right nor as a resource but as a raw material available for development. In fact, the Centro Histórico renewal project actually inverts the liberal relationship between space, security, and the economy through a neoliberal logic that announces that urban renewal brings safety by regulating who inhabits public spaces and what is done in them. Crowds do not bring security to the streets; security is brought to the streets for the sake of the crowds, but only those who can afford it. This is the neoliberal twist: let the market determine who has access to "public" space.

The Centro Histórico renewal project follows a predictable logic, familiar to other urban renewal programs throughout the Americas.[4] From a neoliberal perspective, citizens do not have a right to public space; rather, public space has an economic value that needs to be developed and maximized. The Centro Histórico as an urban renewal program recognizes that the production of semipublic spaces can yield more money and security than Guatemala City's more traditional public spaces, such as the Portal del Comercio, where many of the city's street vendors worked (Greene and Taylor 1988; Kelling 1985; Mastrofski 1988). Development, from the Centro Histórico's perspective, means replacing public spaces supposedly governed by the crowd's protective gaze with upscale cafes, restaurants, and shops secured by private security forces and a more discerning gaze that separates the "haves" from the "have-nots." Renewed and now semipublic spaces, such as the Centro Histórico, foster new environments of consumption, available only to those with the means to participate—that is, the money to shop. Those who "have" consume, or at the very least window-shop; those who "have-not" cannot afford to consume and, in turn, loiter (Friedberg 1994). The same can be said for potential vendors in a semipublic space, such as the Centro Histórico. All are free to participate in the area's renewal, but all must do so through formal channels and with formal shops, with taxes, high rent, and utilities. Amidst this neoliberal vision of public space, the street vendors of Zone 1's Portal del Comercio become criminals who squat on land that is not theirs, rather than citizens who use their streets for their livelihood.

Maximizing and managing Zone 1's economic potential drives the Centro Histórico's development as a semipublic space in postwar Guatemala City. One of the Centro Histórico's own points of departure has been the area's problem with postwar violence. As is noted throughout this volume, postwar Guatemala City's remarkable instability and rising levels of urban violence emerge from a mixture of organized crime, transnational street gangs, and drug trafficking, not to mention the residual effects of a civil war that has left in its wake trained soldiers now struggling to find work in a sluggish economy. One result of this insecurity has been a spatial imaginary (Thomas, this volume) that places violence, criminality, and uncertainty at the very heart of the capital city and in the very center of the city's own center: Zone 1's Portal del Comercio. Securing the city, or at least parts of the city through renewal programs, becomes couched as an economic mandate. Violence is bad for business.

Of course, violence is bad for business; Guatemala's struggling tourist industry tells us this much. The neoliberal logic of urban renewal projects, such as the Centro Histórico, works hard to make intuitive a connection between security, development, and space in a way that ultimately justifies the dislocation of street vendors and their former customers from the Portal del Comercio. It is a new vision of public space as semipublic, which concludes that street vendors do not maximize Zone 1's value and that their former customers also compromise the area's economic stability and general security. Looking at this spatial reorganization through the lens of neoliberal logics of space, security, and citizenship helps to explain why the street vendors did not receive the respect they deserved during negotiations with the municipal government. From the street vendors' perspective, they had a right to use the street as a resource because they are citizens of Guatemala; from a neoliberal perspective, the street vendors' presence could only be tolerated if it did not interfere with the maximization of the Centro Histórico's potential value. Their vending, their stalls, and their customers—their place in their former space—became out of place through the logic of urban renewal.

Conclusions

The Portal del Comercio has changed in important ways. In 2006, at one of its once busy intersections, an old woman taunted municipal workers for displacing the street vendors. Municipal workers relaxed on street corners, while some (ex-)street vendors from the Portal del Comercio loitered, observing the construction at their former place of work and discussing what they should do next. Walking in the middle of it all were several architects and professionals from the Centro Histórico, debating the changes they would make. This relative calm gave way to a public demonstration on October 20, 2006, the anniversary of Guatemala's storied 1944 Revolution. Almost a month after the displacement, representatives from Guatemala's informal economic sector were one of the largest and most organized groups in the public procession. The signs they held displayed slogans against the Centro Histórico and efforts at urban renewal. Marchers beat dolls and piñatas in effigy, some in front of

Zone 1's municipal buildings and others in front of the national palace. However, street vendors, a relatively large subgroup of Guatemala's informal sector, did not participate in the march as a united front. They arrived at different times and in small groups, performing their fragmented uncertainty after having been displaced and disaggregated through the negotiations process earlier that year. Their brokenness existed as a testament to urban renewal's ability to divide.

Today, construction on the Portal del Comercio is complete, and there is not a single street vendor to be seen. Of the forty-eight original street vendors, most now work in the park that the Centro Histórico offered as an alternative, while another twelve work in a different part of Zone 1, far from their original location. The rest have been dispersed throughout the city, not accepting the spaces that they had been assigned during construction. The street vendors note with absolute certainty that earnings in their new locations are considerably less than in their old location at the Centro Histórico. Some feel guilty for having signed the agreement with the municipal government. One of the street vendors explained that the most likely outcome is that the authorities will displace them again, without any respect for them or their trade.

Notes

This essay is dedicated to and in memory of Adolfo Flores (1982–2007) for his years of friendship to one of the authors (Véliz). This essay is also an effort made against social violence and impunity in Guatemala.

1. Many thanks to Lorlene Hoyt 2005 for a number of these critical citations.

2. They organize as la Federación Sindical de Trabajadores Independientes (Independent Workers' Union Federation), which is part of la Central General de Trabajadores de Guatemala (Guatemalan Workers' General Center).

3. Important to note are the contradictions inherent in the liberal model and that these contradictions are evident in the kind of modernity that Barrios envisioned. Liberalism is exclusionary in its own right (Joyce 2003). The promise of an inclusive public space, nonetheless, motivates the street vendors.

4. The work of Paul R. Levy (2001) tells us that there are at least 404 BIDs in the United States and another 400 districts in Canadian cities. In Canada, as in the United States, the BID trend has been met with some resistance (Jacobs 1961). The BID trend, however, extends beyond the North American context to include organizations for management of city centers in Europe, Japan, Australia, South Africa, and Latin America.

Part Two

Guatemala
City and Country

The Security Guard Industry in Guatemala

Rural Communities and Urban Violence

Avery Dickins de Girón

Walking through any commercial zone in Guatemala City, one is struck by the number of armed guards posted outside supermarkets, delivery trucks, and restaurants. Whether they instill a sense of comfort or fear, the individuals behind the guns—most of them rural peasants—symbolize the unequal social and economic conditions in contemporary Guatemalan society. The increasing dependence on private guards for public security has emerged from the legacy of Guatemala's civil war and various political and economic changes. Although Latin American countries have long been characterized by high rates of socioeconomic inequality, the initial "shock" of neoliberal reform and free market economics has disproportionately benefited the elite class, and lower wages and increased unemployment have hurt both rural and urban poor (Gwynne and Kay 2000). The lack of public services and the frustrations resulting from this rising inequality have in turn contributed to a rise in urban violence (Briceño-León 2002; Perez 2005; Strocka 2006). Understandably, the demand for security guards has intensified in the face of this violence.[1]

Simultaneously, Guatemalans have witnessed a failure in the state's ability to provide public security. After years of repressive military dictatorships that culminated in the atrocities leveled against the civilian population during the war, the 1996 Peace Accords mandated a decrease in the size of the military and the creation of a police force dedicated solely to civilian security, the Policía Nacional Civil (PNC). In a country that has relied for so many years on brutal authoritarianism to maintain order, the meager number of police cannot control rising rates of homicides, gang-leveraged extortion, and street crime.

This state of emergency is compounded by widespread corruption within the police force, leading wealthier citizens to employ private guards and thereby find an alternate way to ensure their personal safety and protect their merchandise. The Guatemalan judge María Cristina Fernández García summarizes the situation as follows: "Ever increasing numbers or [sic] people arm themselves or contract private agencies to afford them security. The State does not possess the monopoly of force or the ability to coerce, a situation which it [sic] itself promoted during the war. Every day it tolerates violence coming from private sectors and does not have the capacity to safeguard its people" (Fernández García 2004: 48).

The growth of Guatemala's private security industry echoes Judge Fernández García's statements: in 2000, there were 68 government-registered security agencies in Guatemala; in 2006, this number had increased to 128 registered agencies representing 28,000 guards, plus an additional 60,000 guards working for unauthorized agencies (some of whom use the guise of security guard to conduct illicit activities).[2] Security guards far outnumber state-employed police (approximately 20,000 throughout the country), and the great majority of them are posted in Guatemala City. The growth of the security industry has parallels in several other Latin American countries, where the industry has been widely associated with a decreasing role of the state in public security, as well as in exploitation and human labor rights violations (Gómez del Prado 2007).

In the case of civilian security in Guatemala, a weak state peacekeeping apparatus has become reliant on the privatized security industry, which, in turn, depends on a flexible labor pool willing to accept low wages. The security industry therefore represents a neoliberal response to today's violence, a violence that is also increasingly decentralized and "neoliberalized" (see Benson, Thomas, and Fischer in this volume). The bulk of the labor for security agencies in the capital is provided by men from rural areas, many of whom are Maya. These generally landless men from impoverished communities say that they seek work as security guards *por necesidad* (out of necessity), hinting at the structural conditions that require them to seek wage labor beyond their hometowns. Yet the situation is more complicated, as these men use the flexible nature of the security industry to their advantage, working when they need cash and quitting when the exploitative conditions become unbearable, when a better opportunity comes their way, or simply when they need to take a break (often returning to work in another agency a few weeks later). Moreover, many rural men use employment in the security industry as a means through which to experience urban Guatemala City, and in this sense, working as a guard serves as a bridge to imagined opportunities and possibilities for the future.

Opportunity and Imagination in Neoliberal Guatemala

Security guards constitute a mobile population that inhabits both rural and urban spheres of Guatemala. A large number of men in Guatemala's department of Alta Verapaz, from the rural highlands, leave to seek work on plantations in the departments of Petén and Izabal, the country of Belize, or in the industrial sector in Guatemala City. Included in this migrant population are Q'eqchi' Maya and ladinos (nonindigenous) from other areas of Guatemala who routinely make the decision to work in Guatemala City's security industry. In this essay, I consider the work of the imagination in motivating this decision, and how guards' experiences of the city figure into their novel constructions of identity. Unskilled landless peasants and subsistence farmers have relied on seasonal wage labor, primarily in the form of plantation labor or local agricultural work, throughout the colonial period and during the last two centuries (Adams 2001; de Janvry 1981: 113; Smith 1990; Wilk 1991). Working as a security guard is another version of this long-standing economic strategy, yet it differs from plantation and other forms of wage labor in several important ways: it is a dangerous job that physically reflects the economic and social inequalities of modern Guatemala, creating a fluid and continuous exchange between urban and rural spheres that reconfigures rural identities.

Economic factors serve as the primary motivation for labor migration in Guatemala, yet recent studies have also shown the interrelated importance of discrimination (Odell 1984), political violence (Morrison 1993), and militarization (Smith 1990). The imagination, moreover, is also a deciding factor for rural men who seek work as security guards in Guatemala City. Imagination invokes perceived economic and educational opportunities, but also involves less tangible hopes for a better life and the curiosity of exploring a new landscape. At the same time, this study does not deny the exploitation and discrimination that security guards (like other unskilled workers) endure in the capital. Yet, as Diane Nelson assures in regard to the mujer maya, another exploited figure in Guatemala's economy and public culture, security guards must be considered as more than just victims (1999: 278).

Many of the men who take work in the security industry have never been to Guatemala City or any other urban locale before they are contracted.[3] Some come from towns, but others live in small communities (400 families or fewer) that have no electricity, running water, or direct access to roads. Their intrigue with the city is revealed in their fluent descriptions of paved streets, upscale malls, fast-food restaurants, buses and cars that merge into a dynamic, even exotic, landscape. It is also clear in their emphasis on the educational and employment opportunities in Guatemala City, as well as their focus on the seemingly endless possibilities for entertainment. The capital, therefore, holds an allure for these men that stands in contrast to the communities they call home. This vision of the city as ripe with possibilities emerges out of the structural conditions that define (and constrain) the meaning of "opportunity" for impoverished rural dwellers, combined with individual imaginings, desires, and curiosity. Here, Arjun Appadurai's work on the power of the imagination proves instructive: "More persons in more parts of the world consider a wider set of 'possible' lives than they ever did before . . . What is implied is that even the meanest and most hopeless of lives . . . the harshest of lived inequalities is now open to the play of the imagination" (1991: 197).

Migrating to Guatemala City can open up new possibilities and paths for rural inhabitants with limited options, whether in terms of education, technical or social skills, or the status they gain for having "made it" (if only temporarily) in the city. The allure of the city is not limited to security guards, as surely some of the factory employees, domestic staff, and street vendors who migrate from rural areas have similar hopes and imaginations of what the city holds. Furthermore, the vision of the city as a land of opportunity also has parallels with the ways that transnational migrants view the United States (see Foxen 2007). Yet whereas security guards fluidly travel from their natal communities to Guatemala City and back, other migrants to the capital city commonly set up lives there and become part of the marginalized urban poor (Briceño-León 2002) or work in maquiladoras (offshore textile assembly factories) close to their hometowns (Goldín 2001). Guards' tenure in the city offers a chance to experience urban life, a sort of sojourn that is informed by and informs their position in the larger social context.

Inequality, Seasonal Migration, and Wage Labor in Guatemala

Over half of Guatemala's population live in rural areas and depend primarily on subsistence agriculture, and the majority of these rural dwellers are indigenous (Perez 2005; UNDP 2005). The necessity for subsistence farmers and landless peasants to seek wage labor outside of the local sphere arises from land dispossession and fragmentation and the lack of economic opportunities in rural sectors, all of which are tied to Guatemala's history of socioeconomic inequality. Continued disparities are apparent in the current concentration of land holdings. According to the last agricultural census in 2003, Guatemala has a remarkably high GINI coefficient of 0.785 for land distribution (in which 1 = total inequality and 0 = total equality) (UNDP 2004). This unequal distribution of land took shape through the expropriation of native lands during the colonial period, when Spanish settlers were granted *encomiendas* (parcels of land that included the labor of the indigenous people who lived there), and continued in the nineteenth century, when administrations that had adopted liberal reforms designed to open up Guatemala to capitalist development took possession or forced the sale of communally held indigenous lands for coffee cultivation (McCreery 1990: 106). Those who lost their lands lived and worked on plantations as peons, often as a result of *habilitaciones* (cash advances for labor) that left them indebted to plantation owners into the twentieth century (Goldín 2001; Odell 1984). In general, legal and political structures have facilitated access to land for foreigners and ladinos, and the expropriation of land from indigenous communities.[4]

The concentration of land in the hands of a few Guatemalans figures into current inequalities in education, literacy, and income that disproportionately disadvantage Maya groups (Fischer and Benson 2006: 52). In 2006, Guatemala was ranked by the United Nations Development Programme as having the second-highest level of inequality in Central America,[5] slightly behind Panama. Over 60 percent of Guatemala's population lives in poverty, and 17.9 percent live in extreme poverty; these numbers increase in departments with large indigenous populations, such as Alta Verapaz (84.1 percent live in poverty) and Quiché (84.6 percent live in poverty) (UNDP 2005).

Given the context of high levels of poverty and unequal access to land, peasants in Guatemala have long relied on some form of wage labor to complement subsistence activities, but the patterns and forms of this labor have varied over time and across regions. The traditional route of migration for peasants from the southwestern highlands was to the Pacific coast to work on cotton, coffee, or sugar cane plantations, but alternative wage-generating strategies include local agricultural labor, road-building and other government projects, trade, and craft production (Smith 1990). As demographic pressure increased during the twentieth century, inheritance further divided small peasant landholdings, resulting in an increase in highland-to-coast seasonal migration (Handy 1990: 165; Odell 1984). Carol Smith (1990) estimates that by the late 1970s, 25 percent of the southwestern highland population engaged in seasonal coastal labor.

Peasants in northern Guatemala, the majority of whom are Q'eqchi' Maya, have also engaged in migration for wage labor, but they have traveled to plantations in the northern lowlands and El Salvador, worked throughout Guatemala as iterant peddlers (*cobaneros*), or migrated permanently to Belize or Petén (Adams 2001: 205; King 1974; Wilk 1991). Today, the most common way for smallholding or landless Q'eqchi' to earn wages is to seek local work as a *jornalero* (day laborer), clearing land for cattle or tending a landowner's crops, for which they earn thirty quetzals (four U.S. dollars) per day. Other common options include working for a few months at a time in the *palmeras* (palm plantations) in Sayaxche, Petén, or in Puerto Barrios, Izabal, which pays 900 to 1,200 quetzals (120–160 U.S. dollars) per month; or traveling to Belize to work on citrus plantations. Throughout Guatemala, enlisting in the army provides another option for young men who have completed ninth grade. Army service offers a stable source of income as well as the means to develop skills such as fluency in Spanish.

In addition to these more "traditional" strategies, new forms of wage labor emerged in the late twentieth century as a result of modernization and industrialization. In the 1960s and 1970s, the implementation of Import Substitution Industrialization policies throughout Latin America, designed to reduce dependence on foreign nations, led to the establishment of internally focused manufacturing industries. The boom in industry attracted landless peasants to settle in Guatemala City and led to a new route of migration from the Pacific and northern lowlands to the city (Brown 1996: 170). In the 1980s, the Guatemalan government embraced export-oriented neoliberal policies, embarking on a program to develop "nontraditional exports" including maquila and production of crops such as broccoli and snow peas (Fischer and Benson 2006: 53). The growth of these industries in the 1990s encouraged another wave of rural migration to the city and surrounding central highlands, where their production is concentrated (Goldín 2001: 32–34). In contrast to other forms of migrant labor, including the security guard industry, maquila labor is unique in that it has historically been gendered female (see Thomas, this volume).

Aside from maquilas and production of nontraditional crops for export, however, neoliberal policies have led to a decrease in industry and manufacturing in Latin America, causing a rise in unemployment levels in urban areas, the development of a large informal sector (i.e., street vendors, domestics, and pirates), and the widespread marginalization of urban populations (Briceño-León 2002; Perez 2005). Roberto Briceño-León (2002) identifies this growing inequality as one of the central factors in the rise of violence in urban centers where poor city dwellers are exposed to, yet excluded from, wealthy lifestyles.

Violence in Postwar Guatemala

Despite the signing of the 1996 Peace Accords that formally ended Guatemala's civil war, the level of violence in Guatemala City has grown beyond the control of the state over the last decade. This is due both to an increase in crime as well as a weak police force characterized by poor organization, a lack of funding, and widespread corruption. The level of homicides in Guatemala has risen from an average rate of 18.3 homicides (per 100,000) for the years 1991–93 to 23.9 for the years 1996–98. In 2007, over 6,000 murders were reported to the National Police, representing 17 per day; this is most likely an underestimate (COHA 2009). Homicides are concentrated in the metropolitan area, and the number of women targeted has especially increased in recent years (CIEN 2002: 8; LAPOP 2001, 2006; Sanford 2006). Several survey instruments indicate that even compared to other parts of Latin America, the outlook on crime in urban Guatemala is bleak. Latinobarómetro, a public opinion survey conducted annually among urban populations in seventeen Latin American countries, reports that between 1996 and 1998, at least one member of over 50 percent of Guatemalan households had been assaulted or otherwise victimized by crime in the preceding twelve months. This makes Guatemala the country with the highest level of victimization in Latin America during that period (Gaviria and Pagés 2000: 6; also see CIEN 2002). In a 2004 survey by the Latin American Public Opinion Poll (LAPOP 2006), 12.8 percent of the individuals surveyed in Guatemala reported that they had been victims of crime in the past year, which increased to 19.8 percent in 2006; if only urban areas are considered, these numbers jump to 18.1 percent in 2004 and 25.3 percent in 2006.[6] Nearly 80 percent of those surveyed by LAPOP say that crime is a threat to Guatemala's future.

The increase in crime and violence in postwar Guatemala has also emerged in the context of attempts to reduce the power of the military, which had been nearly unchecked during three decades of military dictators. To make reparations for the terror and human rights violations carried out by the state against civilians during the war, the Peace Accords mandated the creation of the PNC to limit the military's role in civilian "security." Yet in 2004, President Berger's move to integrate military personnel into the PNC as *fuerzas combinadas* (combined forces) indicated the weakness of the police force. In 2006, there were 2,400 soldiers serving in these special units, which led to protests by human rights groups but applause from many of Guatemala City's residents, who were fed up with crime.

In desperation, many Guatemalans have taken their protection into their own hands. Along with the increase in violence, Guatemala has witnessed in recent years a rise in lynchings and social cleansing campaigns directed against supposed gang members, kidnappers, and thieves. Over 500 lynching incidents have been documented between 1996 and 2002, leading to the designation of this period as the "lynching era" in Guatemala (Mendoza 2006). Lynchings are most frequent in rural areas with high indigenous populations and a lack of judicial and police presence, and thus are viewed by locals as punitive (and even preventative) mechanisms leveraged against criminal impunity. While lynch mobs are made up of local residents seeking justice, *limpieza social* (social cleansing) is somewhat more ambiguous. It may consist of vigilante citizens seeking to punish suspected gang members and criminals, but it also provides a cover for state police and parapolice forces to wage violence against citizens without detection. Social cleansing has been on the rise in the last few years in urban as well as rural areas of Guatemala.[7]

In the city, the actual rise in crime and the perception of insecurity motivate capital investments in protection in the form of private security guards or alarm systems (CIEN 2002). As in other Latin American capitals, businesses and residents of Guatemala City who can afford to do so have turned to security guards as a preventative measure. According to a study by Guatemala's Centro de Investigaciones Económicas Nacionales (ibid.), the private sector in Guatemala spent 1.06 percent of the GDP in 1999 on security (this includes a wide array of protective measures, such as alarm systems, purchase of guns, and hiring security guards). The study also found that twenty-six companies that had been especially affected by violence spent approximately US$3.5 million on security in 1999, an average of US$130,000 per business, and Muñoz Piloña claims (interview with author) that the industry moves over US$8 million per year. That a portion of this money ends up in the rural sector has a significant impact on development.

The Security Guard Industry

The requirements to work in the security guard industry in Guatemala are relatively few: applicants must be eighteen, have completed sixth grade, and demonstrate some basic fluency in Spanish (which can be quite variable among rural Guatemalans). Although guards' sixth-grade education is relatively high in the context of their rural communities, it is not high enough to obtain more desirable jobs, as secretaries, teachers, bank tellers, or policemen. Agencies prefer to hire guards with military experience, a policy that links the industry to the reduction of the military. Yet agencies complain about the scarcity of such recruits, which requires them to hire less qualified individuals, who then must be trained. Depending on their experience and the agency, guards usually receive a brief training when they are contracted, ranging from two days to a week. Men in rural communities find out about vacancies in security agencies through word of mouth, radio announcements, and contractors who solicit employees by posting flyers in remote areas with information regarding upcoming interviews in regional centers. Agency contractors continuously seek recruits in impoverished areas, especially Alta Verapaz, Quiché, Baja Verapaz, Jutiapa, and Jalapa.[8] These departments have a high percentage of rural populations, and the first three have high indigenous populations (93 percent, 89 percent, and 59 percent, respectively) (INE 2002).

Guards commonly state that they seek wage labor outside of their rural locales por necesidad because they do not own land (88 percent of those interviewed do not own land, and 35 percent have fathers who are also landless) and have few options to earn wages in rural communities. Guards receive salaries of 1,200–2,600 quetzals per month (160–350 U.S. dollars) (the average of those we interviewed was 1,775 quetzals, or 235 U.S. dollars), which is more than they would receive working as a jornalero or on a plantation. Pedro, a twenty-two-year-old Q'eqchi' Maya man from a hamlet in highland Alta Verapaz has no land of his own. He worked temporarily at a livestock store in a nearby town where he received 900 quetzals (120 U.S. dollars) per month, but as the eldest child and with an eighth-grade education, Pedro hoped to help his parents pay for his siblings' education. He sought work as a guard two years ago and now earns 1,700 quetzals (227 U.S. dollars) per month for providing security outside a Domino's Pizza in Guatemala City. He sends 500 quetzals (67 U.S. dollars) home each month.

Other guards work in the security industry so that they can provide a better life for their children. Ignacio, for example, is from a remote village in northern Alta Verapaz that has no electricity, running water, or secondary school. Because he owns no land, he has struggled to support his wife and five children. In June 2006, he began working as a security guard, which allows him to feed, clothe, and educate his family. Although his wife worries about Ignacio and dislikes the fact that he is away, she emphasizes the need for the income, and views the situation as an improvement. Like Ignacio and Pedro, most guards send a portion of the money they earn to their families (parents or spouse), which goes toward household goods and staples, the education of younger siblings or children, and luxury items such as an electric stove or bed with a mattress. The average amount that the guards interviewed sent home per month was 829 quetzals (110 U.S. dollars), or an average of 46.5 percent of what each earns.

Whereas Pedro and Ignacio had no land of their own, men who own land may also take jobs as security guards. They do so to make ends meet between harvest and planting periods or to make a defined amount of money quickly to invest locally in a specific project such as the construction of a house, opening a tienda (small store), paying off a debt, or investing in some other larger project that requires initial capital they cannot generate at home, such as paying a coyote to take them to the United States. Juan, for instance, is a twenty-two-year-old ladino from Jalapa who owns a small plot of land. He obtained work in the security industry in order to save money to go to the United States, after which he hopes to buy more land and open a store in his hometown.

Why Men Work in the Security Industry

Although the need for wage labor is clear given these men's social conditions, why do they choose to work as guards? This question is important due to the risk the job carries compared to other forms of wage labor available to unskilled rural peasants. In this section, I first lay out the economic reasons men seek work in the security guard industry, and then examine other factors that figure into this decision.

In purely financial terms, the appeal of working as a guard lies in the higher salary and relative ease of labor compared to agricultural work. Guards commonly state that one of the most attractive aspects of working in the security industry is that they are paid quincenalmente (every fifteen days), which they contrast with the irregular nature of income earned from agricultural day labor. Although guards may complain about standing all day long, they describe security work as suave, or easy, compared to laboring in the fields under the hot sun or in the rain. Yet the attractive salary is somewhat compromised by the cost of living in Guatemala City. Almost all of the agencies provide barracks-style housing (that guards refer to as *la cuadra*, literally) that usually includes access to a stove, television, and storage lockers. This housing is initially free, but many agencies quickly charge guards rent, or automatically deduct the cost from the guards' paychecks (encouraging some guards to rent a room elsewhere, which is more expensive but offers more privacy). Although some guards cook, most purchase food from street vendors for about fifteen quetzals (two U.S. dollars) per day, an expense that leads them to complain that they often go hungry in the city, whereas at home they "can eat until they are full." Depending on the cost of travel and the time it takes (round-trip bus fares range from 40 to 300 quetzals, and travel times can be as long as ten hours), guards may go home to visit on weekends, once a month, or once every three months. Between these living expenses and what they send home, guards are left with only a small amount of money, rarely enough to save.

The benefits of working in the security industry are also weighed against the exploitation guards endure, which is similar to maquila, plantation, and other forms of labor in which workers often experience alienation and discrimination. When contracted, new employees are taken to Guatemala City at no cost to them, and they generally receive room and board during their first few days of training in the city. Yet when they receive their first paycheck, guards often find that they have paid for their uniforms and training, which leads some to claim that the contractors "tricked" them. Although guards do not receive advances per se (in the sense of habilitaciones), agencies allow vendors to enter the cuadra to sell clothing and "medicine" (vitamins that promise endurance for their twenty-four-hour shifts). Guards are aware that their purchases will be deducted from the next paycheck, but the price is often much higher than promised, or appears for several pay periods. If an agency is short-handed, supervisors assign guards extra shifts for which they are not always compensated. If guards go to the agency's central office to complain about pay deductions or omissions, they are turned away with no explanation or recourse. The exploitation in some agencies is more overt, including requirements that guards submit their *cédula* (identification papers) to the agency in order to deter them from renouncing their job before finishing their contract.

Moreover, the security guard industry's access to a flexible labor pool institutionalizes worker exploitation. Agencies perceive a limitless supply of workers in rural regions where jobs are scarce, and so invest little in each guard and constantly seek new recruits. Thus, the security guard industry thrives on the flexible workforce that neoliberal policies intend to create and that translates into periodic unemployment and low wages for workers (Gwynne and Kay 2000). Implicit in the idea of a limitless and flexible labor pool is the conceptualization of guards as replaceable bodies, a view that is held by contracting agencies as well as their "clients" (the individuals and businesses that hire guards). This commodification is made even more explicit by the pay structure in which higher salaries are commensurate with greater risk.[9]

Security guards are aware of this exploitation. Rodrigo, a guard from Santa Rosa, clearly stated: "They exploit us, and demand much more work than the payment merits. This is not a profession that helps you get ahead." Guards often view working in the security industry as somewhat of a last resort due to its exploitative and dangerous nature. Ignacio dislikes carrying a gun because it makes him a target for gang violence, and says he would prefer to work in a maquila or cleaning windows in houses. However, he is unsure about how to obtain these jobs, since he has only been in the capital a few months. It is important to note that Ignacio views the security guard industry, symbolized by a gun and almost completely populated by male workers, as a step below the female-gendered maquila industry, which is generally associated with intolerable conditions and high levels of exploitation (although they may be imagined differently by hopeful workers) (see Thomas, in this book). This perception was also apparent in the responses we collected from guards when we asked them to order a set of eleven occupations from most desirable to least desirable. They ranked working in security fourth from the bottom; the three least-desirable jobs were truck driver, farmer, and day laborer (see the table below). Residents of rural communities in Chisec ordered the occupations similarly, but placed security guards third from the bottom, barely ahead of farming. Although family members express concern over the dangerous nature of the job, both guards and their families emphasize the need they have for the income and view it as an acceptable trade-off, as indicated previously by Ignacio's wife.

Working in the security guard industry pays more than plantation work and is easier to obtain than work in a maquiladora, but like factory and plantation labor, it involves exploitation and alienation, similar expenses, and an even higher risk. What tips the balance toward the security industry for many of these men is the flexible nature of security employment. Although the flexibility is most beneficial for employers, guards use it toward their own ends, seeking work when they need it. Due to the large number of agencies that con-

Top Eleven Preferred Male Occupations, Ranked by Security Guards and by Rural Residents, 2006

Ranking (highest to lowest)	Security Guards	Residents of Chisec and hamlets
1	Doctor	Doctor
2	Teacher	Teacher
3	Bank teller	Storeowner/salesman
4	Policeman	Bank teller
5	Storeowner/salesman	Secretary
6	Secretary	Policeman
7	Mason	Mason
8	Security guard	Truck driver
9	Truck driver	Security guard
10	Farmer	Farmer
11	Day laborer	Day laborer

Source: The preferential ranking of male occupations presented in this table is based on surveys administered to 129 individuals, including 51 men who were working at that time as security guards in Guatemala City, 16 family members of guards, and 62 residents of the town of Chisec and small villages in the Chisec municipality.

stantly have vacancies, men who meet the requirements view the industry as an open and easy solution to their needs for wage labor. This is especially true for those who have previously worked as guards and who can directly apply for employment at agencies in the capital. It is just as simple for first-time guards who are recruited in their hometowns by traveling contractors. Because the agencies rarely give time off, when guards want to go home or get "tired" or "bored" of working in security, or if something comes up (e.g., a sickness in the family or the birth of a child), they quit their job, go home, and seek employment in another agency when they are ready to go back to work. This revolving door pattern was substantiated by the guards we surveyed; over one-third have worked in more than one agency, and 12 percent have worked in more than three agencies within the last five years.

Beyond using the flexible nature of the security industry to meet their shifting financial needs, some men view working as a guard as a means to experience Guatemala City. The allure of the city is most apparent among single men in their twenties who have completed secondary school, and thus have the confidence to *salir afuera*, to leave their small communities (where they often know everyone) and explore the urban environment. Although they have certainly heard stories about Guatemala City from relatives and friends, many of the men who work as guards have never been to the city before they contract work as a guard. In addition to seeking a higher salary than what he earned in the livestock store, Pedro sought work as a guard because he wanted to explore the city. Similarly, Mario, a guard from a hamlet near Cobán, explained, "I don't know the capital, but I know everything about my village." His sentiments were echoed by Isauro, who took work in the industry to "meet new people" and "get out of the routine" of life in Chisec where he helps his father cultivate cardamom and corn. For men from small rural communities with limited possibilities and entertainment options, Guatemala City offers "more opportunities to get ahead," a dynamic landscape of "people in movement," and "the chance to meet women."

Some guards relate their initial impressions of the city through a lens of timidity or fear as "everything is different" and "there is so much Spanish," and because they had to learn to navigate the bus system and use escalators. These misgivings and challenges are quickly overshadowed by their descriptions of the "marvelous and tall" buildings and wide boulevards, "beautiful houses," and the abundance of "hospitals, schools, and universities at hand." In their free time, guards visit the airport, go to the zoo, or browse the street markets on 18 Calle, and on Sundays they gather in the Parque Central to lounge on the grass outside the national palace, where they meet other young men and women who work in the city. On a more quotidian level, guards speak of amenities such as running water and concrete floors that provide a sense of comfort they do not enjoy in their rural homes.

Although they are impressed by the urban architecture and city culture, these men are not naively idealistic about urban life. Guards describe the many downsides of the city, including "the number of deaths each day," discrimination, pollution, and a lack of space and freedom. They contrast these aspects of city life with the more tranquil rural sphere where "there are no thieves," "the air is pure and there is less delinquency," and "one can walk freely at night." Like other poor urban residents, guards' social space is often relegated to the underside of the city, as they are excluded from the wealthier sectors that they are charged with protecting. Many guards have been robbed in the street markets in the Trébol and the Terminal, and some guards tell stories of getting into fights with gang members and prostitutes in seedy bars. However, these negative experiences figure into their knowledge of the city and thus represent another notch in their belts of urban know-how.

On one hand, men seek work in the security guard industry because it is one of the few options available to them in a field of constrained choices in which alienation and exploitation are constant variables. On the other hand, the security guard industry cannot be reduced to hegemonic exploitation, because guards co-opt the industry's exploitative flexibility, using it as a means to achieve *algo más* (something better) (Fischer and Benson 2006), or as an avenue to explore urban life. Rodrigo is willing to endure the exploitative conditions he criticizes because the income he earns as a guard will allow him to open a store in his village (and thus own his means of production). Other men, like Ignacio, view working as a guard as a bridge to another (supposedly better) job. And for still others, working in security provides a way to experience living in the city without settling there permanently. For this latter group, the desire to explore the nation's capital figures as a significant factor in their decision to work in the industry, and an element of choice rather than necessity is highlighted in the ways they talk about security guard employment.

Mobility and Novel Conceptions of Rural Life

The flexible employment system in the security guard industry promotes a distinct phenomenon in which guards engage and explore urban lifestyles, yet almost always keep a foot in the door of their rural homes. Although guards spend the majority of their time in the capital when actively employed, the concept of "home" is situated in their rural communities—where their immediate families and most of their personal belongings remain—rather than in the security agency living quarters, where most of them sleep in the city. Guards maintain an almost dual residency through regular trips home to visit their families, which distinguishes them from other urban migrants who carve out a life in the city. While at home, they reassert social ties by helping with household duties and participating in the planting or harvesting of maize, a practice especially important in Maya communities.

The fluidity with which guards move between Guatemala City and their hometowns connects urban and rural populations economically, socially, and ideationally. Following James Ferguson (1999), I avoid the use of dualistic models that contrast "urban" with "traditional" and that imply a transitional trajectory of progress with urbanization as the endpoint. For security guards, the experience of working in the capital motivates the performance of new and somewhat contradictory identities that do not neatly fit a model that might divide out a "modern" and "urban" lifestyle from one that is "traditional" and "rural." In contrast to imaginations of the modern city held by previous generations (see Levenson, in this book), men who migrate to the capital today to work as security guards do not simply understand this as a move into some modern space set apart from the rural life-worlds they previously inhabited. Much like apparel manufacturers, they already view these spaces as interconnected (see Thomas, in this book).

Living in the city forces rural migrants to reconcile their new identities, a process that may be directed toward identity maintenance in the multiethnic urban environment, or toward assimilation. Assimilation to urban culture in Guatemala is associated with *ladinoización*, which specifically refers to the process by which indigenous people adopt aspects of ladino culture (e.g., Spanish language and Western dress). Although dualist models have viewed ladinoización as a step in the transition from tradition to modernity, recent work on pan-Maya activism stresses that being modern in Guatemala today does not necessarily imply ladinoización (Nelson 1999: 196; Fischer 2001). While indigenous guards emphasize the importance of improving their Spanish and gaining other skills and knowledge while living in the city, they do not express a strong desire to "ladinoize." Rather, the experience of urban ladino culture provides them with a sort of cultural capital (Bourdieu 1986) that can be applied in rural or urban spheres. Moreover, the exploitation and discrimination guards experience in the capital informs their understanding of the broader sociopolitical context, which includes both a greater appreciation of rural life and a realization of the exclusion of rural populations. For indigenous guards, this awareness also includes a more explicit understanding of ethnic discrimination.

Besides the money they send, guards take their firsthand knowledge of the city home with them, relaying to their families both the inspiration and disappointment that urban space holds: there are jobs, educational opportunities, and impressive architecture, but food is scarce and crime is high. Based on such descriptions, rural relatives who have never been to Guatemala City alternatively imagine it as "dangerous," "beautiful," and "difficult," yet with "many opportunities to work." Although many family members we interviewed expressed interest in visiting the city, few indicated they would like to settle there, explaining that it would be "impossible" to cook because "there is no leña [firewood]," or that "we would go hungry" due to the high cost of food. Others expressed fears that gangs of robaniños (child stealers) would take their children to harvest their organs or use in satanic rituals. Accusations of child stealing have become a common factor in rural-lynching incidents, even though there is often no evidence to back such claims (Godoy 2006).

Guards' knowledge of the city and the financial contributions they make to their families bring them status in their rural villages (which can also translate to a gain of status for their families). This is particularly true for indigenous guards who are respected for having the confidence and ability to negotiate ladino culture. As Pedro's mother explained in an interview, because her son had attended high school he had the confidence to live in the city, which she contrasted with her grandparents' view that an indigenous person would be killed or robbed if she or he went to the city. She followed this comment with the proud observation that after living in the capital, Pedro had become fluent in Spanish and now talked to strangers (*kaxlan* in Q'eqchi', meaning "foreign," "non-Q'eqchi'") with ease. Similarly, a father from another small Q'eqchi' community expressed envy that his son had the opportunity to work in the city, as his own limited Spanish and lack of education had prohibited him from doing so. Guards enact their status and growing cosmopolitanism through their military-style haircuts, stylish sunglasses, and fashionable jeans and sneakers, all of which mark them as "big fish in the small ponds" of their rural villages.

Yet, this newfound status is tenuous, as not all rural residents are impressed by guards' "hip" styles that convey an attitude of superiority. In particular, guards lose some respect in the eyes of their elders who believe they have become "soft" working in the city. One father lamented that because his son has become accustomed to working *bajo la sombra* (literally "below the shade," i.e., under a roof), he now complains that farming is too difficult. His statement was corroborated by one guard who admitted, "I don't like to work in the fields now," and another who rejects the idea of agricultural work after working in security because, as he put it, "it pays less and you get dirtier." The experience of working as a security guard dissociates these rural peasants from a defining aspect of their elders' identity. Yet the rejection of farming by landless guards might also reflect their difficult position of having no opportunity to control their own means of production. Although it is usually elder community members who express disapproval toward those who work as guards, other community members may look down on guards or even feel threatened by them. Picking up on this, one guard noticed that people avoid him when he goes home, whispering "watch out with the security guy."

Although not all guards experience disapproval in the rural sector, the discrimination they face in the city is more generalized. *Capitalinos* (ladino residents of Guatemala City) refer to the rest of the country as *el interior*, which seems counterintuitive as Guatemala City is the political and operational core of the country. However, this viewpoint underscores capitalinos' view of the capital as the civilized center, defined in contrast to the rural periphery that is imagined as an uncivilized wilderness dominated by nature and characterized by a lack of governmental and ladino presence (see O'Neill, this volume). Because of the predominance of indigenous ethnic groups in rural Guatemala, this geographic sense of superiority is linked to ethnic discrimination by ladinos against Mayas and other ethnic groups.

Indigenous groups in Guatemala have suffered institutional discrimination and racism for centuries and continue to do so today (see Casaús Arzú 2007; Cojtí 2007; Nelson 1999; Otzoy 1996), but Mayan guards from small villages describe the discrimination they experience in the city as more personal and explicit, as it is the first time many have been completely immersed in ladino culture. For example, some store owners at malls instruct indigenous guards to keep out customers wearing *traje* (traditional Mayan dress) as they believe this will deter upper-class *ladinas* from entering the store. The internal structure of security agencies, in which the majority of guards are indigenous and supervisors are most likely to be ladinos, also maintains the ethnic hierarchy.[10] Moreover, even though laws exist against discrimination, the practice is institutionalized by security agency policies that prohibit guards from speaking Mayan languages at their posts or in agency living quarters.

The discrimination guards experience in the capital extends beyond their superiors. Capitalinos use the term *salvaje* ("savage") to refer to indigenous men, a stereotype based on interpretations of precolonial history that stress Maya warfare and blood rituals (recently reinforced by Mel Gibson's film *Apocalypto*), fears of Indian uprisings, and urban explanations of the higher frequency of lynchings in indigenous communities. Simultaneously, indigenous men have been categorized as submissive and docile (qualities desired by plantation *patrones*). An indigenous man in the role of an armed security guard confounds these categorizations: his gun symbolizes masculinity and power, and reinforces the image of indigenous men as violent, yet at the same time it contradicts his supposedly subordinate character. In her analysis of the interplay between gender and ethnicity in Guatemala, Diane Nelson argues that "Mayan men are disempowered along national, ethnic, and gender lines . . . They are discursively feminized vis-à-vis ladino men in a variety of ways" (1999: 204). Many guards relate incidents of being "mistreated" or scolded by capitalinos who refuse to follow instructions (such as submitting their driver's license when entering a gated residence or parking where the guard indicates), which one guard attributed to capitalinos' belief that he does not "know how to do anything." Urban ladinos strip away the indigenous guard's masculine power by questioning his ability to use his gun and asserting their own authority. Most directly, guards are disempowered through interactions with members of the urban elite that they have been charged to protect, who refer to them with pejorative terms such as *indio* (Indian), *idiota* (idiot), or *del pueblo* (from the village). The last indicates the regional aspect of discrimination; while indigenous guards receive the brunt of discrimination, it also extends to ladinos from rural areas who are considered urban outsiders, as revealed in this pointed comment by a ladino guard from Jalapa: "The people who have a lot of money here scorn me [*me desprecia*] because I'm from the countryside."

Guards often contend with discrimination and exploitation in the city, a fact that seems at odds with the status they garner in their rural hometowns. Their experiences and the identities they assume in these disparate settings cannot be neatly separated. Rather, guards are faced with integrating the discrimination and exploitation they suffer in the capital into how they understand their rural lives. The stark contrast between urban and rural society was easily noted by guards: "It makes me sad to see things here [in the capital] because the people have everything, and there is so little in my village." One ex-guard wishfully explained that he would prefer to live in the city rather than in his hometown in Alta Verapaz because "there is nothing here, nothing good, it's very poor," whereas in the capital "everyone has a lot of money." Isauro expressed a broader view, lamenting that in his town "there is no leadership, no good education or vision. People live to pass each day, to sleep and eat each day, and so the community never comes together to make improvements." He explained the lack of collective action with the observation that "people there place too much faith in luck, instead of hard work or studies." His sentiments were echoed by other guards, one, for example stating "the majority of people in my village are illiterate and poor" and so "don't know how take action, or to improve their lives."

Writing in regard to the despair Zambian mineworkers experienced with the decline of the copper industry that forced many of them to return to the rural sector, James Ferguson emphasizes the difference between being unconnected and disconnected, the latter of which "implies an active relation, and the state of having been disconnected requires to be understood as the product of specific structures and processes of disconnection" (1999: 238). In the case of security guards, the experience of actually living in Guatemala City, contrasted with the urban environment they might have imagined and the realities of their rural hometowns, comprises the "active relation" that provides guards with a greater understanding of their place in the broader social context. Because they spend their shifts posted outside high-class hotels, private high schools, posh restaurants and malls, and nightclubs, security guards are uniquely confronted with urban wealth and elite lifestyles—and their exclusion from them. This more tangible awareness of inequality speaks to the "ironic compromise between what they could imagine and what social life will permit" that constrains the realization of opportunities (Appadurai 1996: 54).

This new awareness of inequality does not motivate ladinoización, settlement in the city, or a rejection of urban life. Rather, it informs individual decisions about the future, which do not fit into a neat pattern. Although some guards may be disheartened by their deeper realization of the poverty and inequality in rural Guatemala, many also develop a new appreciation of what rural life offers. After living in the capital for one year, one man was convinced, "There is nothing like my village; it's tranquil and people are friendly to each other," which he contrasted with the dangerous nature of the capital. Others gain greater respect for their families, especially for the cooking and washing their wives and mothers do, and appreciate the "abundance of food." A few stay in the city, looking for algo más, whether it be continuing their education, gaining technical skills that can be applied in the urban or rural sector, or working in a maquila. Thus, working in the capital does not entail a shift from rural to urban existence as suggested by center-periphery dichotomies, but rather represents "a circular process in which people remain oriented to the places from which they have come" (Rouse 2002: 160).

Conclusion

Security guards are in the position of providing physical protection for the elite class, which has become wealthier at their expense via neoliberal policies that favor capitalist entrepreneurs.[11] The ease with which guards are contracted and replaced places them squarely within the flexible labor force composed of unskilled workers willing to work for low wages that neoliberal reforms create in the name of economic growth. Although guards use this flexibility to their advantage—to obtain wages when they need it, to explore the city and gain "skills" in the form of human and cultural capital—their options are limited and constrained by structural forces that have left them with little education, insufficient land, and few opportunities for employment in the local sector. Increases in inequality and violence, coupled with the failure of the state to provide public security in Guatemala, have generated jobs for these men. Yet this "opportunity" carries an irony as the source of labor for the security industry comes from the primarily indigenous, rural population, which bore the brunt of the war. Guards leave the (relatively) peaceful countryside and migrate to Guatemala City to provide protection for wealthy bodies and property, and thus continue a historic pattern of commodification of indigenous, poor, and rural populations. Still, the security guard industry provides examples of the ways in which indigenous and other marginalized Guatemalans employ the resources they have on hand to their advantage. Men take advantage of the security guard industry to expand their economic and other horizons, employment which in turn informs their understanding of their rural communities and of the larger socioeconomic and political structures in which they are enmeshed.

Notes

1. The discussion of Guatemala's security guard industry presented here is based on research conducted in 2006 in Guatemala City and Alta Verapaz. The study consisted of interviews with forty-three men who were working at that time as security guards for legally authorized agencies in Guatemala City; nine men in the town of Chisec, Alta Verapaz, who had retired or were taking a break from working as guards; and sixteen families of guards in their homes in the municipalities of Cobán, San Pedro Carchá, and Chisec in Alta Verapaz. Although some women work as security guards, men comprise the great majority of guards and were the focus of this research. This study was part of a larger research project on development and local economy in Q'eqchi' Maya communities in the Chisec municipality of Alta Verapaz.

I could not have conducted this research without the help of my friend and assistant, Arturo Tiul Coc. My initial idea for this project emerged through conversations with him, and he helped me carry out interviews and enthusiastically accompanied me on our long treks to communities in Carchá and Chisec, continuously offering me insight on the guard industry. Special thanks to my advisor, Edward F. Fischer, for his ideas regarding neoliberal violence in Guatemala, as well as to Kevin Lewis O'Neill, Kedron Thomas, and Thomas Offit who organized the panel where I first presented this research. I also thank Vanderbilt's Center for the Americas for providing funding for this particular research project.

2. The figures from 2000 were reported in the July 26, 2000, edition of Guatemala's *Prensa Libre* newspaper and cited in Fernández García (2004: 48). The 2006 data comes from the article "Rodeados de policías ilegales" on pages 2–3 of the July 16, 2006, edition of the *Prensa Libre*, and were verified in a personal interview with the director of the Gremial de Empresas Privadas de Seguridad (Trade Association of Private Security Companies), Carlos Muñoz Piloña.

3. This is not to suggest that guards and other rural inhabitants in Guatemala live in an isolated world—residents of even remote communities have been exposed to the world beyond their village through newspaper and television images (viewed on televisions powered by generators, or in stores in larger communities with electricity), as well as stories from returning migrants. Rather, as Edward F. Fischer and Peter Benson (2006) and Abigail Adams (2001: 202) have pointed out, they are keenly aware of novel and nonlocal opportunities.

4. Indigenous land access improved somewhat through colonization policies in the 1950s (to settle the northern lowlands of Alta Verapaz and El Petén), as well as more recent titling programs specifically directed toward the indigenous population (Perez 2005).

5. The average GINI coefficient in 2006 for Central America (not including Belize) is .518, and that of Latin America is .525. Bolivia, Colombia, and Brazil show the highest levels of inequality in Latin America with respective GINI coefficients of .601, .586, and .580 (UNDP 2006).

6. The Latinobarómetro survey asked participants if any family member had been a victim of crime in the past twelve months, whereas the LAPOP surveys specifically asked if the individual interviewed had been a victim.

7. See Briceño-León 2002 and Victoria Sanford 2006 for a more detailed analysis of this phenomenon in Guatemala, and Daniel Goldstein, Gloria Achá, and Eric Hinojosa 2009 for a discussion of social cleansing in Bolivia.

8. I was unable to locate any comprehensive data on the departments from which guards come, so this statement is based on interviews with guards and agency personnel.

9. According to the agencies, a guard's level of education influences his salary, but guards claim that one's location figures as a more important factor: guards posted outside of banks receive the highest salaries; followed by those who protect delivery trucks, factories, or warehouses. Those who work in low-risk sites such as malls receive the lowest salaries. Salaries also vary by agency and according to whether or not the guards receive benefits.

10. It is also important to point out here that the security guard industry is a space in which indigenous and nonindigenous guards work side by side and receive the same wages, a space that can thus foster the establishment of friendships not only between ladinos and Mayas, but between Mayas from different ethnic groups. This characteristic, also the case in maquila labor (Goldín 2001: 38), suggests that the social condi-

tions necessitating that individuals work in these industries arise along class rather than ethnic lines.

11. Security guards are also contracted to work in middle-class and working-class areas of the capital and in places frequented by their inhabitants (e.g., banks and fast-food restaurants), and their presence on the street may serve as a deterrent to crime that benefits the general public. My emphasis on the relationship between the elite class and security guards is intended to draw attention to the fact that security services are primarily contracted by wealthy citizens and are aimed at their protection and the protection of property belonging to them.

Guatemala's New Violence as Structural Violence

Notes from the Highlands

Peter Benson,
Kedron Thomas, and
Edward F. Fischer

Anthropologists in Guatemala commonly hear from informants that "things are better now" or "things have improved." Such statements compare the present to the thirty-six-year internal armed conflict in which violence and fear became routine aspects of everyday life (Carmack 1988; Fischer and Benson 2005; Green 1999). Things have changed. Wide-ranging Peace Accords signed in 1996 brought a formal end to the conflict and were hailed with grand speeches filled with grand promises (Jonas 2000; Sieder 1999). When seen in abstract terms, violence seems to have subsided: villages are no longer massacred or destroyed; the average income of the country's indigenous Maya population has risen; and average education levels have increased. But as this volume's introduction notes, living the peace has proven elusive.

One unpleasant irony of our times is that paths of progress and development often carry with them varieties of suffering, inequality, and violence (Ferguson 2006; Kleinman 1999; Sen 1999). The benefits of globalization touted by proponents of free trade have been accompanied by the intensification of insecurity in vulnerable communities worldwide (McGrew and Poku 2007). The waning of one kind of violence has sometimes given way to new kinds of violence or galvanized social residues and collective memories of past traumas and brutalities.[1] In Guatemala, foreign embassy reports and national media emphasize the prominent role of gangs in the new violence and terror.[2] This framing trickles down to influence popular attitudes. "The problem here is *delincuencia*," a Kaqchikel Maya man in Tecpán told us. "It's basically at a national level." However, it is all too easy to pin violence on delinquent if highly organized youth (Taussig 2005)—and besides, political violence continues apace. Politically motivated (and perhaps state-sanctioned) killings continue, as seen in the 1997 assassination of Bishop Juan José Gerardi Conedera and campaign-related killings in recent elections. Yet, impunity is the order of the day (see introduction, this volume). It is widely and credibly believed that the military and law enforcement agencies are tightly connected with drug traffickers and organized crime (Amnesty International 2006).

The ethnographic setting for this study is Tecpán, a town of almost 20,000 located eighty-eight kilometers west of Guatemala City. In the popular consciousness of a town such as Tecpán, closely networked to Guatemala City through market and other social systems, and yet also experientially removed from the dense concentration of violence in the capital city, the idea of delincuencia is a dominant explanatory model (see Thomas, this volume). Delincuencia is used to think about the urban violence that *tecpanecos* read about every day in national newspapers, but, more importantly for our purposes, to also talk about significant social changes occurring in Tecpán amidst the neoliberal order. This essay explores the tendency to blame gangs in highland areas of Guatemala, where the empirical violence faced by people in the capital city takes on mythic proportions. We make several interconnected arguments related to the idiom of delincuencia, first laying out the uneven ways that structural adjustment policies have impacted places such as Tecpán where urban and rural economic systems are tightly intertwined. Then, we explore the events surrounding a popular protest in Tecpán that was clearly focused on addressing some of the difficulties of structural adjustment experienced by many townspeople. Our analysis shows how media and popular interpretations of the protest converted a consideration of the structural dynamics that underpin mass experiences of distress and economic insecurity into a problem of delincuencia. This interpretation played into existing media stereotypes about who is responsible for experiential and material insecurities. Furthermore, the discourse of delincuencia became a useful cultural and moral resource for townspeople struggling to make sense of the fact that the protest turned into an unorganized and violent revolt. As the protest itself came to be framed in terms of the unlawful and incoherent violence of gang members, the event carried symbolic capital for authorities who, in its aftermath, promoted a conciliatory model of proper democratic participation to shore up their own authority and avoid addressing the structural contradictions of neoliberal government that underpinned the protest in the first place.

In the end, we explore how this highland protest reflects a wider process of cultural hegemony that is commonly reproduced on a national level to moralize violence in terms of chaos and unlawful citizenship, partly justifying a resurgence of right-wing political activity. This cultural hegemony was vividly seen in widespread support for a politics of the "iron fist" and platforms centered on militarization (i.e., a tough on crime and delinquency approach) in the 2007 elections.

Market Reforms: A View from the Highlands

Tecpán has a reputation as a progressive and affluent place. In the city proper, about 70 percent of the residents are Kaqchikel Maya. Tecpán's Spanish-speaking, nonindigenous, *ladino* minority has historically exerted disproportionate control over local government and commercial institutions, buttressed by racist ideologies and colonial inequalities. Yet, Tecpán is home to an exceptionally strong indigenous bourgeoisie that has long supported ethnic consciousness, the value of education, and economic experimentation. In the 1990s, this group became increasingly assertive in local as well as national politics (Fischer 2001; Fischer and Hendrickson 2002; Hendrickson 1995).[3] At the same time, Tecpán itself underwent major cultural changes: several large supermarket-style stores opened (one now owned by Wal-Mart); the town's handful of telephone lines was expanded to several thousand; Internet cafes and video rental stores opened; and many households began to tap into cable television lines. Foreign fare became commonplace in town and especially popular among youth.

As in neighboring towns, processes of class differentiation and entrepreneurial economic activity in Tecpán have partially been fostered by (or at least emerged within the context of) the aggressive national program of privatization and liberal economic reform, as well as a new attitude toward Maya peoples that arose in the postwar period. Yet, opportunities for social mobility and economic advancement have gone hand in hand with the partial erosion of economic control and security for many people (Smith 1990). In the countryside, Tecpán has seen a major shift away from traditional milpa (corn and beans) agriculture toward nontraditional export crops, such as broccoli and snow peas. Farmers have sought to earn extra cash by accessing export markets. While some benefit from this and see export production as compatible with traditional agriculture, family life, and community organizing, most farmers report mixed results. Along with quality-control issues owing to import regulations and inspection in foreign markets, there is also the pressure of global competition. Maya farmers have little information about and no control over these forces and are often at the mercy of ruthless local contractors and middlemen. Farmers have sought to mitigate these risks by joining cooperatives and combining export with subsistence production (Fischer 2004; Fischer and Benson 2006; Goldín 1996; Goldín and Asturias de Barrios 2001).

In the urban core, such economic change is also evident. Indigenous families in Tecpán have established a vibrant garment industry with roots in the 1960s, as discussed in greater detail in Thomas's essay (this volume). Most operations are small-scale, family-owned businesses that sell shirts, pants, and sweaters in the capital and rural markets. A surplus of manufacturers grapple for market share and rightfully complain that the Guatemalan state courts foreign capital and puts its own citizens at a competitive disadvantage. Maquiladoras—generally foreign-owned factories where brand-name clothing is assembled for export—were welcomed in the 1980s as part of Guatemala's industrialization and liberalization efforts.[4] Apparel manufacturers fear that the United States–Dominican Republic–Central America Free Trade Agreement (CAFTA), implemented in 2006, locks in maquiladoras' dominance of the export market and allows them to take over domestic sales. They claim maquiladoras drive down prices by selling apparel in Guatemala that was earmarked for export, while foreign-owned retail chains in the highland region sell imported clothing at lower prices than local producers can sustain. Like export farmers, Maya apparel producers have responded to market pressures in numerous ways. Some have created brands based on indigenous symbols, including Maya hieroglyphs and terms from their native Kaqchikel, an entrepreneurial strategy of market differentiation that seeks to capitalize on the revitalization of indigenous identity in the postwar context. Such producers benefit from computer skills and access to financing to support their ventures. Some have incorporated their businesses as legal entities, a process that requires literacy and knowledge of bureaucratic procedures and so is not viable for many producers (Thomas 2006, 2009). In sum, in both agriculture and apparel, economic production is a powerful means of social and class mobility for Mayas. Yet, international and national trade can reinforce or create class hierarchies and community cleavages, and they entail significant pressures related to competition. This context of shifting economic practices and mixed outcomes is one important part of the larger picture of insecurities and inequalities that shape contemporary forms of violence and how people think about and react to them.

Popular Protest

Guatemala has recently seen numerous popular protests over contentious issues from resource exploitation to free trade to the democratic process.[5] On June 10, 2002, thousands of Tecpán's residents marched into the municipal center to protest a new property and estate tax passed down as part of structural adjustment programs mandated by the International Monetary Fund (IMF). The role of collecting and administering the tax was to be devolved from the Ministry of Finance to local municipal governments, a neoliberal approach to improve accountability and transparency while empowering local populations. But this new tax was an added burden for poor agriculturalists from the town's outlying areas. The protest involved anywhere from 3,000 to 45,000 participants, according to local estimates. Whatever the number, it was a remarkable show of public dissent, something that could not have occurred a decade earlier given the climate of fear. Not all protestors were there because of the tax; the demonstration was enlivened by a more general spirit of dissent and dissatisfaction with the town's mainly ladino leadership, especially the mayor. "The mayor treated us poorly. We tried to discuss the tax with him," said one man in an interview a few days following the protest. "We said it was impossible to afford, but he was rude and would not hear our demands."

Marchers carrying banners and documents demanding the mayor's resignation were met in front of his office by a phalanx of local police. Then violence erupted. As locals recount the event, a youth, said to be a gang member, hurled a rock through one of the town hall windows. Others followed, and the protest became chaotic. The municipal building, police station, and mayor's home were torched. Police threw tear-gas bombs into the crowd, who readily recovered and returned them to their senders. Protestors used cell phones to provide family members back home with live reports of the action or to contact each other and organize movements on the spot. Some police were stripped naked and beaten, dragged through the streets. The mayor, protected by bodyguards, fled town as protestors pegged his vehicle with stones and, some said, tried to kill him.

Protest organizers and participants did not want the demonstration to turn violent, except perhaps those eager to loot buildings of televisions and appliances. But "gang members" were not the only ones rioting and torching. Participants told us in interviews that protestors were angry because the mayor had not listened to their complaints for a long while. When the throng approached his house and demanded an audience, the cold shoulder provoked a deeply negative response. "That is why the people got angry," one man said. "Many say it was just gangs acting violently. If the mayor treated the protesters badly when they went to see him, they had their reasons for becoming violent."

Despite the concrete effects of gangs, the category *gang member* functions as something of a scapegoat in contemporary Guatemala. By attributing the cause of violence to delinquent youth, people distance themselves from feelings of complicity and resignation. This is especially important given the moral climate that quickly took shape in the national press afterward. Protesters lamented that the *Prensa Libre* dubbed the well-intentioned protest "chaotic" and portrayed the people of Tecpán as undemocratic rabble rousers. "We were interested in resolving real political issues," said one participant, becoming noticeably upset as he added, "the gangs are to blame, not the protestors. We didn't start the violence in this town, the violence has been here, but we are blamed and we are the ones who suffer." It is useful to think of gangs as a discursive "limit point," a point, within the communicative sphere of Guatemalan civil society, at which violence becomes explicable (Fischer and Benson 2006). Here popular feelings of complicity are disavowed, while responsibility for violence is attributed to a nebulously defined group.

Locals say it is dangerous to walk around Tecpán at night because gangs come out looking for victims. Sometimes there are groups of rough-looking teenagers in the town plaza, and spray paint tags increasingly canvas walls around town. We have heard stories about gangs robbing shoppers and vendors on market day. But to what extent are these groups "gangs"? The lines between gang activity, mischief, and ordinary loitering are blurry and constitute a terrain ripe for anthropological research. We wonder whether these youth consider themselves to be part of a gang and about the social geography of delinquency, petty crime, and gang membership in Guatemala. What are the territorial contours of gang activity? What is the relationship between space and sociality in the constitution of gangs and perceptions of their threat and presence?[6] A decade ago, domestic violence and petty theft were Tecpán's most pressing crime problems, but these days, the perception is that danger levels have risen as a result of an influx of gang activity from Guatemala City. Youths have traveled to the capital to look for employment opportunities not available in the highlands, and many have returned corrupted—this is how elders and families view the situation. Some individuals blame the globalization of Western popular culture for bringing images of gangs and delinquency to the highlands. Others blame a breakdown in moral structure, the erosion of families and declining work ethics. Blame is an ironic partner of reconciliation in postwar times (Benson 2004).

Gangs are no doubt real and their presence menacing. On a national level, some estimates put gang membership higher than that of the national police force (Painter 2007). But they have become larger than life, a synecdoche for violence and insecurity writ large. This mythos reflects a shift in how violence is imagined and talked about in the highlands. A key existential feature of the armed conflict was uncertainty, the experience that things (security, survival, whom to trust) were never clear (Manz 2004; Sanford 2004). With the peace process, this lack of clarity has given way to a climate of assured accusation and directed blame, even though sources of the new violence are much less clear than in the past. Such a climate can be politically useful for various actors because directed blame allows people, such as tecpaneco locals, to distance themselves from and come to grips with violence. Blame can also be useful for state actors because it allows culpable governments to scapegoat segments of the population as singularly at fault, limit the legitimate expression of dissent, and moralize against the eruption of violence among disadvantaged groups.

The Limits of Reconciliation

The category gang member belies the diversity of intentions and social types the mass protest comprised. The majority of protestors were campesino farmers from outlying hamlets. There were also teachers, curious onlookers, aspirant politicians, restless gang members, and other youth. Remarkably, the protest demonstrates the emergence of new political spaces that people have not entered for nearly a generation due to the climate of fear that defined the armed conflict and lingered in the 1990s. Though the tax structure that was the protest's target was implemented as scheduled, many protestors regard the demonstration as a success because it is said to have taught local politicians and others in the ladino population an important lesson about the force of the indigenous community in Tecpán, its capacity to mobilize, and its critical stance with regard to local corruption and political control.

In the months after the protest, there were town hall "reconciliation" meetings in Chimaltenango (the capital of the department of Chimaltenango, where Tecpán is located) between the mayor, protest organizers, and the departmental governor. "We got what we wanted," said one organizer, "a chance at a meeting with the mayor. At least we got that." This is a common phrase, *por lo menos* (at least), used among protestors to describe the meetings. "The protests didn't work out as planned," said another, "but at least we can sit down with the mayor." In this discourse, the opportunity for having a reconciliation process, regardless of the outcome of such meetings, is put forth as the desired goal even though, as it turns out, the deck was already stacked in favor of the powers that be. A discursive limit point establishes a horizon at which critique comfortably rests and political action is deemed a success, even apart from real evidence that social structures are changed. It is often just such a democratic concession—the idea that people *at least* have a chance to participate in a political process—that paradoxically limits the very terms of freedom it purports to enable.

During the meetings, the mayor strategically appropriated the idioms of critique and democratic process that had driven the protest. At one meeting he told protestors, "We are all completely in agreement. You have the right to protest." Then he shifted blame for violence onto the protestors themselves. "But what about those honorable people screaming 'kill him . . . kill him,'" he went on. "I want to work with these honorable people but I don't want to lose democracy." He said that the outburst of violence on June 10 was contrary to democratic principles of deliberative, rational, and communicative action. By association, so were the protestors. "We too want a dialogue," one of the organizers immediately responded, "but with no direct accusations. When you look at the press, it says we have no law here; there is chaos in Tecpán; the organizers are to blame; there is no difference between what we did and what the gangs do." This man, an elderly and outspoken campesino, struggled to justify the eruption of violence in terms of the mayor's failure to listen to the public's voice prior to the protest. He also sought to distance himself and other participants from the violence that had delegitimized that voice in favor of uncontestable ideals of harmony and dialogue. "The same problems we are discussing here right now," he said, "we already met with you about this—"

At this point, the mayor interrupted and moved to the center of the hall, insisting that there was nothing he could do about the tax. "The law is the law and the tax is the tax," the governor said, reinforcing the mayor's position. "The law is *bonito* because it provides the mechanisms for dialogue and equal exchange." Local authorities in Tecpán occupy a "tenuous position between constituent mandates and state authority" (Fischer 2001: 57). The mayor positioned himself as the victim and the protesters appear to blame him, whereas he insisted that his own hands were tied. This pushed the organizers into an apologetic posture. "We are not here to accuse you," an organizer said. "When we're talking we are on an even level. It is a democratic process." Because the organizers did not want to be blamed (by the mayor or the media) for causing violence, they were forced to limit their critique and take on some of the blame that had been shuttled their way by the mayor and his backers.

Discourses and practices of reconciliation are customarily intended to benefit marginalized and victimized groups. Such gestures can also favor established interests, however, when democratic process is strictly framed in terms of harmony, dialogue, and efficiency, which are said to be undermined by acrimonious troublemaking. Such discourse operates as an exemplary form of hegemony that Nader calls "coercive harmony," a controlling process that eschews scrutiny about the fundamental terms of discourse (e.g., ideals such as harmony and dialogue) and encourages active acceptance by opposition (Nader 1997: 712–15). The mayor acquires a privileged rhetorical footing when he positions himself as a victim of undemocratic procedures (namely, violence), while the protestors, if they do not acquiesce to this framing, are seen as stubborn and undemocratic. Consider that the same protestor who was so enthusiastic about the meeting beforehand admitted afterwards: "I am disappointed. The mayor just kept talking about his bad character. Yeah, that's a problem. But we all know that. That's why we protested in the first place. What is he going to do about it? That's my question. Apologies are nice but so are results."

The reconciliation meetings suggest that the constitution of civil society in Guatemala is not a neutral process in which voices are liberated regardless of subject position and in which rational communicative action trumps differences of race or ethnicity and social power. The composition of civil society occurs partly alongside the reproduction of varieties of symbolic violence (e.g., coercive harmony) that empower only certain voices and agitate against the expression of oppositional sentiment if it takes violent form. Charles Hale (2002) has described this sociopolitical context in terms of "neoliberal multiculturalism," calling attention to the ways a discourse of multiculturalism and cultural rights limits the types of claims that indigenous groups can make against the state. Since "recognition" has been achieved, other claims — such as protests that challenge political economic structures that continue to relegate indigenous people to marginalized positions within Guatemalan society—are themselves said to threaten this society's democratic fabric. In the case of the protests in Tecpán, feelings of powerlessness and the threat of changes beyond people's control were crucial to the context in which violence erupted. Practical shortcomings of the reconciliation process reveal a particular linkage of blame and violence that contributes to an uneven distribution of democratic voice and social power in the postwar period, while a blanket ideology of harmony covers over the foundational differences and exclusions upon which Guatemalan civil society is built. If we are willing to concede that coercive harmony is a mode of symbolic violence partly sponsored and fostered by the state, then we must also admit that structured violence against indigenous communities has not come to an end in the postwar period but endures as a legacy of the long history of ethnicized and racialized discrimination in Guatemala.

New Violence and the Iron Fist

In the past decade, Guatemala has seen the resurgence of right-wing political activity involving some of the leading culprits of the genocide. Most prominent was the 2003 presidential run of General Efraín Ríos Montt, the former military dictator. In 1989 he founded the hard-line conservative Frente Republicano Guatemalteco (Guatemalan Republican Front; FRG) party and in 1994 was elected to Congress, where he served as majority leader. In 2003, the FRG government (which held the presidency, a majority in Congress, and great sway over the judiciary) was troubled by corruption scandals involving hundreds of millions of dollars. Ríos Montt began to campaign for president on a platform of greater security (to combat the wave of crime that had swept the country) and an end to corruption. The legality of his candidacy was in doubt, however, because Article 186 of the Guatemalan Constitution bars those who have participated in coups from being president (a military junta brought Ríos Montt to power in 1982). On this basis, the Supreme Electoral Tribunal ruled in June 2003 that he was ineligible to run for president, a decision at first upheld by Guatemala's Constitutional Court. But he continued to campaign. On July 24 the campaign organized mass demonstrations that shut down the capital city and cost millions in property damage. Thousands of rural supporters were bussed in and armed with machetes, sticks, tires, and gasoline by campaign workers wearing black ski masks. The throng was directed to target government buildings and private businesses, a number of which were looted. On what became known as "Black Thursday," Ríos Montt announced to the press that he could not control his supporters, that the people must be heard and their will heeded. In the wake of this event, the Constitutional Court overruled itself and, citing international accords, decided that retroactively applying the 1985 Constitution to Ríos Montt's 1982 actions would violate his human rights.

Ironies of this decision did not go unnoticed in the international community. Ríos Montt's return to power was sharply criticized by human rights advocates and scholars. Human rights monitors hold him largely responsible for the displacement, torture, and death of tens of thousands of noncombatants during the height of the armed conflict. Because the victims were overwhelmingly rural Maya, the United Nations Truth Commission declared the violence a case of genocide. But, paradoxically, in 2003 it was poor Maya peasants (i.e., the very targets of his scorched earth campaign two decades earlier) who formed the base of Ríos Montt's popular support. Much of this support has to do with the fact that as the majority leader of Congress, Ríos Montt cultivated allegiance by pushing through huge subsidies for fertilizer, increases in the minimum wage, and large payments to those who served in the country's notorious army-led Civil Auto-Defense Patrols of the early 1980s.[7]

In June 2003, the Ríos Montt campaign made a stop in a hamlet on the outskirts of Tecpán. Thousands turned out, many because they were promised information about the next installment of payments the government was promising to men (or their widows) who had served in the civil patrols. Ríos Montt arrived in a red helicopter, accompanied by a fanfare of firecrackers and campaign songs. During his speech, he railed against corruption and political patronage: "Who does your mayor work for? Who does your congressman work for? Who does the President of the Republic work for? You, that's right. And so why should you have to enter their offices with your head bowed and hat in hand to beg for a little favor? This is wrong. You are their boss." He stood with Pedro Palma, a former guerilla leader, holding his hand tight, while declaring that "the past is behind us and we must leave it there. We must move forward. Together." Palma, who lived for years in the jungle fighting the Guatemalan Army, appeared unbothered by the irony of running for Congress on the ticket of his former mortal enemy.

But a streak of skepticism, bitterness, and fear has also been evident among rural people. Just one day later, the campaign made an ill-timed stop in Rabinal, a Maya town in the K'iche' region where forensic anthropologists have been working for some time, excavating clandestine graves and identifying victims' bodies in order to document what happened there during the violence and to bring some closure to still-grieving families who never knew for sure the fate of "disappeared" loved ones. On the day Ríos Montt arrived, several bodies were being reburied in marked graves. A group of townspeople arrived at the rally with a coffin painted black and began to jeer at Ríos Montt. He was met with a barrage of bottles, sticks, and rocks. After getting hit on the head with a stone, he retreated to his helicopter holding a handkerchief on his bleeding forehead. Reasoned editorials of the national press highlighted the foolishness of Ríos Montt's Rabinal stop, but also condemned protestors for using tactics of intimidation in a free election. On the other hand, who can really blame them? "I don't care what he says," declared a Maya man at the Tecpán rally, "We remember who he is and what he has done. We have suffered enough. I will never vote for him no matter how much money he promises."

In the end, Ríos Montt's vows to end crime and corruption in Guatemala by using overwhelming force did not carry the day. He finished the presidential race in third place.[8] However, his campaign has had an enduring impact. In the 2007 presidential election, security was a dominant buzzword. Leading presidential candidates, including the runner-up Otto Pérez Molina, adopted a "tough on crime" platform. They portrayed themselves in stump speeches and on roadside billboards as eager to stamp out violent crime and potentially utilize coercive power in the process. Pérez Molina, also a former military general, garnered 47 percent of the vote. Amidst other candidates focused on security issues—one party promised "Seguridad Total" and another "Security, Welfare, Justice"—Pérez Molina's Partido Patriota (Patriotic Party) stood out with its promise to bring an "iron fist" (*mano dura*). In conversations with a number of Maya, we found support for the Partido Patriota, even among people well aware of Pérez Molina's role during the armed conflict, when he oversaw military operations in the department of El Quiché, where some of the worst atrocities took place. "We have no other choice," asserted a thirty-two-year-old Maya woman. "As a *capitalina* [a resident of Guatemala City] I support whichever candidate will clean up the streets and bring security."

If "a culture of fear" exists in Guatemalan political life, as Piero Gleijeses (1988: 4) has said, it does not necessarily need to be understood as an enduring national psychological character rooted in the conquest. Here it seems a strategic part of a political platform specially framed to overcome the seeming paradoxes of resurgent military leadership in the highlands and marshal political support among unlikely allies. The winner of the 2007 election, Álvaro Colom, ran on a Left-Center platform that included social programs to end corruption as part of a broader vision of what security means. His party now faces the difficult task of addressing conditions of structural violence that pervade Guatemalan society, which have been largely ignored in right-wing political discourse, mass media, and everyday talk. The Partido Patriota's campaign propaganda encouraged citizens to believe that targeting gangs and delinquents is the key to bringing order. Again, gangs are singled out and blamed for many of Guatemala's problems, as they offer a quick and sensible explanation for violence. This has become a handy scapegoat, one actively promoted by politicians.

Historicizing Violence and Popular Conservatism

Someone assaulted on his or her daily bus commute experiences that violent act as an episode caused by a gang member or otherwise delinquent individual. Yet, to adequately understand such episodes and develop effective social responses, it is perhaps advisable to forgo this tendency to pin praise or blame on individual actors and focus on underlying systemic conditions that may not be immediately visible when violence occurs. They are not "ethnographically visible," to use Paul Farmer's (2004) words. Guatemala's new violence is not adequately understood apart from important historical and societal factors. Against the backdrop of decades of counterinsurgency warfare and embodied memories of trauma and terror, popular support for "iron fist" platforms looks less like categorical support for a new militarized state and more like an understandable desire to no longer live with insecurity.

Thinking about the paradoxes of violence and popular conservatism in contemporary Guatemala, Angelina Snodgrass Godoy (2002) examines the case of vigilante justice, which blurs the distinction between victim and victimizer, popular mobilization and mob rule. She describes an incident that occurred in the department of El Quiché in 1999. Thousands gathered to witness the execution of four men suspected of robbing a local merchant. The men were rounded up by an enraged local mob and stood before a "hastily convened" public tribunal. Police and human rights authorities were held at bay, and the sentence was immediately carried out. According to the United Nations, there were nearly 500 lynchings in Guatemala from 1996 to 2001. Resocializing this violence, Godoy notes that lynchings are undoubtedly a legacy of state terror and that the sociopolitical and moral climate in which lynchings occur demands new ways of conceptualizing violence and its social origins. Against a tendency to view violence as something that afflicts or is perpetrated by an individual (or group) in isolation, Godoy argues that "certain forms of massive violence," such as the country's armed conflict, "cause a type of social trauma that is more than the sum of the individual traumas suffered." Drawing on in-depth ethnographic interviews with Mayas, Godoy implicates "uniquely sociological effects of state terror, which affect not only individuals but the social spaces they inhabit" in the social production of new violence. Lynchings, she argues, are a manifestation of embodied trauma that has become collective experience in many communities. Since lynchings can be explained in light of historical forces and sociological factors, Godoy argues, the new violence is a complicated scenario in which the state simultaneously is and is not the primary force behind human rights abuses (Godoy 2002: 641–42).

Guatemala City has not become a locus of intense and routine violence in a vacuum. The city's violence has historical roots, despite the tendency of the mass media, politicians, and ordinary citizens to look for more immediate explanations. The devastating earthquake in 1976 and Ríos Montt's scorched earth campaigns of the early 1980s dislocated rural communities and created massive unplanned squatter settlements on the outskirts of the capital. Even today, about 25 percent of the city's residents live in what state authorities define as "precarious settlements." In slums of squalid housing lacking basic services, gang membership now thrives as an ordinary social arrangement. An enormous underclass experiencing high unemployment in the formal sector has turned to thriving informal economies, often linked to organized crime (Morán Mérida 1997).[9] Across the country, market liberalization has coincided with a decline in formal sector employment. Meanwhile, the state responds to pressures from the IMF and World Bank by reducing social service expenditures and lifting price controls on basic necessities, which leaves many Guatemalans vulnerable to poverty, chronic unemployment, health problems, crime, and violence (Chase-Dunn 2000; Green 2003: 52; Pérez Sáinz 1996).

In light of these conditions, more fully explored in the introduction to this volume, the predicament of Guatemala's urban violence seems like a symptom of historically shaped conditions and structural problems (e.g., a legacy of state violence; deep socioeconomic inequality; the penetration of extractive industries; the erosion of political and social infrastructures; and disparate access to health care, education, and life chances) rather than simply the product of itinerant youth, organized crime, and other stereotyped and pathologized subsets of the population (Thomas and Benson 2008). This is not to say that gangs and organized crime are uninvolved in the new violence. Quite the contrary—these groups have emerged and continue to thrive amidst societal conditions shaped by state policies, extranational political influence, and global economic restructuring. The degree to which the state and its agencies are complicit in the new violence remains unknown and is a topic of ongoing inquiry and scrutiny. But explanations that narrowly focus on gang activity understandably resonate within a context in which the state no longer has a monopoly on coercive force. Violence is "neoliberalized" (Fischer and Benson 2006) or "democratized" (Godoy 2006), transferred into the hands of private entities such as urban gangs, rural mobs, or the hired security forces discussed by Dickins de Girón (this volume).[10] The bulk of the murders that occur in Guatemala City are not carried out by the thinly veiled heavy hand of the military or secret police. Popular fears about being robbed and terrorized that circulate in Tecpán are not, from a phenomenological standpoint, linked to state actors. When dissent and aggression are directed toward state actors or private entities, as seen in the case of vigilante justice or popular protest, local communities are blamed as solely responsible perpetrators. The state and its partners transcend accusation (Goldstein 2004). This sociopolitical context deflects attention from the reality of politically motivated violence and the state's likely links to organized crime. It also provides a platform for "tough on crime" policies and the promotion of the idea that troublesome local communities impede economic and democratic development.

Democratized Violence as Structural Violence

Interpretive ethnographic methods are often incapable of establishing causal associations between individual experiences of violence, social events, and broad-scale structures, such as market reforms. But the very pursuit of such causal associations often relies on disaggregating violence and the market as separate variables. For example, Robert H. Holden (1996: 435–59) argues that endemic violence in Central America tends to be theorized reductively as a simple byproduct of political and economic conditions in the region. His remedy is to look at political violence as an independent variable that can be documented across more than a century of regional history. Our analysis suggests that it is likewise imprudent to read violence, whether in the form of popular protest in Tecpán or everyday forms of violence and crime seen in Guatemala City, as a simple experiential corollary of neoliberal reforms. But treating violence as an independent variable risks naturalizing its enduring presence as a static form linked to regional psychological character. Violence does not simply mirror market processes. Yet, market processes are fundamentally a part of the abiding sociopolitical contexts in which violence takes shape and is interpreted in often dangerous ways by people who experience and participate in it. Appreciating moral and cultural meanings of blame in contemporary Guatemala pushes us to apprehend how concrete historical processes and structures of uneven social and economic power partially give rise to new forms of violence and the explanatory model that blames a certain form of embodiment—gang membership—as the circumscribed root of the problem. It must be acknowledged that the dominant explanatory model of violence in Guatemala, focused on delincuencia, reflects a model of neoliberal government that is the moral and legal basis of market reforms. This model is a model of citizenship that pins praise or blame for social conditions on individual actors and discounts the influence of history by pathologizing behaviors rather than attempting to understand them as deriving from complicated contexts of experience and social change.

We find it useful to conceptualize Guatemala's new violence in light of a social theory that has been advanced in medical anthropology. The concept of "structural violence" (Farmer 2004; Farmer et al. 2006) has been used to emphasize the systemic constitution of much violence and suffering. Violence is typically thought about in terms of physical harm, and responses most often seek to pin praise or blame on individual actors or groups, a tendency Paul Farmer calls "the erosion of social awareness" (2004: 308). The theory of structural violence emphasizes how institutional and structural factors contribute to social conditions in which various forms of violence and suffering can thrive. Farmer's work insists upon a causal relationship between historical conditions and political economic structures and the prevalence of certain public health and social problems. "Structural violence," Farmer writes, "is violence exerted systematically—that is, indirectly—by everyone who belongs to a certain social order" (307). This kind of critical medical anthropology can be linked to a richer cultural appreciation of the sociopolitical contexts in which people experience and respond to violence and suffering (Benson 2008a, 2008b, n.d.). An analogy is found in Katherine Newman's (2005) recent work on school shootings in the United States. She argues for the analytical power of sociological and anthropological approaches over psychological explanations. Rather than drawing direct causal links, Newman explores a number of key variables (e.g., mass media influence, community and family fragmentation, mental health) that are linked in various ways and differentially across settings to a particular kind of violence. These variables together constitute social conditions that enable violence, and they partly reflect the lived effects of the contemporary economy (Storper 2004).[11] This kind of structural violence perspective is also important for scrutinizing the extent to which dominant explanatory models of violence reflect the very market logics that, at least partly, contribute to violence in the first place. Our analysis of the Tecpán protest reveals the value of cultural anthropology in complementing a structural violence account because it elucidates the forms of moral reasoning that are used to make sense of violence on multiple levels and at the expense of a robust social understanding of violence's contextual origins.

This essay conjectures that the myriad forms of violence found in post-conflict Guatemala are partly the result of waves of capitalist restructuring, including the effects of urbanization processes coupled with the retraction or continued lack of state services. The essay also interprets popular concep-tions of violence in Tecpán, centered on the bogeyman of urban delinquency, as themselves partly constituted in relation to market processes linked to a certain kind of democratization. This combination of neoliberalism and lib-eral government creates a dangerous moral order in which, on the one hand, large segments of the population experience physical and economic insecuri-ties, and, on the other hand, feel empowered to support punitive policies as the optimal pathway for ameliorating these insecurities. If lasting peace and a robust democratic civil society are to be achieved, then those structures that systematically place poor and vulnerable populations, such as the indigenous Maya majority and the urban and rural poor, in harm's way will need to be re-organized in ways that address root causes of violence, including those causes found in policies promoted as solutions to violence, poverty, and the country's other woes.

Guatemala is a dangerous place. Equally dangerous are patterns of re-sponse that have arisen in the postwar period. The "iron fist" seems like a commonsensical approach: militarize the streets and round up the bad guys. Guatemalans are scared and want to live in safe communities. But violence and insecurity are multifaceted problems. Political and social responses that do not attend to postwar violence as a broad-scale condition in which en-demic poverty, rapid structural adjustment, and a lack of law enforcement are clustered risk compounding rather than ameliorating violence and insecurity. The iron fist approach does not address root causes of violence, including deepening inequalities linked to structural adjustment policies or desperation and despondence among populations victimized by armed conflict. Rather, it and other responses that emphasize punitive measures and the assignation of blame onto individuals (responses which are evident among Mayas as much as ladinos) reorganize violence as something that the state and private secu-rity forces can legitimately use to establish a sense of security. Given that this situation would resemble the long internal armed conflict, a crucial part of the ongoing peace process involves the implementation of programs that cut to the heart of violence's social origins and transform the sociopolitical context of accusation.

Notes

1. On violence and memory in postwar Guatemala, see *testimonios* by Rigoberta Menchú (1984) and Víctor Montejo (1992). See also Linda Green 1999, Victoria Sanford 2004, Beatriz Manz 2004, and others on postwar memory projects and collective experiences of trauma in the aftermath of the armed conflict.

2. On sensationalist media accounts of gang activity and violence, see Caroline Moser and Alisa Winton 2002 and Winton 2004. For a comparison with the Nicaraguan case, see Dennis Rodgers 2006.

3. The broader context of indigenous activism in Guatemala in the 1980s and 1990s is also explored in Kay B. Warren 1998 and Warren and Jean Jackson 2002.

4. On the growth of the *maquila* sector in Guatemala, see Linda Green 2003; Liliana Goldín 2001; Juan Pablo Pérez Sáinz 1996; and Kurt Petersen 1992.

5. The discussion of popular protest in this section and the discussion of reconciliation meetings in the next section are a revised and updated version of a more extended discussion found in Peter Benson 2004 and Edward F. Fischer and Benson 2006.

6. Researchers are beginning to investigate such questions in Guatemala and other parts of Central America (see Portillo 2003; Rodgers 2006; and Winton 2004).

7. Organized in Civil Auto-Defense Patrols, villagers were charged with protecting their towns from "subversives," often given quotas of suspects to hand over to the local military garrison for "questioning" (see Carmack 1988; Montejo 1992). The civil patrols were responsible for thousands of extrajudicial killings (as the Guatemalan legal code delicately phrases it), working with the army to instill a quotidian terror in Guatemalans that we can scarcely imagine, even in this age of terrorist threats. Yet, the civil patrollers were also victims, forced into their position under the threat of persecution and death themselves. Poor Maya farmers were forced to turn on their neighbors and friends, also poor Maya farmers. It is for this suffering that the Guatemalan Congress, led by Ríos Montt (who, twenty years earlier, oversaw the expansion of PACs and sanctioned their atrocities), authorized compensating former civil patrollers with cash payments. The payments were to be disbursed in three parts. The first payout of 5,000 quetzals (about 640 U.S. dollars, a year's income for a poor farmer) per claim was made in April 2003. Over 600,000 applications were filed, but only the 250,000 whose names appear in the official but incomplete government registry of patrollers were eligible for payment. Even still, this represented a half billion dollar cost that Guatemala could ill afford, and the program was frozen in 2004.

8. Ríos Montt's loss in the 2003 presidential campaign did not end his political

career. In the 2007 national election, he won a congressional seat with the Guatemalan Republican Front.

9. Thanks to Kevin Lewis O'Neill for this citation.

10. Less affluent segments have resorted to neighborhood watch groups that eerily recall the civil patrols of the war era (Kincaid 2001; Moser and McIlwaine 2004: 188).

11. In other contexts as well, anthropologists have highlighted experiences of economic insecurity wrought by structural adjustment as a conduit of violent behavior in groups and individuals (e.g., Bourgois 1995; Godoy 2002; Klima 2002; Moodie 2006, 2007).

Spaces of Structural Adjustment in Guatemala's Apparel Industry

Kedron Thomas

Although Guatemala's long internal armed conflict officially ended in 1996, levels of violence, especially varieties of violence that cluster in urban areas, are on the rise. This essay explores how urban violence influences the everyday lives of indigenous Maya entrepreneurs who make and sell nontraditional clothing in highland markets and the capital city. The conclusions are based on eight months of ethnographic fieldwork among apparel workshop owners and employees in Tecpán, a large, predominantly Kaqchikel Maya town located about eighty kilometers from Guatemala City.[1] I argue that the ways in which urban space is imagined and experienced among *tecpaneco* apparel producers are related to class differentiation in Tecpán and shifting opportunities linked to Guatemala's entrance into international trade and legal agreements. Apparel producers in Tecpán both participate in and contest a spatial imaginary that portrays Guatemala City as dangerous. Many avoid the capital city streets when possible, in spite of the market potential that the city holds, and associate urban life with violence and insecurity (see O'Neill, this volume; Dickins de Girón, this volume). Nonetheless, some producers have been able to establish useful connections with urban markets and official power structures in the capital city. To understand the relationship between market processes, class structures, and urban space, Ghassan Hage's (1996) concept of the "spatial imaginary" proves helpful, emphasizing how particular kinds of space, such as the nation or the city, are thought to have particular qualities and how senses of community and belonging are often mapped onto geographical spaces. A political-economy approach, in which space is understood as networks of association that structure market systems (Harvey 1989), is also important to this analysis. Bridging the ethnography and phenomenology of spatial imaginaries and the political economy of spatialized market relationships is ultimately an advantageous yet underappreciated method for understanding space and spatial experience (Escobar 2001: 153).

In the past decade, Guatemala has ratified several international treaties, including the World Trade Organization Agreement on Trade-Related Aspects of Intellectual Property Rights (TRIPS) and United States–Dominican Republic–Central America Free Trade Agreement (CAFTA), which have resulted in the adoption of economic policies that benefit multinational capital more than domestic clothing manufacturers. These policies include the criminalization of brand piracy—the unauthorized use of registered trademarks and brand names, a practice that has been widespread for decades in Tecpán and other towns where nontraditional clothing (i.e., T-shirts, jackets, sweatshirts) is made.[2] Some producers, mainly those whose class position already affords them a competitive advantage, have abandoned piracy in favor of new strategies, including the use of unique brands, formalization, and organization into marketing associations. They take advantage of connections to formal distribution channels and business services, government institutions, and educational opportunities in Guatemala City, opportunities that are not available to most apparel producers.

The realities of differential class positions and uneven resource distribution that structure market access are obscured when entrepreneurs who benefit from urban connections talk about their relative success in terms of a moral division between those who engage in brand piracy and those who do not. "Pirates," gangs, and other marginalized groups are commonly blamed by officials as well as ordinary people for the country's social and economic ills, including urban violence. In line with this discourse, apparel producers who have formalized their operations often view those who copy popular brands as immoral and illegal. At the same time, smaller-scale producers who traffic in pirated brands—i.e., those labeled pirates—are disadvantaged by levels of fear, crime, and violence that make the capital city a place to be avoided. The case study presented here, which explores processes of class differentiation and industrial restructuring in Tecpán, is fruitful ground for theorizing how cultural representations of urban space, including stereotypes about violence and delinquency, influence market strategies amidst the complex impact of international trade and legal frameworks.

The Neoliberal Apparel Industry

Spatial imaginaries evident among Tecpán's apparel producers have taken shape amidst global restructuring of the apparel industry and a regional process of spatialization associated with the rise of maquiladoras (garment assembly factories that are generally foreign owned), informal economic activities, and everyday violence in and around Guatemala City. The neoliberal economic restructuring that has swept Latin America over the past three decades has reorganized global production chains, linking cheap industrial labor in places such as Guatemala with United States and European consumers in new ways (Bonacich et al. 1994; Ong 1991). When the World Bank and International Monetary Fund (IMF) began promoting an export-led development approach in the 1970s, apparel production was one of the first export sectors introduced in many Asian and Latin American countries. Most clothing sold in the United States now travels a circuit: textiles produced in American, European, or Asian factories are imported to maquiladoras in tariff-free zones in Latin America, the Caribbean, or other parts of Asia where a low-wage labor force cuts, assembles, finishes, and packages garments which are then exported to the United States for distribution and retail sale. The movement of cloth along this commodity chain has not only reorganized capital and labor relations on a global scale, but has also affected economic, social, and spatial relations in the places where apparel production happens.

Export-led development is part of a larger neoliberal program in which communal lands are often privatized and agricultural markets opened to foreign imports, leading to massive job loss in domestic agriculture and patterns of rural dislocation and transnational migration, as discussed in greater detail in Avery Dickins de Girón's essay (in this book). Economic restructuring that began in Guatemala in the 1980s has resulted in declining formal sector employment, both public and private, leaving the vast majority of Guatemalans engaged in informal sector activities, including piracy. At the same time, under pressure from the World Bank and IMF the Guatemalan state has reduced social service expenditures and lifted price controls on basic necessities. These changes have left many Guatemalans vulnerable to poverty and chronic unemployment, health insecurities, crime, and violence (Chase-Dunn 2000; Green 2003).

It is in this context of broad-scale restructuring that the maquila boom took place in Guatemala. State-sponsored violence diminished in the 1980s; democratic reforms promised relative peace and stability. Though some factories had opened earlier, it was during this transitional period that significant numbers of foreign investors came to view Guatemala, with its low wages, low rates of unionization, and lax regulatory structures, as a favorable environment for industrial production. Maquila expansion, fueled mainly by capital from the United States and South Korea, was rapid (Petersen 1992). The number of factories nearly doubled between 1992 and 1996. By the mid-1990s, 130,000 Guatemalans were employed in almost 500 textile and garment factories, and 99 percent of their products were exported to the United States (Traub-Werner and Cravey 2002). By 2005, Mexican and Central American maquiladoras supplied nearly 20 percent of all apparel sold in United States stores (Abernathy, Volpe, and Weil 2005).[3]

Most maquiladoras opened either on the outskirts of Guatemala City or along the initial fifty or so kilometers of the Pan-American Highway as it stretches westward into the highlands. The highway was the preferred location for manufacturers seeking ready access to urban infrastructure (i.e., transportation and other business services) as well as vast labor pools in the central highlands, especially unmarried women and young girls who make up the overwhelming majority (between 70 and 80 percent) of maquila workers. Many highland residents affected by structural adjustment policies migrate to the capital and surrounding towns in search of factory employment (Goldín 2001) despite the notoriously poor working conditions and labor abuses common to maquiladoras (Ross 1997).

Along the highway, the movement of migrant women and men into newly industrialized towns influences material and symbolic relationships between rural and urban areas. In a study of maquila labor in Guatemala, Liliana Goldín (2001) emphasizes that the shift to factory employment in the central highlands reshapes family-level and community-level social dynamics. One important change is the "pseudo-urbanization of rural life" (ibid.: 36). In addition to the incipient proletarianization of youth working in the maquila sector, Goldín records a sentiment among highland townspeople that the benefits and ills of city life have accompanied the construction of maquiladoras along the highway. Workers migrating to industrializing towns may have imagined them as "ripe with possibilities" and opportunities, as do rural migrants moving to Guatemala City to work in the security industry (see Dickins de Girón, this volume). Yet, when migrant laborers move to centers of garment production, locals complain about drunken workers, rising crime, and gang activity. Gangs are commonly associated with Guatemala City and represent the "worst of urban life" coming to a small town (Goldín 2001: 37).

Townspeople attribute emergent security issues to urbanization rather than to broad-scale processes of dislocation and industrialization. A spatial imaginary that associates danger with urban life provides a cultural lens through which structural adjustment is interpreted as moral decline and community instability.

Apparel Production in Tecpán

It is commonly assumed that Maya men and women are employed in apparel production only as low-wage laborers in maquiladoras or purveyors of finely woven traditional garments. This myth overlooks the world of indigenous apparel entrepreneurs who manufacture and sell T-shirts, pants, jackets, and sweaters for domestic consumption. Tecpán is a hub in Guatemala's domestic apparel industry. An hour's drive from Guatemala City on the Pan-American Highway, just beyond the maquiladoras, Tecpán is a short distance from highland markets and urban shopping centers. A handful of indigenous families, part of the town's Kaqchikel Maya majority, began manufacturing and selling nontraditional clothing on the domestic market in the 1960s. A decade later, Guatemala's internal armed conflict was intensifying in the rural highlands. The apparel industry in Tecpán suffered during this time, with many entrepreneurs and community leaders fleeing to the capital or "disappearing" (Fischer and Hendrickson 2002). Not until the peace process began in the late 1980s did the local apparel industry take off, part of a larger context of Maya resurgence in the postconflict period (Warren 1998).

Apparel production contributes significantly to Tecpán's economy. According to local estimates, there are as many as five hundred Maya-owned garment factories and workshops in and around Tecpán. Most consist of a few knitting and sewing machines housed in a spare room of the owner's home. The largest producers own high-capacity machines and employ dozens of workers. They manufacture stylish clothing to sell in regional marketplaces and to national distributors. Local residents are proud of the booming industry. They commonly brag about how tecpanecos clothe the rest of the country and attribute the town's relative economic strength to the industry. The growth of apparel manufacturing has led to the establishment of a slew of textile and thread suppliers around town as well as machinery importers and embroidery and screen-printing shops. Nearly every family has a connection to the industry in some respect. A gendered division of labor positions male heads of households as factory owners and salespeople, while young men from rural hamlets are often employed as machinery operators. Young women are more often employed at sewing machines or in handwork, finishing, and packaging. Entire families are sometimes employed in the workshops, and the industry has grown largely through apprenticeship and kinship connections.[4]

Although the number of garment workshops continues to grow, demand for domestically manufactured clothing may be waning. Maya producers in Tecpán complain that the Guatemalan state, as in many developing countries, courts foreign capital and puts its own citizens at a competitive disadvantage. Some fear that CAFTA, which expanded and made permanent duty-free measures in the agriculture, manufacturing, and textile and apparel sectors, locks in maquiladoras' dominance of the apparel export market and threatens the local labor pool. Alberto Ixim, a Maya man who began manufacturing children's knitwear in the 1980s, has these concerns. Don Alberto has done rather well in the apparel business. He sells bulk quantities of sweaters, children's knitwear, and blankets in the highland markets to several distributors, who are his customer base. Don Alberto is increasingly concerned that maquiladoras pose a threat to Tecpán's industry. His worries have a lot to do with the encroachment of maquiladoras up the Pan-American Highway. "If they move closer to Tecpán—the closest one right now is about thirty kilometers away—they will take employees from us. Everyone hears how they exploit workers, but they also give workers more benefits." As young people in Tecpán observe, maquiladoras promise year-round employment, guaranteed benefits, and steady cash flow, enticements not generally available to workers in the local apparel industry.

Don Alberto has also noticed a rise in "gray market" clothing available in the highland markets he visits once per week to sell his products. "You see a lot of shirts that are made in the maquiladoras, and they sell for 12 to 15 quetzals [about two dollars] instead of 20 or 30 like the same clothes made here." These items are usually overruns or imperfect stock sold at a fraction of the retail price (McDonald and Roberts 1994). Don Alberto has seen that the influx of these goods lowers prices for him and his neighbors. Producers also frequently complain about foreign imports sold in highland markets and foreign-owned retail chains gaining market strength throughout the region. The stores, they claim, sell imported clothing at prices lower than Tecpán's producers can sustain. In 2005, for instance, Wal-Mart acquired controlling interest in the largest retail holdings corporation in Central America. The multinational giant currently has 145 retail outlets in Guatemala, including a Dispensa Familiar in Tecpán that sells groceries, clothing, and other consumer goods, just a block from the town center where the outdoor municipal market has served as a regional commercial hub for centuries (Fischer and Hendrickson 2002).

Don Alberto, like other producers in Tecpán, also worries that CAFTA could mean the end of brand piracy, a staple of the domestic market. Manufacturers themselves report that as much as 80 percent of apparel production in and around Tecpán involves the use of pirated brands such as Nike, Lacoste, Disney, and Abercrombie & Fitch. Manufacturers say that pirated logos, labels, and tags are easy to obtain. Local embroidery shops reproduce the most popular labels with varying degrees of verisimilitude. Many producers travel to markets or other factories in the departments of Totonicapán or Sacatepéquez or Guatemala City to purchase copied tags and labels in bulk. They can sometimes participate in gray market exchanges by purchasing tags, size stickers, and embroidered logos that have been smuggled out of maquiladoras. Still, the variable quality of the clothing and logo reproductions and the low prices at which these garments are sold mean that brand piracy in Tecpán remains distinct from a "counterfeit" market, in which consumers may be convinced that they are buying an item whose manufacture has been authorized by the trademark holder (Phau, Prendergast, and Chuen 2001: 46–47).

The piracy market has been a boon to Tecpán's apparel manufacturers, as Guatemalan consumers and even tourists scramble to purchase knock-offs.[5] Producers face new challenges as the globalization of markets threatens informal, pirated production. Processes of liberalization that shifted industrialized apparel production away from United States and European factories have made international intellectual property rights (IPR) protections a crucial mechanism for ensuring profitability in these regions (Correa 2000). The Guatemalan government has overhauled its IPR protections and developed new enforcement mechanisms in order to comply with international trade agreements.[6] In the official view, pirates now belong to the criminal underside of the international economy, trading on the symbolic capital associated with global brands without returning profits to those who hold the rights.

Modern Pirates and the Politics of Blame

In the Guatemalan media, *piratas* (pirates) who hawk unauthorized reproductions of copyright-protected and trademark-protected materials are portrayed as lawbreakers — "mercenaries of illegality," as one national newspaper calls them. They are viewed as participants in an underground market that threatens the ostensibly more legitimate business interests of multinational corporations, the integrity of Guatemala's economy, and the state's modernist aspirations. Pirates who are fully integrated into the contemporary global economy and work with the latest technologies of mass reproduction and circulation are said to be antithetical to Guatemala's legitimate participation in the international community, as defined according to an official globalized view of economic development and progress (see Portes and Schauffler 2004). The *Prensa Libre*, one of the country's major dailies, reports, "They don't need to decipher maps or plunder ships to find the treasure that makes them millionaires. We are talking about the modern pirates . . . who cost the Guatemalan state millions in lost taxes."[7]

Official, media, and popular explanations for rising levels of violence and insecurity in Guatemala often blame youthful delinquents, gangs, and organized crime, a discursive process that conflates structural problems having to do with neoliberal reforms and democratic shortcomings with the cultural problems of unsavory social figures (Benson, Fischer, and Thomas 2008). Many apparel producers from Tecpán travel each week to sell their goods to distributors in Guatemala City. Some of these goods are then sold in the streets of Zone 1 (see the essays by Offit and by Véliz and O'Neill, in this book). The social and spatial proximity of street vendors hawking pirated goods to street crime (e.g., pickpocketing, mugging, and assault) leads to the lumping of piracy into a generalized portrait of violence as an intractable part of urban life. The political effect of a framing that defines piracy as opportunistic and criminal is to detract attention from state policies that contribute to rising levels of economic insecurity that underpin and sustain the market in cheap, pirated goods. The state and military have flexed their muscles through sporadic, well-reported crackdowns on piracy, confiscating the illegal compact discs, DVDs, and name-brand clothing sold in Guatemala City streets.[8] According to several vendors, the police resell these pirated goods for a profit.[9]

National discourses regarding piracy that generally lump this practice together with delinquency and criminality overlook the everyday context in which piracy production occurs. Open sales of apparel featuring pirated brands as well as pirated software, CDs, and DVDs in municipal markets and city streets contradict the notion that piracy is an underground practice that the state must somehow root out. Many people who own apparel workshops in Tecpán regard the selection of brand names and logos as an important part of the design and marketing process. There is little discourse regarding the legality of copying trademark-protected brands except among a certain class of producers, ordinarily those who do not participate in the piracy market. Apparel producers capture more than a brand name when they sew a global logo onto a sweater. Brands are powerful social symbols and organizing structures of modernity (Coombe and Herman 2004; Miller 1997). The dominant meanings and values associated with fashion brands are the outcome of what Roland Barthes (1990) calls "the fashion system," constituted in the continual flow of recognizable styles and their constituent parts, including brand names, across producers and consumers.[10]

Brand pirates in Tecpán are thus pirates of modernity in two senses. They tactically poach logos to capture a bundle of values having to do with "fashion," participating in a form of signification that some have characterized as a "hallmark of the late modern" era (Coombe 1993: 413). In this sense, they pirate modernity itself. Modernity is not simply an empirical, historical condition, but more broadly a set of attitudes and expectations that privilege what is perceived to be Western or cosmopolitan, as well as those rhetorics of progress that accompany the development of a world economic system (Appadurai 1996). Producers in Tecpán take a measure of pride in their knowledge of the latest fashion trends. One producer commented, "The popular brands sell fast and that is the only way to earn a living. Last year, it was Tommy Hilfiger, Winnie the Pooh, and Spiderman. Every child wanted Spiderman on his shirt, his jacket, his backpack. This year, it's Lacoste. If I don't keep up with what they want, I can't make it in this business." But modernity can also be fruitfully understood in terms of the highly rationalized institutional arrangements and market logics that organize contemporary social and economic networks (Giddens 1990). In this sense, pirates are caught in a thoroughly modern predicament. They are relegated to the wrong side of international legal and trade agreements that globalize a narrow understanding of property rights, beneficially used by corporations in conjunction with nation-states to determine who can legitimately produce fashion, who can consume it, and who cannot. A "predicament of culture" (Clifford 1988) facing pirates is the tension between an experience of being a subject of modernity from the perspective of globalizing legal and trade regimes and being an agent of modernity in the local, entrepreneurial context.

Local Responses to Industry Changes

In addition to protecting corporate investment and promoting economic development, trademark law is hailed by proponents as a mechanism for establishing consumer rights and norms against lying and deception (Bone 2004). Arguments in favor of the institutionalization and expansion of this legal doctrine are often couched in terms of the spread of democracy, progress, and prosperity (Bettig 1996), a deep entanglement of Western values with legal and economic principles. These values shape debates over trademark protections in international arenas and also pervade local settings where they are sometimes embraced and sometimes contested by those with something at stake in their application.

In Tecpán, garment manufacturers have responded in a variety of ways to the criminalization of piracy and market pressures of trade liberalization. For many producers, piracy remains a routine part of the manufacturing and marketing process. Others depart from local norms of piracy and have adopted new practices and strategies. Some manufacturers have created their own brands, for instance, using indigenous symbols and signs from classic Maya hieroglyphs to terms from their native Kaqchikel. This entrepreneurial strategy of market differentiation builds on the revitalization of indigenous identity in Guatemala's postconflict context. The Pérez family, for example, runs a workshop that produces sweaters sold in boutiques and retail chains in Guatemala City. The operation is overseen by two brothers. Their father was an early purveyor of sweater production in the 1970s. Their workshop houses four knitting machines and a few sewing machines. The Pérez family uses the Kaqchikel term for a woven textile, kem, on the tags sewn into each sweater. For this family and other producers, Maya identity has become an authorized and objectified economic strategy, a way to capitalize on what differentiates indigenous apparel manufacturers from maquiladoras and foreign-based firms, as well as neighbors who engage in piracy (Thomas 2006).

New economic strategies of unique branding have been accompanied by the rise of an actively demarcated moral divide between brand pirates and those who use their own brands. One of the Pérez brothers asked, "What if someone started using our brand [Kem] to sell their clothes?" He continued, "It wouldn't be fair. It would be a crime." He adopts the language of trademark protectionism and sees local, perhaps neighboring, producers as a threat to brand sovereignty. Producers such as him often view themselves as morally superior because they obey the law, engage in official regulatory channels, and do not pirate. I asked another producer who manufactures children's clothing why he has registered his factory with the state tax administration and why he uses the family name, Jiatz, as a brand. He replied: "Most people do not know that piracy is illegal, but some know and just don't care." As we talked in the cutting and assembly room of his workshop, his wife and two young men from neighboring hamlets speedily stitched together the front and back sections of toddler-sized pants. He continued, "We put our own name on our clothing. Some people think that their garments will sell faster if there is a cartoon, maybe Mickey Mouse or Spiderman, on the tag. For us, we depend on higher quality to keep our customers." He then added, "There is also the ethical question. It would be a crime to use someone else's brand. It's a question of what is right and wrong."

Reflexive moral sensibilities regarding piracy, linked to localized judgments about competitors, are crucial components of the process by which economic and legal reforms are taking root in this corner of the apparel industry. The integration of IPR law into the legislative codes of developing nations is characterized by legal scholars and economists as a process of "harmonization" (Blakely 2000). Anthropologists have shown, however, that the movement of legal frameworks across borders more often involves a difficult and unpredictable process of translation and transformation. Intellectual property rights are "never fully successful in being everywhere the same" because of the productive frictions that attend to movement across disparate political and cultural contexts (Tsing 2004: 10; Hirsch and Strathern 2004; Vann 2006). In Guatemala, it is not simply the case that people are following or ignoring trademark laws as they are implemented. Rather, the law becomes a charged social and cultural terrain where people construct moral positions and craft strategies of market differentiation, exclusion, and expansion.

Spatial Imaginaries, Urban Violence, and Market Connections

Local ethical debates taking shape around piracy highlight how trademark law and associated values influence moral sensibilities and business practices in Tecpán's apparel industry. What is covered over in claims about pirates who "just don't care" about piracy's illegality, as the children's clothing manufacturer put it, is the extent to which market and class structures determine whether or not one has access to alternative marketing strategies and emergent market opportunities. Who benefits from the globalization and liberalization of Guatemala's apparel industry, including new opportunities for exporting goods to the United States and other countries and also capitalizing on domestic market segments, depends heavily on access to resources. For apparel manufacturers, these resources include education, private loans, and machinery as well as connections to officials, institutions, and formal markets in Guatemala City. Spatial imaginaries that organize how producers relate to urban space intersect with the uneven distribution of cultural and economic capital, as well as social capital (i.e., networks), in Tecpán. In turn, the risks and opportunities associated with free trade, urban space, and the criminalization of piracy are unevenly distributed among Tecpán's apparel manufacturers.

From the earliest days of garment production in Tecpán, the capital city has been an important trading center. As with many other families, Don Alberto's parents got their start in the apparel trade by selling baby clothes in Guatemala City markets. They bought a knitting machine in the early 1970s and made hats and blankets at their home in Xenimajuyu', a small hamlet outside Tecpán. Alberto's father would leave the village late at night in order to arrive early in Guatemala City on market days. Alberto's mother, Doña Eugenia, explained, "It was much safer back then. There were not as many cars on the roads and we didn't fear robbers. Not like today. My husband would walk up and down the path from Xenimajuyu' to Tecpán. He would carry the hats and blankets in a bag. Then, he would ride to Guatemala City to sell to *mayoristas* [wholesalers] and some of the hats would go to El Salvador." Her eyes lit up when she talked about the little hats she made on their rusty machine ending up in another country. "There was no market for baby clothes around here back then because everyone made their own. But in El Salvador, they didn't make these things so we could always sell what we made." At that time, the capital served as an international trading post for the Central American market. In many such stories, Guatemala City is remembered as a vibrant center of economic life and a gateway to distant places.

Things have certainly changed, as Eugenia points out (see also Camus's and Levenson's essays in this volume). The distinction she makes between the days when her husband did not fear walking the dark streets of Tecpán or riding into the capital in the twilight hours and the level of violence today is striking, perhaps even surprising, when one considers the rest of her story. In 1982, at the height of the genocide, Alberto's father was killed not far from their rural home. His body was discovered in the woods outside Xenimajuyu'. Eugenia moved her family into Tecpán's semiurban core and eventually built a small house, where she continued to make children's clothing and sell it in Guatemala City to support her family. Alberto's father was one among many in the region to meet this fate, most at the hands of soldiers, state-sponsored death squads, and armed civil patrols acting on government orders (CEH 1999). Fear and threat are not something new for Eugenia and her family; what have changed are the spatial coordinates of violence. During the largely rural conflict, urban spaces provided something of a refuge for many Maya people (see the introduction, this volume). In Eugenia's talk of the new forms of violence that threaten travelers along the Pan-American Highway and in the capital city streets, it is as if the promises of the city, and of the 1996 Peace Accords, had failed miserably. Rather than steady improvement in the general welfare and security of the population, the postconflict era has seen the rise of new forms of violence that are perhaps more amorphous if no less threatening (see Fischer and Benson 2006). Eugenia's story reveals a spatial ordering of insecurity that now associates the capital city and even Tecpán's urbanizing core with danger, and rural space with safety and security (see O'Neill, this volume).

Others in Tecpán share Eugenia's fears about the city. A number of workshop owners refuse to sell in Guatemala City because of the level of crime and violence. Producers who do not own their own vehicle depend on public transportation to access markets, and public buses are often hijacked and robbed. "It's just not worth it," I heard from one workshop owner who makes and sells women's sweaters. "If you don't have your own car, it's not worth it to ride the bus into the capital. Everything will be stolen from you and you can't do anything about it." Another producer said, "Even if you make it to La Terminal with your packages, you might get attacked in the street. It's not safe." Perhaps playing up the difficulties of his job as a small-scale manufacturer, this producer nonetheless echoes the sentiments expressed to me by many others. Producers commonly say they prefer to sell to wholesalers in highland market towns where the bus rides are safer even if one has to worry about hairpin turns and brake failure on the steep hillsides.

The rising level of crime and danger in the capital city is certainly real. Apparel producers in Tecpán have experienced bus robberies and witnessed violence in urban markets and streets. At the same time, stories and rumors passed among workshop owners and employees resonate with sensationalized media reports that propagate a "climate of fear" (Godoy 2006). National discourses in which urban life is portrayed as chaotic, crime-ridden, and threatening serve the immediate interests of both media organizations relying on fear and gore to boost circulation figures and politicians using scare tactics to garner votes for their "total security" platforms (common in the 2007 national election), which advocate an iron fist solution to crime and violence (Thomas and Benson 2008; Benson, Thomas, and Fischer, this volume). The visions of urban space promoted in such discourses have come to form a hegemonic spatial imaginary in contemporary Guatemala. The concept of spatial imaginaries has been fruitfully employed by anthropologists to understand how spatialized categories of belonging like the "nation" matter for the constitution of identity politics and anti-immigrant sentiments (Anderson and Taylor 2005). Writing about spatial imaginaries in Australia, for example, Ghassan Hage (2000) explores how racist ideologies of exclusion and marginalization, as well as multicultural discourses of "tolerance," rely upon a spatial logic whereby immigration issues are framed as matters of national and community-level territorial defense. In Guatemala, conservative ideologies of neoliberal development and antidemocratic, militarized security are justified in terms of a spatial logic that associates "the city" with crime bosses, gangs, drug traffickers, and other blameworthy individuals who are said to be the root of postconflict economic and social problems.

The stories of urban violence that circulate among apparel producers share this same spatial imaginary even though producers themselves are often scapegoated as pirates in media stories and official reports. Some apparel producers, however, also talk about the city in terms of business opportunities. What separates those who see market potential in the capital and those who see only danger is often a matter of class position. Producers who do not participate in piracy generally have entrepreneurial relationships with state institutions. They are registered with the state tax administration and use receipts for purchasing and sales transactions, keep financial records, and pay business taxes. The incorporation and formalization process requires knowledge of bureaucratic procedures and some degree of literacy. Producers who formalize their operations have generally benefited from educational opportunities, often in the capital city, that prepared them for formal market dealings. This is not an option for most Maya producers, who generally have low levels of education.

Another strategy that apparel producers use in response to economic restructuring, trade liberalization, and the criminalization of piracy is organization into trade associations. The Pérez family and about twenty other producers have sought to form a production and marketing association, much like a cooperative. They view this association as a necessary step toward expanding their reach in the domestic market and preparing the way for export contracting. The group formed as a direct response to Guatemala's entrance into CAFTA. In 2006, when the trade agreement was implemented, several producers paid to attend a series of seminars in Guatemala City on CAFTA's implications for the textile and apparel industries. They met with officials from Guatemala's export promotion agency (a public–private partnership) who walked them through the rules and regulations for exporting apparel to the United States and other foreign markets. The Pérez brothers and their colleagues returned from these meetings with the idea for a marketing association through which several dozen producers could collectively secure an export contract.

The question of who is invited to participate in this marketing opportunity and who gets excluded is a point of contention among manufacturers in Tecpán. Association organizers tend to disparage the informality and piracy that dominate the local apparel industry. They envision a cooperative endeavor in which only formal, legal producers will be allowed to participate, and comment that the people who traffic in piracy are unprofessional and not suited to the new demands of the free trade environment. Again echoing the media reports cited above, this small group of entrepreneurs characterizes pirates as shady characters who produce low-quality goods and who traffic in informal markets. Among those outside the group, talk frequently turns to the big plans and big money that the association stands to make.

The association members are not the only producers who benefit from urban connections. Producers who have the safety of their own automobiles and the machinery and labor to produce at sufficient quantities explained to me that working with distributors and retailers in Guatemala City is more lucrative than selling to wholesalers in the highland markets. Some have secured regular contracts with retail stores to produce branded clothing. Others have contracts with distributors who work from office buildings set above the fray of piracy and crime. Unlike wholesalers in the highlands and street vendors in the capital, these distributors contract for specific quantities to be delivered on fixed dates. If a producer does not meet quality standards and contractual obligations, she or he may lose the business. But distributors in the city pay on delivery or in scheduled installments, whereas wholesalers in the rural marketplaces demand credit and pay only as the goods are sold. The latter arrangement can make it difficult for apparel manufacturers to keep cash on hand to buy production inputs, save money for capital improvements, or keep employees on staff full time, especially during the rainy season (May to October) when sales are generally slower. As a result, those who sell in highland markets commonly face cash flow deficits, have to invest in employee recruitment and training with each new season, and sometimes depend on other sources of income to supplement their earnings from garment production.

For apparel producers struggling to make sense of postconflict insecurities and survive market pressures, spatial imaginaries regarding rural and urban space "provide a seemingly orderly map for orienting oneself amidst the disorder of social life" (Guano 2004: 72). Many apparel manufacturers in Tecpán have ceded urban space to thieves and gangs, refusing to participate in markets there because of perceived dangers. For others, including marketing association members and those who have formalized their businesses, urban space figures prominently in plans for entrepreneurial success. For those with sufficient economic and educational resources, access to automobiles, and business and official connections, the city takes shape both perceptually and practically as a somewhat exclusive entrepreneurial space, even if the threat of crime and violence still looms large. These class and market advantages, which permit some producers a different relationship to the city, are hidden from view when decisions about whether or not to participate in piracy and informal markets are couched in terms of moral integrity and a principled commitment to working through official (public and private) business channels. Such ethical stances allow well-positioned producers to distance themselves from the worlds of piracy and informality so often targeted in national discourse as sources of economic and social decline and insecurity.

Conclusion

Spatial imaginaries in Guatemala have historically linked urban space, ladinos (nonindigenous), and modernity on the one hand; and rural space, indígenas, and tradition on the other (Fischer and Brown 1996: 10–11). Diane Nelson's (1999) work on "Maya-hackers" documents how Maya cultural and political activists negotiate these binaries, which can be both empowering and belittling. Such binaries are the basis for claims about cultural continuity and ethnic identity, and yet also the source of prevailing stereotypes and patterns of discrimination (Fischer 1999; Fisher and Hendrickson 2002). Nelson is interested in the hybrid cultural forms and social strategies that define how Maya actors engage with the state. Writing specifically about activists and public intellectuals, she says that Maya-hackers are "decoding and reprogramming such familiar binary oppositions as those between past and future, between being rooted in geography and being mobile, between being traditional as opposed to modern . . . between mountain shrines and mini-malls, and between unpaved roads and the information superhighway" (1999: 249–50).

This essay extends the analysis of how such binaries are constituted, challenged, and reinscribed by emphasizing the distinctly spatial dimension of these divisions in the context of neoliberal restructuring and legal reform. The daily production and marketing practices of tecpaneco apparel manufacturers challenge tidy dichotomies such as traditional versus modern and rural versus urban. Piracy producers traffic in powerful symbols of modernity in the form of global brands. Tecpán's apparel industry is interwoven with Guatemala City's public and private sectors, global trade, and international legal structures and fashion systems. Yet, rising levels of violence in urban areas and a ubiquitous discourse that attributes various forms of physical, economic, and social insecurity to processes of urbanization ensure that a conceptual divide between rural and urban space remains significant for apparel producers just as it does for many Guatemalans. The conditions of insecurity that proliferate in neoliberal cities disrupt commonly held expectations of modernity that link urban space with progressive social services and stable institutions (Ferguson 1999; Lewinson 1998). In Guatemala, the discursive pairing of urban space with informality, crime, and violence is now a powerful cultural and political resource. It informs a spatial imaginary appropriated in national campaigns and media reports and also evident in emergent moral divisions between differently positioned apparel producers in Tecpán.

Notes

1. Between 2006 and 2008, I conducted ethnographic interviews with twenty-five workshop owners and employees and spent time in their businesses and homes, and in marketplaces. This research forms part of an ongoing investigation of the apparel industry in Guatemala's central highlands.

2. Brand piracy is a public and generally accepted practice in Guatemala, and Tecpán is a well-known center of clothing production. Nonetheless, my research design takes into account potential legal, social, and economic threats to individual piracy producers. The names of piracy producers were not recorded during interviews, and names and identifying characteristics have been changed in this essay to protect informants' identities.

3. Despite the rapid expansion of the maquila sector in Guatemala, factory employment is far from secure. In the late 1990s, nearly 100 maquiladoras closed and moved operations elsewhere (Goldín 2001), a trend that has continued in recent years.

4. A similar pattern of industry growth was reported in Omar Ortez's (2004) study of the domestic apparel industry in the department of Totonicapán.

5. Guatemala ranks fifth in Latin America and first in Central America in sales of pirated goods. Carlos Menocal, "Guatemala es paraíso de la falsificación," *Prensa Libre*, August 7, 2005.

6. These changes were principally mandated by the TRIPS Agreement, which Guatemala implemented in 2000. The legislative implementation of CAFTA in 2006 included additional IPR laws.

7. Menocal, "Guatemala es paraíso de la falsificación."

8. Francisco Mauricio Martínez, "Negocios de película," *Prensa Libre*, October 3, 2004.

9. On the problem of police corruption, see Camus (this volume). Camus also notes that the politics of blame in relation to Guatemala's rising levels of insecurity follow the pattern of centuries of discrimination against the country's indigenous population. Gang members, for instance, are often assumed to be and classified as indigenous, and indigenous migration into the city is viewed as a root cause of crime and violence. That many apparel vendors and merchants, including Don Napo (Offit, this volume), and apparel producers, including those from Tecpán, are indigenous may be important in this regard.

10. In my ongoing research, I am examining local cultural logics behind style choices and aesthetic preferences, building on the work of ethnographers who have usefully examined fashion in cultural context (see Hansen 2004).

Hands of Love

Christian Outreach and the
Spatialization of Ethnicity

Kevin Lewis O'Neill

Amidst the continued privatization of social services, the hemisphere's second-lowest tax revenue (next to Haiti), and the lowest tax collection base in Central America (Sridhar 2007; USAID 2006: 73), the practice of Christian charity in postwar Guatemala has become increasingly important. Who else but churches provide basic services to Guatemala's poor? The practice of Christian charity, however, is not without consequences — cultural and political. This essay explores two such consequences. They are the observable facts that the practice of Christian charity (1) divides and connects as well as (2) orders and ranks Guatemala City and country. This two-part observation rests on the fact that neo-Pentecostal megachurches, congregations of growing political importance (O'Neill 2009, 2010a), tend to direct their charitable interventions toward Guatemala's rural indigenous rather than Guatemala City's indigent, and that this decision to serve those in the country as opposed to the city evidences a shared moral geography with an agreed-upon sense of place.[1]

By *place*, neo-Pentecostalism evokes two interrelated meanings: "Place understood as both a location in space and a rank in a system of social categories (as in the expression 'knowing your place')" (Ferguson 2006: 6). Neo-Pentecostal charity, first, places the biblically deserved in the country as opposed to the city. From a neo-Pentecostal perspective, the city is a site of delinquency (laziness, thievery, and corruption), while the countryside is a locus of pure biblical need. Second, neo-Pentecostal charity ranks the rural indigenous as less developed and, in turn, more deserving of Christian charity than the urban poor. Neo-Pentecostalism, that is, tends to make the rural indigenous a charitable priority *over* and *above* the urban poor, while also contributing to the framing of both populations as less developed than (as ranked *below*) megachurch congregations.

These divisions and rankings emerge in a range of megachurch settings, during formal and informal interviews as well as public sermons. Yet, these divisions and rankings crest most clearly in a series of images produced by Manos de Amor—the philanthropic wing of El Shaddai, one of Guatemala City's most influential neo-Pentecostal megachurches. El Shaddai has a church community of more than 25,000 congregants, a main auditorium that seats over 6,000 people, 31 incorporated satellite churches throughout the Guatemalan countryside, and a sophisticated transnational media network that links radio and television programming to informal cassette economies and print media. Simply put, El Shaddai sits proudly atop Guatemala's remarkable shift in religious affiliation (Althoff 2005; García-Ruiz 2004). Once overwhelmingly Roman Catholic, Guatemala is now more than half charismatic or Pentecostal Christian (Pew Forum on Religion and Public Life 2006).

Distributed in El Shaddai's Sunday bulletins, Manos de Amor, or "Hands of Love," presents the church's urban congregation with photos of their organization feeding, clothing, and caring for Guatemala's indigenous communities. They distribute these images every Sunday in the church's weekly bulletin. They are images meant to update the El Shaddai community on Manos de Amor's philanthropic work, but they are also images intended to invoke compassion—to inspire a donation. For the El Shaddai community, these images provide some of the most potent, even iconic, representations of the biblically deserved—the orphan, the widow, and the stranger—that currently shape urban neo-Pentecostal understandings of, and responses to, the Guatemalan interior. The production of these images and the short texts that frame them speak directly to issues of ethnicity, place, and deservedness in postwar Guatemala, as well as to a changing relationship between Guatemala City and country. In a sentence, these images teach congregants (both *ladinos* [nonindigenous] and the urban indigenous alike) what the rural indigenous need and what the urban congregant's responsibility (and relationship) is to the interior.

The overarching message advanced is that the urban churchgoer is distinct from (yet forever responsible for) the rural indigenous. The discourse splits city from country while also insisting that the capital city and the country are interrelated. This ironic tension sits at the very center of this essay. Rather than perpetually disconnected, urban neo-Pentecostals understand the city as in constant relationship to the country vis-à-vis Christian charity. Interestingly, even astoundingly (and oftentimes ironically), neo-Pentecostalism is not only the social imaginary that divides city from country but also the glue that holds the two together for urban residents.

This observation about interconnectedness through divisions makes sense when placed into conversation with George Simmel's (1997) work on bridges and doors. Simmel suggests that bridges and doors are not just material constructions but also images of boundaries that both separate and connect. Bridges and doors speak to the human desire to connect while also marking the reality of separation: "Without bridges connecting separated places in our practical thoughts, needs and fantasies, the concept of separation would have no meaning" (Houtum and Struver 2002: 143). Bridges that connect one locale to another also mark the two as separate. Nothing could be truer about Manos de Amor; the organization reinforces the idea that the Guatemalan countryside is an entirely different kind of place than the capital while at the same time announcing to the urban faithful that they are responsible for (and, in turn, in constant relationship to) the rural countryside. This essay assesses this tricky relationship—the idea that neo-Pentecostal charity both divides and connects, as well as orders and ranks, Guatemala City and country.

Divided yet Interconnected

Present-day Guatemala City is neither an ancient nor a beautiful metropolis.[2] Aesthetically, Guatemala City has been set apart from the rural interior because the capital (in contrast to a lush countryside) has long been a gray and ugly city—flattened by earthquakes, unplanned development, and violence. Its narrow, congested streets with their squat architecture, sprawling developments, and shortage of public space belie an itinerant life that has produced many—but maintained few—monuments, memorials, and museums. The capital, as history notes, currently stands in its fourth location because of moves prompted by natural disasters. From 1543 to 1776, the third capital of Guatemala, La Antigua, was the cultural and economic center of what is today known as Central America; yet, its location proved fatal. Vulnerable to natural disasters, such as floods and volcanic eruptions, two massive earthquakes in 1773 destroyed the city, driving residents to present-day Guatemala City, or La Nueva Guatemala de la Asunción, in 1776.

The construction of the new capital, like all Latin American cities under

Spanish rule, followed the ordinances established by Spain's Felipe II in 1573; a Plaza Mayor was built along with ordered city streets. But the 200 years that separated Felipe II and Guatemala City's construction provided room for improvisation. The city's buildings, for example, drew very little inspiration from colonial, baroque, or neoclassical styles of architecture, choosing instead more modern, even functionalist, approaches. The constant fear of earthquakes kept the buildings modest, sturdy, and single storied, and the city's cathedral was completed slowly (finished in 1815) and without its planned towers. Furthermore, developers never properly prepared the capital to accommodate its eventual growth. Urban congestion became more of a problem as the city continued to grow, from 11,000 in 1778 to 55,728 in 1871 (Gellert and Pinto Soria 1990: 32).

Following Guatemala's independence from Spain in 1821, and until the beginning of its liberal period in 1871, the capital experienced very few modifications, remaining a relatively undersized capital city. By the end of the nineteenth century, however, modern urbanization in Guatemala City began with the reorientation of the national economy toward the cultivation of coffee. The city's infrastructure developed rapidly, and new barrios were built to accommodate a rapid influx of immigrants from Guatemala's rural departments. Banks, municipal buildings, and commercial agencies emerged by way of function and utility (rather than beauty and grandeur). Early efforts at liberalization prized factories over cathedrals. Yet, a rather different phase of development followed the election of President José María Reyna Barrios in 1892. With images of Paris in mind, Barrios constructed some of Guatemala City's major avenues that still stand today (e.g., La Reforma); he also attempted to beautify an otherwise drab city with gardens, parks, a replica of the Eiffel Tower, and Guatemala City's own Temple Minerva. His goal was for Guatemala City to become a "tropical Athens" and to be known throughout the world as "Little Paris" (Peláez Almengor 1994).

A series of earthquakes in 1917 and 1918 devastated Barrios's Parisian dreams. The city's reconstruction period began soon thereafter, but cholera and political instability frustrated every effort. After President Manuel Estrada Cabrera was overthrown in 1920 amidst a crumbled cityscape, construction once again prized function over splendor as migrants from the countryside entered the city looking for food, work, and shelter. The city's population swelled to 112,086 in 1921 while the capital's waning infrastructure both limited and defined its urban development. Political instability (1920–31) ultimately gave way to corruption under President Jorge Ubico (1931–44), which subsided briefly when voters elected Juan José Arévalo as president in 1944. When the 1954 coup sparked Guatemala's civil war, Guatemala City had more than quadrupled in size since President Barrios amidst a stretch of history that left little time for sustainable urban development, let alone attractive public works projects. Architecturally, the city was still reeling from the 1917 and 1918 earthquakes when it underwent yet another moment of destruction and reconstruction with the 1976 earthquake. Following that quake, thousands migrated from rural areas to the capital looking for refuge; finding little, the organized reconstruction period began alongside informal attempts by Guatemala City residents to build shelter from whatever materials were available.

Thirty years later, Guatemala City has once again doubled in size, with people moving to the city on a daily basis. Infrastructure remains a problem as public transportation and water systems struggle to keep up with the city's demands. All of this strain amidst a history of construction, destruction, and reconstruction has left Guatemala City without Spanish architecture, towering churches, and cobbled streets lined with "local color." Polluted with diesel fumes, the capital currently stands as a city once built (and continually rebuilt) with an eye toward industrial function over beauty.

Guatemala City's gray facades and smoggy atmosphere contribute to an imagined divide, drawn along the lines of color as well as culture — not to mention class and ethnicity. Roughly half of Guatemala's population is indigenous. For many, this demographic fact calls to mind the colorful traje (traditional dress) that the postwar Maya movement celebrates and that the Guatemalan tourist industry continues to market. In contrast to rural areas that are as much as 80 percent indigenous, however, the capital has been overwhelmingly ladino/a: 99.1 percent ladino/a in 1930, 98.2 percent ladino/a in 1960, and 96.4 percent ladino/a in 1990. While there are now a reported 1 million indigenous people living in or around the capital city, this historical trend perpetuates an imagined division between the "culture-less" (and colorless) ladinos of the capital, with their "sophisticated" sensibilities and stylized Spanish, and the "culture-full" (and colorful) indigenous of the countryside, with the kind of linguistic and ethnic diversity that has long excited tourists, artists, and anthropologists alike.

This kind of imagined imbalance between grayness and color has led to a neat division between city and country — a division that has dissuaded both Guatemalans and ethnographers from seeing "culture" in Guatemala City. Diane Nelson makes this point in A Finger in the Wound (1999), noting that ladinos have for far too long been understood as without culture (in much the same way that whiteness becomes deracialized in the United States), while Guatemala's indigenous communities are understood as a wellspring of alterity. The dissection is one that authors have long reproduced. The travel writer Paul Theroux describes Guatemala City from his hotel balcony: "Guatemala City, an extremely horizontal place, is like a city on its back. Its ugliness, which is a threatened look (the low morose houses have earthquake cracks in their facades; the buildings wince at you with bright lines) is ugliest on those streets where, just past the last toppling house, a blue volcano's cone bulges . . . [The volcano's] beauty was undeniable, but it was the beauty of witches" (cited in Lutz and Collins 1993: 114). Another travel writer adds: "Guatemala City is a rough place . . . The buildings and infrastructure are more or less intact, but the city is tired and world-weary. It lays supine in the highlands valley, beaten down by earthquakes, volcanic eruptions, civil war, revolution, economic devastation, and dictatorship. The city is hungover. Its eyes squint at the sun. It groans with depression and exhaustion."[3] This kind of division between urban blight and the natural (even supernatural) "beauty of witches" in nature contributes to the idea that Guatemala City is set apart from the rural and apparently magical countryside that is its backdrop. Using Guatemala City as an example of an impenetrable fortress of high culture, Jean Franco notes that "the [Latin American] city, once imagined as the polis, had long been an image of repression and confusion, . . . a panopticon surveyed by the all-seeing eye of a dictator as in the Guatemala City of Miguel Ángel Asturias's El Presidente" (2002: 11). Set apart, literally above the rest of the country like a guard who stands watch in his tower, Guatemala City has long been imagined as above the rural highlands.

At the same time, travel literature on Guatemala's rural areas does not disappoint. Collectively, the story is of a paranormal, maternal world of mystery that is laced with a lush jungle setting. The dominant narrative actually begins at the very edge of Theroux's description, at the foot of blue volcanoes. Martín Prechtel writes:

> The Indian girl was like an archaic Mayan clay figurine coming alive before my eyes. She was dressed in traditional clothing, her eyes both gentle and untamed, her long black hair carefully coiffured. Her appearances bespoke a ten-thousand-year-old pool of ancestral Mayan women. Her luxurious red and purple *huipil*, made by her own hand on a back strap loom, belied other secrets embodied within. Her hips were wrapped and bound by an indigo *murga*, a tubelike ankle-length skirt held fast by a wide sash where she tucked her little things: her comb,

her money, weaving pick, and so on. Three large holes in her earlobes were laced with hanging shanks of red and violet yarns from which were suspended old Spanish *piastres* and *reals*, seventeenth-century silver. (1998: 78)

Alongside objectifying his subject (the girl "was like an archaic Mayan clay figurine") and sexualizing her with a peculiar interest in the young lady's hips and "untamed eyes," important here is the author's use of color: clay, black, red, purple, indigo, red, violet, and silver. This kaleidoscope of culture paints a radically different portrait than the one commonly drawn of Guatemala City. While the countryside literally explodes with color—in travel literature, through indigenous-made and marketed textiles, and in Guatemalan tourist brochures—Guatemala City continues to be portrayed in and through shades of gray, as hungover. As one popular travel guide explains: "The best part about Guatemala City is leaving" (Lonely Planet 2001: 114).

The last thirty years of Guatemalan history, however, perforate this imagined divide. The 1976 earthquake not only sent indigenous migrants from rural areas to the capital city but also contributed to the escalation of the then low-level civil war. At first, the armed conflict peppered Guatemala City's streets with bombs and forced disappearances; yet, the earthquake quickly contributed to a new kind of struggle that placed rural indigenous communities between two armies (Stoll 1993). As the violence moved from the city to the country, refugees relocated from the country to the city, once again poking holes in the shared belief that the capital city was an exclusively ladino/a place.[4] There has also been a continued spike in the number of Guatemalans, indigenous and ladinos alike, who have left Guatemala for the United States as undocumented migrants. International labor circuits tend to use the capital city as a "first step" in the journey from the countryside to the United States. These international circuits have developed alongside intranational labor circuits that bring the indigenous from rural areas to the city for days at a time— to work as private security guards or to hawk wares in the city's informal economy. In the capital for two or three days of work, these migrant workers return to their families in, for example, Huehuetenango or Chichicastenango only to later return to Guatemala City for another stretch of time (Dickins de Girón, this volume). Public buses brimming with rural migrants, their bodies dangling from the bus doors, shuttle between the countryside and the capital city. Their very travel evidences the fact that the city and the country are not distinct entities—although they have become imagined as such—but are rather interrelated social formations. So too are a range of other bridges and doors, in the words of Simmel: cell phones, political campaigns, gangs, and private security industries.

Another development that breaks any easy divide between Guatemala City and country has been the establishment of neo-Pentecostal church networks.[5] These networks use the capital city as a kind of headquarters for the satellite churches that dot rural *departamentos*. El Shaddai, for example, has dozens of active satellite churches in the Guatemalan countryside. They sprinkle the nation, from the mountainous regions of Totonicapán to the lakeside vistas of San Marcos, from the jungles of Petén to the semiurban regions of Chimaltenango, from Retalhuleu of the Pacific coast to the commercial center of southwest Guatemala known as Quetzaltenango. Tethered together by an apostolic network, these smaller churches minister to indigenous communities in their respective languages. Connected by Internet, radio, and television broadcasting, El Shaddai's rural communities keep in constant contact with their urban "mother ship" by participating alongside fellow congregants with live audio broadcasts of important sermons and conferences. Pastors and church leaders from rural areas also travel to the capital city for training sessions, workshops, and meetings about church growth, while pastors and church leaders from the capital city return the favor for special events in the departamentos. And through Manos de Amor, El Shaddai's main church in Guatemala City also organizes mission trips to the countryside to aid those El Shaddai communities in need of basic social services. This constant flow of ideas and people, faith and action, money and skills, picks at the imagined divide between city and country—between drabness and color, between ladino/a and indigenous. Neo-Pentecostal Christianity contributes to the formation of Guatemala City and country as interrelated spatial formations that draw on (and pull at) each other. Philanthropic interventions, moreover, suggest a new kind of relationship forming between these imagined worlds—one that announces, at one and the same time, that the capital city is different from but nonetheless in constant relationship to the countryside. This relationship is clearly observed through the images and texts that Manos de Amor produces and distributes to the El Shaddai congregation.

Viewing the Country from the City

Every Sunday at 8:00 a.m. and 11:00 a.m., El Shaddai opens its megachurch doors to thousands of believers. The church's expansive parking lot obscures the fact that the vast majority of churchgoers come by public buses that snake

through the city and dock at the church's front gates. El Shaddai's unbeliev-
able growth since the late 1980s has literally bent bus routes to its front doors,
forcing drivers to remap their routes to meet public demand. The 82 bus, for
example, toddles from Zone 2 through Zone 1's historic center, up through
Zone 4's efforts at urban renewal, and right on past Zone 10's shopping centers, to the open arms of El Shaddai in Zone 14, where hoards of people walk
patiently into the front doors, past the church lobby, and into their seats. For
those who arrive a little late for service, they are greeted as soon as they take
their first step from the bus to the pavement with rolling waves of high-energy
music, the density of which grows with every step toward the church (O'Neill
2010c). Along the way, somewhere in between the lobby and the main auditorium, a volunteer hands each churchgoer a glossy Sunday bulletin. Six to eight
pages in length, the bulletin announces the service's theme as well as items
for sale at the bookstore and other upcoming events. Sandwiched somewhere
among these announcements and advertisements, there is an entire page devoted to the work of Manos de Amor.

Each Manos de Amor page tells a story and teaches a lesson through images
and text. Although there exist innumerable interpretations of any given set
of Manos de Amor images, the stories reported are overwhelmingly about
need—about how poor indigenous communities in rural Guatemala need
roofing materials, need better trained teachers, need food items, or need
medical care. At the same time, these images also deliver a lesson that is directed toward El Shaddai's viewing public—toward those who linger on these
colorful announcements during the less exciting moments of Sunday service,
on their bus rides home, or while relaxing in the late evening or early morning. The images teach the model viewer how to read the country from the city
and, in the process, how to understand the city as in constant relationship
to the country. They promote a limited universe of ideas about ethnicity and
class and how ethnic difference should be placed within postwar Guatemala.
To study these images is in fact to hear a powerful voice in an ongoing cultural
discussion about charity, space, and ethnicity in Guatemala—about the place
of the country's deserved. The most basic assumption here, moreover, is that
these narratives and images are not clear-cut representations of poverty (or
even indigenousness), but a much more complicated kind of cultural work.

Deservedness is the first of three lessons derived from these images. With
whom is God concerned? The answer is biblical for Manos de Amor—the
orphan, the widow, and the stranger (e.g., Exodus 22:21–24; Leviticus 19:34;
25:35; Psalm 10:14; Deuteronomy 10:18; Proverbs 15:25). One Manos de

Amor administrator—I will call her María—explained during an interview: "We are called to help our neighbor. We read in Isaiah 58 that you need to 'share your bread with the hungry, and bring the poor and homeless into your house; when you see the naked, cover them.' Isaiah 58 is our base. It's our fundamental principle." This sense of responsibility to the biblically deserved repeatedly comes to the fore in El Shaddai Sunday bulletins—in the text and in the images produced by Manos de Amor and distributed every week to a viewing public. The story of Zacarías Cuc Tuc is but one example.[6]

Zacarías is a five-year-old indigenous boy from the highlands of Cobán whose story embodies Manos de Amor's philanthropic mission: to transform Guatemala one child at a time.[7] Images begin to tell the story. The largest of the pictures introduces Zacarías, with his big smile turned upward despite the frowning scar on his forehead. A row of smaller pictures anchors the narrative with scenes of recovery: Zacarías with his father at the hospital, Zacarías bandaged but with friends, Zacarías again with his father, and Zacarías with his classmates. Zacarías's face tells a story of not just hope and childlike wonderment but also sincerity and potential. His scar cuts across his shaved scalp, interrupting the portrait's soft composition with a brute concern that ideally gives way to curiosity. Answering the very question that such a dramatic image raises, the text explains that Zacarías suffered a terrible fall. A student in one of El Shaddai's rural elementary schools, Zacarías was taken by his teacher to a local emergency room, where it was determined that his skull had been severely fractured and that he would need to be taken immediately to a better-equipped hospital. There, doctors operated on Zacarías as his fellow classmates and family members prayed for his speedy recovery.

The Manos de Amor page also reports that one intercessor received a direct message from God, who explained to him that Zacarías would one day preach in not just one but two languages. This prophecy, the text continues, reassured the faithful that the boy's life was in God's hands. At the same time, Zacarías's own father, a "true believer," was confident that the surgery would be successful—that his son would not only survive but also that his intelligence would not be affected in any way. All of these predictions seem to come true as the Manos de Amor announcement concludes its story by assuring the viewer that the surgery was a success—although Zacarías still needed to take expensive medication to fully recover. María added in an interview: "The boy is doing well. It's been a year and he's doing well. I was able to visit him after his operation and things were okay, but by now he has had a year of treatment, and he's taking a medication called Epamin. The doctor actually said that the medicine carries the risk of seizures, but thank God he didn't have any of those. He's fine." The message, advanced by the Manos de Amor announcement and confirmed by María, was that Zacarías received the care that he so desperately needed with the help of Manos de Amor.

The lesson is that Zacarías is emblematically deserving—of money, of medication, of a future. To this end, the unmistakably endearing photos of Zacarías and his healing wound are an effective pedagogical tool. As noted by scholars elsewhere, images of children are frequently used to convey hope; the face of a child oftentimes becomes the ambassador of hope during charitable solicitations (Malkki 1997). Especially for philanthropic agencies, who market an idea of deservedness alongside Christian charity's moral imperative to help, children become symbols of goodness and seeds of world peace. Children suffer unjustly, but they also see a truth that adults, jaded by their years, cannot. They are emissaries of not just tranquility but also the future (Bornstein 2001: 601). In this sense, following the work of Liisa Malkki, children are depoliticizing agents; they erase the complexities of life to reveal the simplicity of need (1997: 17). The story of Zacarías, it is safe to say, functions in this exact way. Manos de Amor markets Zacarías as intuitively deserved of charity because he is not just poor, but also because he simply did what so many other children do every day: he fell. The story is one of simple needs, one that is far less complicated than the stories wrought by, for example, alcoholism, gang involvement, and Guatemala City's informal economy.

Having determined who is deserving, Manos de Amor advances a second lesson—the geographical place of the deserved. Zacarías lives in the countryside rather than Guatemala City. The placement of the deserved in the Guatemalan countryside mirrors the kinds of division that James Ferguson observes in Zambia, where "Ethnographies from the 1950s provide many examples of moral thinking that opposed moral 'village women' to immoral 'town women'; rural generosity to urban selfishness; rural cooperation and social ties to urban competition and monetary ties; and, most generally, rural morality to urban immorality" (1992: 81). This kind of dissection of city from country has become heightened in Guatemala's postwar context, where urban violence now threatens the welfare of the nation through both organized crime and drug trafficking. Delincuencia is the word used by both believers and nonbelievers alike to describe the capital city; the word hints at the moral dimensions of Guatemala City's separation from the rural highlands. In response to Manos de Amor's decision to work in the countryside as opposed to the city, María added: "Regrettably, la delincuencia in the capital has been increasing. It really has been getting stronger. So you can imagine the risks that a child faces by living in the streets of the capital. It's the kind of risk that children in the rural areas do not know. They have no idea. Thank God. They are guarded, more protected. Maybe there are other risks, like house fires, but the children in the rural areas definitely do not live amidst as much delincuencia as people do here in the capital." Zacarías, María continued, has needs, but they are needs that are straightforward and pure; Zacarías is "guarded" and "more protected." His life is simple.

Guatemala City is also the seat of the government, which neo-Pentecostals agree is more corrupt than other parts of Guatemala. The moral constitution of the capital city, in short, is weak when seen through neo-Pentecostal eyes. Rural areas, however, remain less complicated and far simpler. Many congregants even describe the Guatemalan countryside and the rural indigenous as childlike, as full of potential but nonetheless underdeveloped. This analogy allows capitalinos (capital city residents) to depoliticize and even infantilize the indigenous, making rural Guatemala a place that needs simple things to make life better: food, medication, small amounts of money, and building materials, for example. Much of this narrative rests on the second lesson, the idea that the deserved—these prototypical orphans, widows, and strangers—live outside of the city and in a more primitive setting.

Manos de Amor communicates to urban congregants through weekly solicitations that the place of the deserved is the countryside. On one particular Sunday, for example, Manos de Amor announced that a rural elementary school in Río San José simply needed more money for a teacher.[8] The parents of this community had constructed a school with their own hands, building the structure out of nothing into something, from a simple plot of land to a modest schoolhouse. But, the community still lacked the money to retain a qualified instructor. The three photos that animate the solicitation in the Sunday bulletin depict a scene far different than those at the El Shaddai megachurch in Guatemala City. Rather than tiled floors, drywall, and an urban backdrop punctuated by megachurch glamour, the pictures document dozens of indigenous children standing barefoot in colorful traje on a dirt floor under a tin roof. The pictures, taken at the school during the rainy season, with its thick morning fog, also suggest that these children live somewhere far away from the capital. The contrast becomes even more apparent with El Shaddai's own advertisements for its own capital city elementary school.[9] Also appearing in the weekly bulletin, oftentimes next to solicitations made by Manos de Amor for rural school children, these advertisements depict smiling ladino/a (not indigenous) children, with crisp white T-shirts (not colorful trajes).

The contrast, while strange from a certain perspective, is quite naturalized from another. Akhil Gupta comments on anthropological conceptions of space in a way that speaks to the imagined distance between Guatemala City and country: "Concepts of space have always fundamentally rested on . . . images of break, rupture, and disjunction. The recognition of cultures, societies, nations, all in the plural, is unproblematic exactly because there appears an unquestionable division, an intrinsic discontinuity, between cultures, between societies, etc." (1988: 1–21 cited in Malkki 1992: 28). The division between Guatemala City and country rests on this kind of break. Furthermore, this kind of cultural placement—the idea that the deserved exist in rural areas while less deserving ladinos occupy the capital city—leads (conceptually speaking) to a kind of ecological immobility that many capitalinos share. Arjun Appadurai explains: "Natives are not only persons who are from certain places, and belong to those places, but they are also those who are somehow incarcerated, or confined, in those places" (1988: 37). Urban neo-Pentecostals and middle-class capitalinos in general tend to echo this kind of ecological incarceration. The director of a small nongovernmental organization (NGO) that works to train community-based NGOs in Guatemala City, for instance, sighed during an extended conversation about philanthropic intervention. She explained that capitalinos are a huge obstacle to sustainable development. They believe, she explained, that the poor live outside of the city, not within it, and that the urban poor can thus be relocated from the city to rural areas since they belong in the mountains.

This kind of worldview, be it international or intranational, obviously flattens the politics of migration as well as the emotional and infrastructural complexity of resettlement. The imagined simplicity and effectiveness of its philanthropic interventions allow Manos de Amor to market Christian charity successfully to its congregants. While the felt complexity of urban politics paralyzes many neo-Pentecostals, sending them to their knees in prayer, modest donations can really impact rural communities. Just one week after the publication of the above solicitation for the rural schoolteacher, Manos de Amor delivered another message to its congregation: thank you.[10] Reprinting the same pictures, the Manos de Amor page announced that God had provided a quick answer to their prayers. A Guatemala City Bible study group had taken up the responsibility not only to pay a schoolteacher's salary, but also to provide funds to strengthen the schoolhouse's own sagging structure.

Simple problems with simple solutions helped to place the biblically deserved in Guatemala's rural areas rather than in the city.

The third and final lesson that Manos de Amor communicates to El Shaddai's urban congregation is that neo-Pentecostals in the capital exist in constant relationship to the rural indigenous. This is by far the most surprising recalibration of city and country. While many are eager to dub the city and the country as of two entirely different universes, neo-Pentecostalism links these distinct social formations through the language of Christian membership and responsibility. El Shaddai's founding pastor, Dr. Harold Caballeros, spoke at a public event, forming an image of the city and the country as one: "We are Guatemalans, but what really is a Guatemalan? Do leaders hold the same concept of Guatemalans in [the village of] Santa María, the same concept of Guatemalans in a barrio, the same sentiment in the city? Some say that [the identity of] those in the high classes is close to what it's like in Miami, while other [Guatemalan] towns are closer to Africa." The distinctions that separate Guatemalans from Guatemalans are class-driven, but also laced into geographic locales. The idea of Santa María sparks images of the rural indigenous, while the "high classes" akin to those in Miami direct the imagination to the capital city's business sector. Dr. Caballeros continued by leaning on the metaphor of space to communicate a need for unity: "We Guatemalans are so distant from each other in terms of the formation of citizenship and the formation of identity. What better than the work of believers, what better than the link of the gospel, to dissolve these sentiments and polarization . . . We need to pursue a national consensus, and we have the tools to clean up [the polarization] — the gospel, love, and forgiveness, allowing us to construct this identity." Dr. Caballeros makes clear that collapsing this radical polarization begins with extending outward, linking city and country through, among many other things, Christian charity.

Manos de Amor encourages this kind of outreach through its images and texts, allowing congregants to participate in the bridging of two regularly disassociated regions with small donations. Project updates let the El Shaddai congregation know that their donations (big and small) make a difference. One Manos de Amor page exudes the message of success with a large photo of laughing indigenous boys and girls. The headline announces, "the advances of our new school."[11] The text then tells a story brought to life by three more pictures. They show children being children — learning, playing, and laughing with their friends and family. More importantly, the school has allowed the children "to be able to know God in a personal way." This rural elementary school not only became a house of learning but also a house of worship because of the charitable support and missionary work that Manos de Amor stewards from the capital city.

Another, possibly less focused, Manos de Amor announcement echoes this particular message of success.[12] With images of indigenous men having their teeth screened by Manos de Amor dentists, of mothers and daughters in traje holding donated clothes, and long lines of people waiting to visit Manos de Amor doctors, the bulletin announces that Manos de Amor makes a difference in the countryside. A long list of rural departments is the first of only two sets of text that accompany these photographs. A passage from the Bible is the second text. The first list includes the regions of Tucurú, Chimaltenango, Huehuetenango, Quetzaltenango, and Totonicapán. The biblical passage that accompanies this list is Psalm 41:1–3: "Happy are those who consider the poor, the Lord delivers them in the day of trouble. The Lord protects them and keeps them alive; they are called in the land. You do not give them up to the will of their enemies. The Lord sustains them on their sickbed; in their illness you heal all their infirmities." Those in the capital maintain a charitable relationship with the countryside and reap great rewards, such as the idea of empathetic Guatemalans that might one day be accountable to each other through charitable outreach.

Ranking the Deserved

Neo-Pentecostal philanthropic intervention places deservedness in the country as opposed to the capital, mapping biblical need onto the rural indigenous. Christian charity makes Guatemala's countryside the geographical place of the deserved. Yet, place is not simply a matter of location, but also an issue of value and verticality—of being ranked within a cultural system. Louis Dumont's *Homo Hierarchicus* tells us this much: "Hierarchy [is] the principle by which the elements of a whole are ranked in relation to the whole, it being understood that in the majority of societies it is religion which provides the view of the whole, and that the ranking will thus be religious in nature" (1980: 10).[13] The practice of Christian charity ranks certain groups as higher, or lower, than others—as not just more or less deserving, but also more or less developed; more or less modern; more or less proximate to God. The images and sets of ideas that Manos de Amor produce and distribute by way of Sunday bulletins hints at this cultural ranking, as do the kinds of philanthropic intervention that the organization pursues. As this section notes, Manos de

Amor's promotion of hygiene among rural indigenous communities is one effort (among many others) at ranking the rural indigenous as less developed, less modern, and less proximate to God than capitalinos. Hygiene is so very illustrative of this process because hygiene invokes Mary Douglas's (1966) observation that "dirt is matter out of place" as well as the Christian cliché that "cleanliness is next to godliness" (an axiom popularized through the sermons of John Wesley, the eighteenth-century Anglican minister).[14] The spatial dimensions of both phrases are instructive when thinking through, and listening to, Manos de Amor's ranking of the indigenous in Guatemala's rural areas—as below capitalinos in terms of both spiritual and economic development but also above the urban poor in terms of righteousness.

Manos de Amor's Christian commitment to hygiene is not subtle; the narrative unabashedly exposes the organization's Christian compulsions as well as some of its most basic (and, at times, base) assumptions. Responding to a question about lice within indigenous communities, one Manos de Amor spokesperson explained: "Lice is dirty. Absolutely. As we know, there are values that slow down progress. There are values that limit the development of a culture and a population [such as dirtiness], and values that promote [development]. One of those values [that promotes development] is the use of a schedule. Punctuality, responsibility, cleanliness—these are the values of efficiency, of progress, of one's level of development. And so, dirt for the indigenous represents a great obstacle for them." Manos de Amor leadership, however, fully understands that dirt does not make itself. As Mary Douglas usefully argues, conceptions of dirt are relative: "There is no such thing as absolute dirt: it exists in the eye of the beholder" (1966: 2). What is so egregious to the very Christian sensibilities that Manos de Amor attempts to impart is that many of the indigenous do not recognize themselves as dirty. The spokesperson continued: "They are accustomed to it. And since they are accustomed to dirt, they don't see the need to clean themselves. They see it as a total waste of time. Totally. And so the most interesting goal [for us] is to change the way that they think." Manos de Amor, alongside building projects and clothing drives, educates the rural indigenous, providing them with not only a sense of dirt, but also new regimes of self-governance so that they may tend to their newfound filth.

Protestant efforts to indoctrinate the indigenous with Christian modes of purity and danger stretch throughout colonial times, but they took on an eerily familiar, if not entirely modern, form during Guatemala's liberalization period. Edward Haymaker, Guatemala's second Protestant missionary, arrived in 1887 with a set goal: "When the people of Guatemala begin to develop [the country] along modern lines, when they learn sanitation, motherhood, education, thrift . . . Guatemala will be one of the greatest little countries in the world" (Garrard-Burnett 1997: 41). Identifying the rural poor as "The Great Unwashed," Haymaker published Christian pamphlets on health and hygiene, all for Guatemala's salvation and development.[15] The two goals were hardly distinct. In the 1880s, President Justo Rufino Barrios injected Protestant Christianity into the Guatemalan context to bolster efforts at liberalization. As Virginia Garrard-Burnett notes, Protestant Christianity seemed "the ideal vehicle" to advance Barrios's liberal agenda (1997: 38). The religion would "civilize" Guatemala by undercutting Roman Catholicism and Maya spirituality while also contributing to the country's own efforts at industrialization, not only with a "Protestant work ethic," but also with a more hospitable atmosphere for German and North American Protestants interested in business opportunities. With the nineteenth-century French sociologist Auguste Comte and Social Darwinism fresh in his mind, Justo Rufino Barrios saw Protestant Christianity as a means "to create a modern, unified nation from a mix of ethnicities, languages, classes, customs, and conflicting bonds of loyalty and association" (ibid.: 35). Central to this modernization fantasy was, and still is, a vision of the human as autonomous, rational, and free—the Enlightenment's very own philosophical anthropology, which pushes past magic and religion to stake its claim on science and democracy.

Christian hygiene existed (and still exists) as one small but ever important part of this modernization project. Hygiene provides an incredibly mundane, deeply routinized, marker of Christian civility; it exposes not simply exterior enactments, but more importantly, the quality of one's interior will (O'Neill 2010b). Mary Douglas cites the penitential of Archbishop Theodore of Canterbury: "If without knowing it one eats what is polluted by blood or any unclean thing, it is nothing; but if he knows, he shall do penance according to the degree of pollution" (1966: 75). The Christian predicament of knowing better—of understanding the difference between "earth" and "dirt," as Jonathan Z. Smith would argue (1993)—places the moral responsibility for cleanliness as well as advancement squarely on the shoulders of the learned.[16] As the Manos de Amor spokesperson makes transparent, "Since [the indigenous] are accustomed to dirt, they don't see the need to clean themselves." This Christian logic makes Manos de Amor's commitment to dental hygiene, among a range of other hygienic prescriptions, rather telling. As innocuous practices, brushing and flossing, using Manos de Amor's widely distributed "bags of personal hygiene" (filled with soap, toothpaste, and floss), attempt to shape the indigenous into modern citizens through regimes of self-governance. Complimentary brushes and paste, alongside Christian goodwill, recruit the indigenous into regimes of self-regulation that ultimately aim for a more advanced nation-state. With instructions on how to brush gently in semicircular motions, Manos de Amor's promotion of dental hygiene contributes to the production of Christian citizens who not only have a greater awareness of their own inner terrain, but also the means by which to observe and clean that terrain—to actually scrub it with soft bristles. To quote Douglas: "Dirt offends against order. Eliminating it is not a negative movement, but a positive effort to organize the environment" (1966: 2). Christian charity not only marks the rural indigenous as "matter out of place," to invoke Douglas once again, but also inculcates them with an array of self-governing rationalities to attend to the very filth they have been taught to see.

During a public presentation of Manos de Amor's charitable activities, a spokesperson walked a small group of El Shaddai capitalinos through some of the many ways in which the organization supports the rural indigenous. While explaining that the organization educates the indigenous to understand that taking baths, "even if they make you shiver," is proper and good, one photo among many confirmed the organization's spatial commitments. The photo is of a small, rural classroom with ten students and an instructor. The colors are muddied—dull blues and greens straddle the room's browns and grays. Yet, red boxes of Colgate toothpaste, obvious donations from Manos de Amor, pop the scene. They break the photo's balance as the children stretch upward and toward the camera, leaning their smiling faces at the model viewer. Of particular importance is that the children lean forward and upward toward the camera, their shiny boxes of toothpaste pulling them from their seats and toward somewhere else. Their bright smiles suggest that Manos de Amor's commitment to dental hygiene is working—maintaining white teeth and producing auto-regulating citizens.

While it would not take a great deal of analytical effort to conclude that the photo's composition has everything to do with a tall cameraperson and decidedly short subjects, who are most likely elated to have not only received something free, but also a short break from schoolwork, the photo nonetheless exists as a cultural artifact. The photo communicates a logic that is still present and operative in postwar Guatemala. The image evidences the rank of the biblically deserved. Urban congregants, to explain, are the photo's implied viewer; the rural indigenous, moreover, are the photo's obvious subjects.

Additionally, the rural indigenous in this photo literally look up, reach toward, and lean forward—all in the direction of the implied capital. The directionality of it all—the photo's implied verticality and value—is meaningful even if unintentional.

President Justo Rufino Barrios, as mentioned before, studied the works of Auguste Comte, who was one of the first to argue that society matures much like an organism and that not all societies have developed along the same timeline.[17] Different parts of the world, Comte reasoned, are at different stages of development. In a related point, Comte concluded that individuals pass through three stages of development and that each of these stages has a distinct mindset. Children are devout, even magical, believers. Adolescents become metaphysicians; they are enamored with fate and first causes. Adults, however, are positivists. They rely on science and reason. Societies, Comte then leaps, follow the very same stages of development, constantly moving upward and outward—away from childish magic and adolescent metaphysics and toward a mature realism. Understanding Guatemala's fragmented society as literally at different stages of development, Justo Rufino Barrios hoped that Protestant Christianity would propel his compatriots beyond Maya spirituality and Roman Catholicism and toward liberal secularism (Garrard-Burnett 1997). Protestant Christianity, for Barrios, was not an end but a means; he did not want his country to be Protestant, per se, but to have Protestant Christianity provide his citizens with enough forward momentum to not just surpass magic but also catapult all of Guatemala beyond religion altogether.

Manos de Amor's photo of stretching schoolchildren, kids apparently lurching from one place to another, underscores the directionality of not just Justo Rufino Barrios's use of Protestant Christianity, but also of Manos de Amor's own efforts at Christian charity. As Mary Douglas notes: "When we honestly reflect on our busy scrubbings and cleanings in this light we know we are not mainly trying to avoid disease" (69). Dental hygiene does not simply keep teeth clean, but also works to raise the indigenous up—to rank them while also providing the tools for the indigenous to advance themselves. Responding to these interpretations of space, of seeing strained efforts at progress in the photo itself, a Manos de Amor spokesperson commented: "We want to untie them from their yoke of slavery; we see them as enslaved by their paradigms and their ways of thinking. Really. The same tradition, the same history, the same . . . The history and their past; their traditions enslave them. So for me [the work of Manos de Amor] is a way to liberate them from slavery and break them free from the yoke of oppression."

Explaining that rural communities receive incredible amounts of support from international groups, but that the support nonetheless keeps the indigenous poor, the spokesperson continued: "It is more important that they meet their potential, their [inner] wealth and that they see all of this in themselves. I want them to see the responsibilities that they have. If not, they are not going to progress beyond where they are now or how they now think. They just won't." The language of progress, of moving forward and upward, easily latches onto Christian temporalities of salvation, of beginning with the Christ event here on earth and ending with judgment up there in heaven. Modernity, salvation, democratization, secularism—the accepted goals of supposed developing nations—begin low and aim high; they advance societies upward and outward. Manos de Amor, by way of dental hygiene (among other projects), aims to advance the rural indigenous in the same way.

Ranking, however, is a relational practice. Urban congregants who rank the rural indigenous also rank themselves along the way. Edward Said makes this argument in his seminal work *Orientalism* (1978), explaining that "the relationship between Occident and Orient is a relationship of power, of domination, of varying degrees of complex hegemony" (6). The East forever exists in material and discursive relationship to the West—making the production of the East also very much about the production of the West. The same can be argued about Manos de Amor. By ranking the biblically deserved as lower—as less developed, as less modern, as less clean—than urban congregants, those who attend El Shaddai's urban megachurch come to understand themselves as cut from a different cloth, so to speak—as literally set apart.

Another spokesperson, responding to yet another question about why Manos de Amor does not do work in the capital city, explained: "We work *there* [in the countryside] because we are only a few people and we cannot be everywhere. We work *there* because we feel that we are called by God to work *there*. We said, we can do something as a church over *there* in the mountains where they don't understand our Spanish. So that's where we want to work" (emphasis added). The spokesperson's repeated use of *allí*, or *there*, is telling. Beyond signifying the actual distance between the capital and more rural areas, or the literal difference between *here* and *there*, her use of the adverb also denotes a moral distance, suggesting that the urban congregation is *up here* while the rural indigenous is not just "over there in the mountains" but also *down there*, "where they don't understand our Spanish." The spokesperson continued: "That was our first challenge. It was 'Let's go and do something.' Then, after figuring out that we could do something, we wanted to make a lasting change.

We are a church that talks a lot about changing communities, so we wanted to put what we believe into practice. [The countryside] has been a laboratory for us [Ha sido todo un laboratorio]."

The spokesperson's notion that the countryside exists as the church's laboratory evokes regrettable images of colonialism, of experimenting on "lesser" societies in the hopes that they might "catch up." The image of Manos de Amor as a collection of well-intentioned mad scientists with Christ on their side, in fact, taints the promise of Christian charity with a naked self-assessment of Christian charity's own practice, calling to mind the words of Joseph Conrad. Conrad wrote on the theme of colonialism but nonetheless speaks to the practice of Christian charity: "[It] is not a pretty thing when you look into it too much. What redeems it is the idea only. An idea at the back of it; not a sentimental pretence but an idea; and an unselfish belief in the idea—something you can set up and bow down before, and offer a sacrifice" (1995: 52).[18] Manos de Amor believes in the idea of Christian charity, with all of charity's tendencies to rank the rural indigenous below urban congregants; however, this belief smoothes over an otherwise uncomfortable inclination to help at all costs. The spokesperson continued: "We enter [a community] and we begin working. We don't have a specific goal. We only know that we have entered a place where there is an opportunity to help. It's all about serving and helping the community we enter. And then we stay there, returning often, because they want something, and so we do more and more. We ask them: 'What do you want to change?' And they often say 'nothing.' And so we help them move forward. Why? Because God commands us. We feel a love for them, for Guatemala, and for God. God saves them." From a neo-Pentecostal perspective, Christian charity saves the rural indigenous; yet from a perspective that is more critical, from a perspective best understood as anthropological, the practice of Christian charity also ranks those who participate within a hierarchy of strict divisions—either as volunteers or as deserving; either as below or as above; either as here or as there; either as arrived or as "not yet."

The Gift out of Place

Marcel Mauss's The Gift (1990) dissects the nature of gift giving and exchange, noting that the obligation to give and receive gifts demonstrates alternating expressions of generosity and respect. Mauss's most important observation, at least for this essay, is that gift giving is a moral practice that establishes enduring social relationships between communities. The gift is not a simple object, or commodity, but is representative, even constitutive, of society. Giving a gift maintains social relationships between communities while also binding them to one another. In postwar Guatemala, philanthropic intervention as gift bridges the city and the country while also reinforcing the division between the two. A collage of ethnographic vignettes make up one final observation about the place of the biblically deserved in postwar Guatemala and the kinds of responsibilities that this moral geography lends to those Christians who live in the capital.

The first vignette begins with a walk through a depressed part of Guatemala City with three neo-Pentecostals. En route to a Bible study group, we walked along with a sense of purpose until two small children approached us with candy in their hands. Their faces were pointed upward toward me, their eyes as doelike as they could make them. They asked us to buy the candy, explaining that the money would support a local charity. Francisco, the group leader I was walking with, quickly turned the two around, spinning them on their heels and said, "Thanks but no thanks." I asked him what the problem was. He muttered to me that I could buy the candy, but only if I wanted candy. I should simply not expect the money to go to a charity.

The second moment came during an extended interview in one of Guatemala City's upscale malls. Seated in a food court, Pedro and I chatted about the power and efficacy of prayer when a middle-aged woman approached us with child in hand. She pressed a sheet of paper toward us, explaining that it was a prescription for medicine that she desperately needed. Pedro had extolled the work of Manos de Amor in prior interviews, filling my notebook with stories of his own volunteer activities with Guatemala's indigent. But here, he avoided eye contact with the woman and shook his head. He later explained to me that we could have given the woman food, but that her solicitation for money was probably bogus. "You never can tell," he quipped.

The third scene came as I stepped out of a public bus and onto church grounds. It was Sunday morning, and I was walking through El Shaddai's parking lot to attend service. A woman I had interviewed several months earlier approached me, hailing me as her brother in Christ, and asking me about my research. I explained that everything was progressing nicely, but then turned the conversation to her. She was a single mother with three children. She explained to me that times were hard and that she could not make rent. She repeated this fact several times, eventually asking me if I could help her and her children. As I gave her the equivalent of five U.S. dollars, what struck me was my own lack of confidence. Having been instructed by my urban informants for several months that those who ask for money in the streets are untrustworthy—are working a scam that my gringo sensibilities just cannot register—I questioned my own relationship with this woman. As she thanked me, we entered the church together, her with five dollars and me with an unsettled sense of whom to trust and whether I had been taken for a ride. At the very least, I knew that Pedro and Francisco would not have been happy with me. They would have scolded me, arguing that the money would have been put to better use if given to Manos de Amor. Perhaps it would have been.

What emerges from these three vignettes (selected from dozens of similar instances) reinforces some of the lessons that Manos de Amor communicates to its viewing public about the place of the deserved, while also saying something about the needy (and gifts to the needy) that are literally out of place. In short, there is an obvious and observable disconnect with the giving practices of El Shaddai congregants. I found that urban neo-Pentecostals tend to be dismissive of Guatemala City's own widows, orphans, and strangers, but compassionate to those Manos de Amor brings to life in El Shaddai bulletins. Dozens of reasons explain the divide. For one, Manos de Amor has earned a certain level of trust with the El Shaddai congregation. Guatemala has seen an explosion in the number of NGOs and not-for-profit projects, including many used for tax evasion.[19] In contrast, Manos de Amor offers a welcome degree of transparency. Congregants know that their donations will have an effect. Another reason is the context in which congregants often donate their money—during church services. Manos de Amor "passes the hat" in between jubilant praise and worship sessions; congregants have mentioned that they are most willing to give when they feel themselves filled by the Holy Spirit. This explains, in part, why believers may be less inspired to give in the dusty streets of Guatemala City, late at night or during a long commute home. Yet another reason may simply be the complexities of walking through Guatemala City with a gringo who is forever a target for panhandlers.[20]

Amidst all these reasons for such a giving divide, there is still something more interesting at work. As discussed, Manos de Amor's moral geography tends to place Guatemala's biblically deserved in the countryside as opposed to the capital and rank the rural indigenous as *below* capitalinos but *above* the urban indigent, bending congregants' hearts (and giving practices) toward poor indigenous communities and away from Guatemala City's own needy. This kind of philanthropic intervention establishes a social relationship and hierarchy between city and country that not only reinscribes stereotypical characterizations of urbanites and country folk, but also links city to country in ways not previously seen. At the same time that this new relationship between urban congregants and the country's rural areas becomes more enmeshed through gifts, there is an obvious disconnect taking place as well. If Christian charity encourages neo-Pentecostals to become emotionally and financially invested in the country's biblically deserved, then there is also an observable disengagement that continues to form when it comes to helping urban congregants' most proximate neighbors, those who walk (or even sleep) in the streets of Guatemala City.

A striking example came while I was traveling by bus to a Bible study group one night. I rode with Julio, a trusted informant. We huddled together in a slow-moving, fume-congested bus that was lit only by a few Christmas lights that cast a red haze throughout the cabin. Suddenly, a man called for everyone's attention. He waved one hand in the air while using his other to brace himself up against a seat. He was sick. With his shirt unbuttoned, a colostomy bag dangled from his side, half-filled with waste. In a loud voice, he began to preach over the engine about God's mercy and about his own struggles with sickness, accidents, and near death. He was poor, he insisted, and his tired face did not suggest otherwise. As he spoke, Julio nudged me in the ribs. Julio was obviously taken by this dramatic scene—an incredibly performed plea for help that mixed Christian faith with a broken body. Taken by the sight— the roar of the engine, the man swaying with every gear shift, and the soft red lights—my own thoughts drifted to the philosophical work of Emmanuel Levinas, who reflects on "the face of the poor, the stranger, the widow, and the orphan" (1969: 251). The face for Levinas commands us all not just to feed the hungry with "a gift of the heart, but of bread from one's mouth, of one's own mouthful of bread" (1978: 74). His hyperbolic ethics is embarrassingly arrogant as well as productively impossible and one that I failed to meet, as I handed the man some coins.[21] Julio, however, did not move for his pockets. He instead stared straight ahead as the man walked up and down the bus, asking for small gifts. Yet, later, Julio would celebrate the man's faith to a surprising extent and note throughout the night (during the actual meeting, but also afterward) how incredible this man's faith was and how dramatic his story had been. Julio was sincerely touched.

On our way home, after hearing just how much of an impression this poor man had on Julio, I asked why he did not simply pass along one or two coins. The amount, I said, was not the issue so much as the gesture of giving. One centavo could have been enough. Julio's reaction to my question was one of moral ambivalence. This is not because I proved to be more ethical or compassionate than Julio (as Julio's own dedication to Manos de Amor is commendable) but because I saw the sick man with different eyes. While I assessed the event through an admittedly romantic moral vocabulary, one that ethnographers often assume far too often, Julio kept true to the idea that Guatemala's widows, orphans, and strangers do not ride public city buses. Rather, the truly deserved live in Guatemala's rural countryside. Julio, turning to me, remarked that his money was better off in the hands of Manos de Amor. The sick man simply existed somewhere outside of his moral grid.

Notes

1 For more on the concept of moral geography, see Philip Thomas 2002 as well as James Ferguson 1992; John Comaroff and Jean Comaroff 1987; and Raymond Williams 1973.

2. The following history of Guatemala City is based on the work of Gisela Gellert (1995); Gellert and J. C. Pinto Soria (1990); Gellert and Silvia Irene Palma Calderón (1999); Stephen Webre (1989); Óscar Guillermo Peláez Almengor (1994); René Arturo Orellana (1978); AVANCSO (2003); Santiago Bastos (2000); Manuela Camus (2002); Augusto Gordillo Castillo (1995); Amanda Morán Mérida (1997); Edward Murphy (2004); Irma Alicia Velásquez Nimatuj (2002); Ileana Contreras Pinillos (1977); and Carol Smith (1984).

3. Michael J. Tottens, "In Guatemala City," Middle East Journal, November 25, 2003, web pages at Middle East Journal, www.michaeltotten.com, visited May 2010, printouts on file with author.

4. Santiago Bastos and Manuela Camus have produced a series of joint studies of Maya migrants to the capital (1995, 1997, 1998; see also Camus 2002) that document emerging urban Maya identities.

5. Here, I rely on the scholarship of Ulf Hannerz and his understanding of how "boundary-crossings" and "long-distance cultural flows" contribute to the production of community. Of particular interest is his sociological understanding of networks: "In more sociological terms, the habitat of an agent could be said to consist of a network of direct and indirect relationships, stretching out wherever they may, within or across national boundaries" (1996: 46). See also Hannerz 1992.

6. See El Shaddai's Sunday bulletin ¡Feliz Día Papá!, June 18, 2006.

7. Ibid.

8. See El Shaddai's Sunday bulletin ¡No te puedes perder!, July 23, 2006.

9. See El Shaddai's Sunday bulletin Jesús: La razón de la navidad, December 23, 2006.

10. See El Shaddai's Sunday bulletin Concierto de exaltación, July 30, 2006. See also El Shaddai's Sunday bulletin ¡Inscríbete ya!, September 17, 2006.

11. See El Shaddai's Sunday bulletin *¡Inscríbete ya!*.

12. See El Shaddai's Sunday bulletin *Los pasos del hombre son ordenados por Dios*, February 4, 2007.

13. It should be noted, at least briefly, that Dumont in this quote addresses the Indian caste system and not Christianity and that Dumont's analysis has received two major strands of criticism. The first is that Dumont addresses traditional rather than contemporary Indian societies. The second is that Dumont's association of an individual with his or her caste does not hold up to ethnographic scrutiny. See Andre Béteille 1986; and Brian Morris 1994.

14. Kathryn Lofton (2008) notes that "even within Wesleyan lore, cleanliness was a minor thesis, as Wesley's own 1764 treatise, *Primitive Physick*, devoted no special part to bathing, despite its comprehensive discussion of home remedies."

15. "The Great Unwashed" as a term has a lively history within the Western context, usually attributed to recent immigrants, non-Christians (i.e., the unbaptized), or those considered uncivilized. See, e.g., Marilyn Thornton Williams 1991. Williams notes that "Public baths were one of the many solutions proposed by nineteenth-century American reformers when they were faced with the numerous social problems presented by unprecedented urban growth and congested slums" (2). Kathryn Lofton adds: "White women and men did their white washing (of clothes, of stainless steel, of selves). Ivory bars lay track to anyone, anywhere that desires that which the product assures: 'to cleanse without injuring.' The 'do no harm' Ivory bar became a symbolic sidekick to the history of Protestant missions, American expansions, and the widespread medicalization and sanitization of American culture" (2008).

16. In *Map Is Not Territory* (1978), Jonathan Z. Smith discusses working on a small farm: "I would have to rise at about a quarter to four and fire up the wood burning stove, heat a pan of water and lay out the soap and towels so that my boss could wash when he awoke half an hour later. Each morning, to my growing puzzlement, when the boss would step outside after completing his ablutions, he would pick up a handful of soil and rub it over his hands. After several weeks of watching this activity, I finally, somewhat testily, asked for an explanation: 'Why do you start each morning by cleaning yourself and then step outside and immediately make yourself dirty?' 'Don't you city boys understand anything?,' was the scornful reply. 'Inside the house it's dirt; outside, it's earth'" (291).

17. See, e.g., Lewis Coser 1977; Frank Elwell 2006.

18. Michael Taussig cites this very quote from Conrad in his *Shamanism, Colonialism, and the Wild Man* (1987: 16). My use of Conrad here builds on Taussig's reading to suggest how colonialism as a horrifically violent experiment in domination actually persisted because it was understood in a certain era as good—as progress. Although the association is uncharitable for Manos de Amor, there are obvious parallels between Christian efforts at charity and colonialism.

19. See, e.g., Jennyffer Paredes, "Q67.33 millones cobra OIM en comisiones," *Prensa Libre*, September 11, 2006.

20. If anthropology's reflexive turn has proven anything, it is that the anthropologist cannot remove him or herself from the equation (Clifford and Marcus 1986; Rosaldo 1989). When dealing with informants' giving practices on the streets of Guatemala City, I was surely approached more often than my informants (I was even sometimes approached by my informants) for money. While from one perspective this could be seen as an epistemological wrinkle in the study, the predicament (the "gringo factor") opened up productive avenues to speak about giving and deservedness in Guatemala City.

21. In regards to "productively impossible," the work of Emmanuel Levinas allows for an ethically informed ethnography premised upon an acknowledgment of risk and uncertainty over researcher control or reflexivity. See Peter Benson and O'Neill 2007.

References

Abernathy, Frederick H., Anthony Volpe, and David Weil. 2005. *The Future of the Apparel and Textile Industries: Prospects and Choices for Public and Private Actors.* Cambridge: Harvard Center for Textile and Apparel Research.

Acevedo, Anabella. 2006. Extraños paraísos urbanos. In *IX Festival del Centro Histórico Municipalidad de Guatemala,* 11. Guatemala City: El Ministerio de Cultura.

Adams, Abigail E. 2001. The Transformation of the Tzuultaq'a: Jorge Ubico, Protestants and Other Verapaz Maya at the Crossroads of Community, State, and Transnational Interests. *Journal of Latin American Anthropology* 6(2):193–233.

Adams, Richard N., ed. 1970. *Crucifixion by Power: Essays on Guatemalan National Social Structure 1944–1966.* Austin: University of Texas Press.

Althoff, Andrea. 2005. *Religion im Wandel: Einflüsse Von Ethnizität auf die religiöse Ordnung am Beispiel Guatemalas.* Wittenberg: Martin-Luther-Universität Halle-Wittenberg.

Amnesty International. 2006. Guatemala City: No Protection, No Justice: Killings of Women in Guatemala. *Amnesty International* 34(19):1–23.

Anderson, Kay, and Affrica Taylor. 2005. Exclusionary Politics and the Question of National Belonging: Australian Ethnicities in "Multiscalar" Focus. *Ethnicities* 5(4):460–85.

Annis, Sheldon. 1987. *God and Production in a Guatemalan Town.* Austin: University of Texas Press.

Appadurai, Arjun. 1988. Putting Hierarchy in Its Place. *Cultural Anthropology* 3(1):36–49.

———. 1991. Global Ethnoscapes: Notes and Queries for a Transnational Anthropology. In *Recapturing Anthropology: Working in the Present,* edited by R. G. Fox, 191–210. Santa Fe: School of American Research Press.

———. 1996. *Modernity at Large: Cultural Dimensions of Globalization.* Minneapolis: University of Minnesota Press.

———. 2000. Spectral Housing and Urban Cleansing: Notes on Millennial Mumbai. *Public Culture* 12(3):627–51.

Asociación de Investigación y Estudios Sociales (ASIES). 2003. *Proceso de modernización y fortalecimiento del sistema de justicia: Avances y dificultades, enero 2002–junio 2003.* Guatemala City: ASIES.

Asociación para el Avance de las Ciencias Sociales en Guatemala (AVANCSO). 1996. *Por sí mismos: Un estudio preliminar de las "maras" en la Ciudad de Guatemala*. Guatemala City: AVANCSO.

———. 2003. *El proceso de crecimiento metropolitano de la Ciudad de Guatemala*. Guatemala City: AVANCSO.

Auyero, Javier. 2001. Introducción: Claves para pensar la marginación. In *Parias urbanos: Marginalidad en la ciudad a comienzos del milenio*, edited by L. Wacquant, 9–32. Buenos Aires: Manantial.

Barthes, Roland. 1990. *The Fashion System*. Berkeley: University of California Press.

Bastos, Santiago. 2000. *Poderes y quereres: Historias de género y familia en los sectores populares de la Ciudad de Guatemala*. Guatemala City: Facultad Latinoamericana de Ciencias Sociales.

Bastos, Santiago, and Manuela Camus. 1995. *Los Mayas de la Capital: Un estudio sobre identidad étnica y mundo urbano*. Guatemala City: Facultad Latinoamericana de Ciencias Sociales.

———. 1997. *Sombras de una batalla: Los desplazados por la violencia en la Ciudad de Guatemala*. Guatemala City: Facultad Latinoamericana de Ciencias Sociales.

———. 1998. *La exclusión y el desafío: Estudios sobre segregación étnica y empleo en Ciudad de Guatemala*. Guatemala City: Facultad Latinoamericana de Ciencias Sociales.

Beall, Jo, and Sean Fox. 2006. *Urban Poverty and Development in the 21st Century: Toward an Inclusive and Sustainable World*, Oxfam Research Report. London: Oxfam GB.

Benjamin, Walter. 1998. *The Arcades Project*. H. Eiland and K. McLaughlin, trans. Cambridge: Harvard University Press.

Benson, Peter. 2004. Nothing to See Here. *Anthropological Quarterly* 77(3):435–67.

———. 2008a. El Campo: Faciality and Structural Violence in North Carolina Farm Labor Camps. *Cultural Anthropology* 23(4):589–629.

———. 2008b. Good Clean Tobacco: Philip Morris, Biocapitalism, and the Social Course of Stigma in North Carolina. *American Ethnologist* 35(3):357–79.

———. n.d. *"In the Company of Innocence": Growers and the Changing Face of Big Tobacco*. Princeton: Princeton University Press.

Benson, Peter, Edward F. Fischer, and Kedron Thomas. 2008. Resocializing Suffering: Neoliberalism, Accusation, and the Sociopolitical Context of Guatemala's New Violence. *Latin American Perspectives* 35(5):38–58.

Benson, Peter, and Kevin Lewis O'Neill. 2007. Facing Risk: Levinas, Ethnography, and Ethics. *Anthropology of Consciousness* 18(2):29–55.

Berman, Marshall. 1988. *All That Is Solid Melts into Air: The Experience of Modernity*. London: Penguin.

Béteille, Andre. 1986. Individualism and Equality. *Current Anthropology* 27(2):121–34.

Bettig, Ronald V. 1996. *Copyrighting Culture: The Political Economy of Intellectual Property*. Boulder: Westview Press.

Blakely, Timothy W. 2000. Beyond the International Harmonization of Trademark Law: The Community Trade Mark as a Model of Unitary Transnational Trademark Protection. *University of Pennsylvania Law Review* 149(1):309–54.

Bonacich, Edna, Lucie Cheng, Norma Chinchilla, Nora Hamilton, and Paul Ong. 1994. *Global Production: The Apparel Industry in the Pacific Rim.* Philadelphia: Temple University Press.

Bone, Robert G. 2004. Enforcement Costs and Trademark Puzzles. *Virginia Law Review* 90(8):2099–185.

Bornstein, Erica. 2001. Child Sponsorship, Evangelism, and Belonging in the Work of World Vision Zimbabwe. *American Ethnologist* 28(3):595–622.

Bossen, Laurel H. 1984. *The Redivision of Labor: Women and Economic Choice in Four Guatemalan Communities.* Albany: University of New York Press.

Bourdieu, Pierre. 1984. *Distinctions: A Social Critique of the Judgement of Taste.* R. Nice, trans. Cambridge: Harvard University Press.

———. 1986. The Forms of Capital. In *Handbook of Theory and Research for the Sociology of Education,* edited by J. G. Richardson, 241–58. New York: Greenwood Press.

———. 1999. *The Weight of the World: Social Suffering in Contemporary Societies.* Palo Alto, Calif.: Stanford University Press.

Bourgois, Philippe. 1995. *In Search of Respect: Selling Crack in El Barrio.* Cambridge: Cambridge University Press.

Brantingham, Paul J., and Patricia Brantingham. 1984. *Patterns in Crime.* New York: Macmillan.

Briceño-León, Roberto. 2002. La nueva violencia urbana de América Latina. *Sociologias* 4(8):34–51.

Brookings Institution. 2007. *The Impact of Globalization on the World's Poor.* Washington, D.C.: Brookings Institution.

Brown, R. McKenna. 1996. The Mayan Language Loyalty Movement in Guatemala. In *Maya Cultural Activism in Guatemala,* edited by Edward F. Fischer and R. McKenna Brown, 165–77. Austin: University of Texas Press.

Burrell, Jennifer. 2005. Migration and the Transnationalization of Fiesta Customs in Todos Santos Cuchumatán, Guatemala. *Latin American Perspectives* 32(5):12–32.

Caldeira, Teresa. 2001. *City of Walls: Crime, Segregation, and Citizenship in São Paulo.* Berkeley: University of California Press.

Camus, Manuela. 2002. *Ser indígena en Ciudad de Guatemala.* Guatemala City: Facultad Latinoamericana de Ciencias Sociales.

———. 2005. *La colonia Primero de Julio y la "clase media" emergente.* Guatemala City: Facultad Latinoamericana de Ciencias Sociales.

Canadian Red Cross. 2006. *Facts and Figures: Guatemala 2005.* Web pages of Canadian Red Cross, www.redcross.ca, visited May 2010, pages on file with author.

Caplow, Theodore. 1949. The Social Ecology of Guatemala City. *Social Forces* 28(2):113–33.

Carey, David, Jr. 2008. Hard Working, Orderly Little Women: Mayan Vendors and Marketplace Struggles in Early-Twentieth-Century Guatemala. *Ethnohistory* 55(4): 579–608.

Carmack, Robert M., ed. 1988. *Harvest of Violence: The Maya Indians and the Guatemalan Crisis*. Norman: University of Oklahoma Press.

———. 1995. *Rebels of Highland Guatemala: The Quiche-Mayas of Momostenango*. Norman: University of Oklahoma Press.

Casaús Arzú, Marta Elena. 2007. *Guatemala: Linaje y racismo*, 3rd ed. Guatemala City: F&G Editors.

Castillo, Augusto Gordillo. 1995. Historia urbana de la Ciudad de Guatemala en 1935: Una aproximación al comercio. In *Memoria del segundo encuentro nacional de historiadores del 4 al 6 de diciembre de 1995 de Guatemala*, 111–56. Guatemala City: Universidad del Valle de Guatemala.

Cattelino, Jessica R. 2004. The Difference that Citizenship Makes: Civilian Crime Prevention on the Lower East Side. *PoLAR: Political and Legal Anthropology Review* 27(1):114–37.

Centro Histórico. 2006. *Un centro histórico para vivir*. Manifiesto. Guatemala City: Municipalidad de Guatemala.

Centro de Investigaciones Económicas Nacionales (CIEN). 2002. *Estudio sobre magnitud y costo de la violencia en Guatemala*. Guatemala City: CIEN.

———. 2006. *Economía Informal: Superando las barreras de un estado excluyente*. Guatemala City: CIEN.

Chajón, Aníbal. 2007. *De la Calle Real a la Sexta Avenida, vida cotidiana en la Ciudad de Guatemala*. Guatemala City: El Centro de Estudios Folklóricos de la Universidad de San Carlos de Guatemala.

Chase-Dunn, Christopher. 2000. Guatemala in the Global System. *Journal of Interamerican Studies and World Affairs* 42(4):109–26.

Chesluk, Benjamin. 2004. "Visible Signs of a City Out of Control": Community Policing in New York City. *Cultural Anthropology* 19(2):250–75.

Chua, Amy. 2004. *World on Fire: How Exporting Free Market Democracy Breeds Ethnic Hatred and Global Instability*. New York: Anchor Books.

Ciencia y Tecnología Para Guatemala (CITGUA). 1991. *Asentamientos precarios y pobladores en Guatemala*. Guatemala City: CITGUA.

Clifford, James. 1988. *The Predicament of Culture: Twentieth Century Ethnography, Literature, and Art*. Cambridge: Harvard University Press.

Clifford, James, and George Marcus. 1986. *Writing Culture: The Poetics and Politics of Ethnography*. Berkeley: University of California Press.

Cojtí, Demetrio. 2007. Indigenous Nations in Guatemalan Democracy and the State: A Tentative Assessment. *Social Analysis* 51(2):124–47.

Comaroff, John, and Jean Comaroff. 1987. The Madman and the Migrant: Work and

Labor in the Historical Consciousness of a South African People. *American Ethnologist* 14(2):191–209.

Comisión para el Esclarecimiento Histórico (CEH). 1999. *Guatemala: Memoria del silencio.* Guatemala City: CEH.

Conde Prera, Hugo Arnoldo. 1989. *Baja Verapaz: Sultana de las rosas.* Guatemala City: Óscar de León Palacios.

Conrad, Joseph. 1995 [1902]. *Youth / Heart of Darkness / The End of the Tether.* New York: Penguin Classics.

Contreras Pinillos, Ileana. 1977. *Desarrollo histórico urbanístico de la Zona 1 de la Ciudad de Guatemala de 1776 a 1976.* Guatemala City: Universidad de San Carlos de Guatemala.

Coombe, Rosemary. 1993. Tactics of Appropriation and the Politics of Recognition in Late Modern Democracies. *Political Theory* 21(3):411–33.

Coombe, Rosemary, and Andrew Herman. 2004. Rhetorical Virtues: Property, Speech, and the Commons on the World-Wide Web. *Anthropological Quarterly* 77(3):559–74.

Correa, Carlos. 2000. *Intellectual Property Rights, the WTO, and Developing Countries: The TRIPS Agreement and Policy Options.* London: Zed Books.

Coser, Lewis. 1977. *Masters of Sociological Thought: Ideas in Historical and Social Context.* New York: Harcourt Brace Jovanovich.

Council on Hemispheric Affairs (COHA). 2009. *Guatemala: Central American Crime Capital.* Web pages of COHA, www.coha.org, visited May 2010, printouts on file with author.

Davis, Mike. 1990. *City of Quartz: Excavating the Future in Los Angeles.* London: Verso.

——. 2006. *Planet of Slums.* New York: Verso.

de Janvry, Alain. 1981. *The Agrarian Question and Reformism in Latin America.* Baltimore: Johns Hopkins University Press.

de Soto, Hernando. 1987. *El Otro Sendero: La Revolución Informal.* Bogotá: Editorial Oveja Negra.

Douglas, Mary. 1966. *Purity and Danger: An Analysis of Concepts of Pollution and Taboo.* New York: Praeger.

Dumont, Louis. 1980. *Homo Hierarchicus: The Caste System and Its Implications.* G. Weidenfeld, trans. Chicago: University of Chicago Press.

Ehlers, Tracy Bachrach. 1990. *Silent Looms: Women and Production in a Guatemalan Town.* Boulder: Westview Press.

Ellison, James. 2006. "Everyone Can Do as He Wants": Economic Liberalization and Emergent Forms of Antipathy in Southern Ethiopia. *American Ethnologist* 33(4): 665–86.

Elwell, Frank. 2006. *Macrosociology: Four Modern Theorists.* Boulder: Paradigm.

Escobar, Arturo. 2001. Culture Sits in Places: Reflections on Globalism and Subaltern Strategies of Localization. *Political Geography* 20(2):139–74.

Espinosa, Lair, and Edgar Hidalgo. 1994. *Una experiencia de participación comunitaria en las áreas precarias de la Ciudad de Guatemala.* Guatemala City: UNICEF.

Eyerman, Ron, and Andrew Jamison. 1991. *Social Movements: A Cognitive Approach*. University Park: Pennsylvania State University Press.

Falzon, Mark-Anthony. 2004. Paragons of Lifestyle: Gated Communities and the Politics of Space in Bombay. *City and Society* 16(2):145–67.

Farmer, Paul. 2004. An Anthropology of Structural Violence. *Current Anthropology* 45(3):305–25.

Farmer, Paul E., Bruce Nizeye, Sara Stulac, and Salmaan Keshavjee. 2006. Structural Violence and Clinical Medicine. *PLoS Medicine* 3(10):449.

Felson, Marcus, and L. E. Cohen. 1980. Human Ecology and Crime: A Routine Activity Approach. *Human Ecology* 8:398–405.

Ferguson, James. 1992. The Country and the City on the Copperbelt. *Cultural Anthropology* 7(1):80–92.

———. 1999. *Expectations of Modernity: Myths and Meanings of Urban Life on the Zambian Copperbelt*. Berkeley: University of California Press.

———. 2006. *Global Shadows: Africa in the Neoliberal World Order*. Durham: Duke University Press.

Fernández García, María Cristina. 2004. *Lynching in Guatemala: Legacy of War and Impunity*. Web pages of the Weatherhead Center for International Affairs, Harvard University, www.wcfia.harvard.edu, visited May 2010, printouts on file with author.

Fischer, Edward F. 1999. Cultural Logic and Maya Identity: Rethinking Constructivism and Essentialism. *Current Anthropology* 40(4):473–99.

———. 2001. *Cultural Logics and Global Economies: Maya Identity in Thought and Practice*. Austin: University of Texas Press.

———. 2004. The Janus Face of Globalization: Economic Production and Cultural Reproduction in Highland Guatemala. In *Pluralizing Ethnography: Comparison and Representation in Maya Cultures, Histories, and Identities*. J. Watanabe and E. F. Fischer, ed., 257–90. Sante Fe: School of American Research Press.

Fischer, Edward F., and Peter Benson. 2005. Something Better: Hegemony, Resistance and Desire in Guatemalan Export Agriculture. *Social Analysis* 49(1):3–20.

———. 2006. *Broccoli and Desire: Global Connections and Maya Struggles in Postwar Guatemala*. Palo Alto, Calif.: Stanford University Press.

Fischer, Edward F., and R. McKenna Brown, eds. 1996. *Maya Cultural Activism in Guatemala*. Austin: University of Texas Press.

Fischer, Edward F., and Carol Hendrickson. 2002. *Tecpán Guatemala: A Modern Maya Town in Local and Global Context*. Boulder: Westview Press.

Foxen, Patricia. 2007. *In Search of Providence: Transnational Mayan Identities*. Nashville: Vanderbilt University Press.

Franco, Jean. 2002. *The Decline and Fall of the Lettered City: Latin America in the Cold War*. Cambridge: Harvard University Press.

Friedberg, Anne. 1994. *Window Shopping: Cinema and the Postmodern*. Berkeley: University California Press.

Frisby, David, and Mike Featherstone. 1997. *Simmel on Culture: Selected Writings.* London: Sage.

Garcés de Mancilla, María Cecilia. 2003. Hablando del otro: Categorías y estereotipos racistas en Guatemala. El caso de estudiantes de diversificado y cuatro centros educativos en la Ciudad de Guatemala. Tesis de Licenciatura en Antropología. Universidad de San Carlos de Guatemala.

García-Ruiz, Jesús. 2004. Le néopentecôtisme au Guatemala: Entre privatisation, marché et réseaux. *Critique Internationale* 22:81–94.

Garrard-Burnett, Virginia. 1997. Liberalism, Protestantism, and Indigenous Resistance in Guatemala, 1870–1920. *Latin American Perspectives* 24(2):35–55.

———. 1998. *Protestantism in Guatemala: Living in the New Jerusalem.* Austin: University of Texas Press.

Gaviria, Alejandro, and Carmen Pagés. 2000. *Patterns of Crime Victimization in Latin America.* Washington, D.C.: Inter-American Development Bank.

Gellert, Gisela. 1995. *Ciudad de Guatemala: Factores determinantes en su desarrollo urbano (desde la fundación hasta la actualidad).* Guatemala City: Facultad Latinoamericana de Ciencias Sociales.

Gellert, Gisela, and Silvia Irene Palma Calderón. 1999. *Precariedad urbana, desarrollo comunitario y mujeres en el área metropolitana de Guatemala.* Guatemala City: Facultad Latinoamericana de Ciencias Sociales.

Gellert, Gisela, and J. C. Pinto Soria. 1990. *Ciudad de Guatemala: Dos estudios sobre su evolución urbana (1524–1950).* Guatemala City: Universidad de San Carlos de Guatemala.

Giddens, Anthony. 1990. *The Consequences of Modernity.* Palo Alto, Calif.: Stanford University Press.

Gleijeses, Piero. 1988. *Politics and Culture in Guatemala.* Ann Arbor: Center for Political Studies, Institute for Social Research at the University of Michigan.

Godoy, Angelina Snodgrass. 2002. Lynchings and the Democratization of Terror in Postwar Guatemala: Implications for Human Rights. *Human Rights Quarterly* 24(3):640–61.

———. 2006. *Popular Injustice: Violence, Community, and Law in Latin America.* Palo Alto, Calif.: Stanford University Press.

Goldín, Liliana R. 1996. Economic Mobility Strategies among Guatemalan Peasants: Prospects and Limits of Nontraditional Vegetable Cash Crops. *Human Organization* 55(1):99–107.

———. 2001. Maquila Age Maya: Changing Households and Communities of the Central Highlands of Guatemala. *Journal of Latin American Anthropology* 6(1):30–57.

———. 2005. Labor Ideologies in the International Factories of Rural Guatemala. *Latin American Perspectives* 32(5):59–79.

Goldín, Liliana R., and Linda Asturias de Barrios. 2001. Perceptions of the Economy in the Context of Non-traditional Agricultural Exports in the Central Highlands of Guatemala. *Culture and Agriculture* 23(1):18–31.

Goldstein, Daniel M. 2004. *The Spectacular City: Violence and Performance in Urban Bolivia*. Durham: Duke University Press.

Goldstein, Daniel M., Gloria Achá, Eric Hinojosa, and Theo Rocken. 2009. La Mano Dura and the Violence of Civil Society in Bolivia. In *Indigenous Peoples, Civil Society, and the Neo-liberal State in Latin America*, edited by Edward F. Fischer, 43–63. New York: Berghahn.

Gómez del Prado, José Luis. 2007. *Consejo de Derechos Humanos: Intervención oral del Grupo de Trabajo sobre La Utilización de Mercenarios como medio de violar los derechos humanos y de obstaculizar el ejercicio de los pueblos a la libre determinación*. Web pages of Office of the High Commissioner for Human Rights, United Nations, www.ohchr.org, visited May 2010, printouts on file with author.

Graham, Stephen, and Simon Marvin. 2001. *Splintering Urbanism: Networked Infrastructures, Technological Mobilities, and the Urban Condition*. New York: Routledge.

Grandin, Greg. 2000. *The Blood of Guatemala: A History of Race and Nation*. Durham: Duke University Press.

Green, Linda. 1999. *Fear as a Way of Life: Mayan Widows in Rural Guatemala*. New York: Columbia University Press.

———. 2003. Notes on Mayan Youth and Rural Industrialization in Guatemala. *Critique of Anthropology* 23(1):51–73.

Greene, Jack, and Ralph B. Taylor. 1988. Community-Based Policing and Foot Patrol: Issues of Theory and Evaluation. In *Community Policing: Rhetoric or Reality?*, edited by J. R. Greene and S. D. Mastrofski, 195–224. New York: Praeger.

Guano, Emanuela. 2004. The Denial of Citizenship: "Barbaric" Buenos Aires and the Middle-Class Imaginary. *City and Society* 16(1):69–97.

Gupta, Akhil. 1988. Space and Time in the Politics of Culture. Paper read at the Eighty-seventh Annual Meeting of the American Anthropological Association. Phoenix.

Gupta, Akhil, and James Ferguson. 1997. *Culture, Power, Place in Critical Anthropology*. Durham: Duke University Press.

Gwynne, Robert N., and Cristóbal Kay. 2000. Views from the Periphery: Futures of Neoliberalism in Latin America. *Third World Quarterly* 21(1):141–56.

Hackworth, Jason. 2006. *The Neoliberal City: Governance, Ideology, and Development in American Urbanism*. Ithaca: Cornell University Press.

Hage, Ghassan. 1996. The Spatial Imaginary of National Practices: Dwelling–Domesticating/Being–Exterminating. *Environment and Planning D* 14(4):463–85.

———. 2000. *White Nation: Fantasies of White Supremacy in a Multicultural Society*. New York: Routledge.

Hale, Charles. 2002. Does Multiculturalism Menace? Governance, Cultural Rights and the Politics of Identity in Guatemala. *Journal of Latin American Studies* 34(3):485–524.

———. 2005. Neoliberal Multiculturalism: The Remaking of Cultural Rights and Racial Dominance in Central America. *PoLAR* 28(1):10–28.

———. 2006. *Más Que Un Indio: Racial Ambivalence and the Paradox of Neoliberal Multicultur-alism in Guatemala.* Santa Fe: School of American Research Press.

Hamilton, Sarah, and Edward F. Fischer. 2005. Maya Farmers and Export Agriculture in Highland Guatemala. *Latin American Perspectives* 32(5):33–58.

Handy, Jim. 1990. The Corporate Community, Campesino Organizations, and Agrarian Reform: 1950–1954. In *Guatemalan Indians and the State: 1540 to 1988*, edited by C. A. Smith, 163–82. Austin: University of Texas Press.

Hannerz, Ulf. 1992. The Global Ecumene as a Network of Networks. In *Conceptualising Society*, edited by A. Kuper, 34–56. London: Routledge.

———. 1996. *Transnational Connections: Culture, People, Places.* London: Routledge.

Hansen, Karen. 2004. The World in Dress: Anthropological Perspectives on Clothing, Fashion, and Culture. *Annual Review of Anthropology* 33:369–92.

Harvey, David. 1989. *The Condition of Postmodernity: An Inquiry into the Origins of Cultural Change.* London: Blackwell.

———. 2005. *A Brief History of Neoliberalism.* Oxford: Oxford University Press.

Hendrickson, Carol. 1995. *Weaving Identities: Construction of Dress and Self in a Highland Guatemala Town.* Austin: University of Texas Press.

Hirsch, Eric, and Marilyn Strathern, eds. 2004. *Transactions and Creations: Property Debates and the Stimulus of Melanesia.* New York: Berghahn Books.

Hochleutner, Brian R. 2003. BIDs Fare Well: The Democratic Accountability of Business Improvement Districts. *New York University Law Review* 78(3):374–404.

Holden, Robert H. 1996. Constructing the Limits of State Violence in Central America: Towards a New Research Agenda. *Journal of Latin American Studies* 28:435–59.

Houston, Larry. 1997. BIDs: *Business Improvement Districts.* Washington, D.C.: Urban Land Institute.

Houtum, Henk van, and Anke Struver. 2002. Borders, Strangers, Doors and Bridges. *Space and Polity* 6(2):141–46.

Hoyt, Lorlene. 2004. Collecting Private Funds for Safer Public Spaces: An Empirical Examination of the Business Improvement District Concept. *Environment and Planning: Planning and Design* 31(3):367–80.

———. 2005. Do Business Improvement District Organizations Make a Difference? Crime in and around Commercial Areas in Philadelphia. *Journal of Planning Education and Research* 25(1):185–99.

Instituto Nacional de Estadística de Guatemala (INE). 2002. *Guatemala Census.* Web pages of INE, www.ine.gob.gt, visited May 2010, printouts on file with author.

———. 2006. *Encuesta Nacional de Condiciones de Vida.* Web pages of INE, www.ine.gob.gt, visited May 2010, printouts on file with author.

Jacobs, Jane. 1961. *The Death and Life of Great American Cities.* New York: Random House.

Johnston, Francis E., and Setha M. Low. 1995. *Children of the Urban Poor: The Sociocultural Environment of Growth, Development, and Malnutrition in Guatemala City.* Boulder: Westview.

Jonas, Susanne. 2000. Democratization through Peace: The Difficult Case of Guatemala. *Journal of Interamerican Studies and World Affairs* 42(4):9–38.

Joyce, Patrick. 2003. *The Rule of Freedom: The City and Modern Liberalism*. London: Verso.

Kelling, George L. 1985. Order Maintenance, the Quality of Urban Life, and Police: A Line of Argument. In *Police Leadership in America*, edited by W. A. Geller, 296–308. New York: Praeger.

Kincaid, A. Douglas. 2001. Demilitarization and Security in El Salvador and Guatemala: Convergences of Success and Crisis. *Journal of Interamerican and Studies and World Affairs* 42(4):39–58.

King, Arden R. 1974. *Coban and the Verapaz: History and Cultural Process in Northern Guatemala*. New Orleans: Tulane University Middle American Research Institute.

Kleinman, Arthur. 1999. Experience and Its Moral Modes: Culture, Human Conditions, and Disorder. In *The Tanner Lectures on Human Values*. Vol. 20, edited by G. B. Peterson, 355–420. Salt Lake City: University of Utah Press.

Klima, Alan. 2002. *The Funeral Casino: Meditation, Massacre, and Exchange with the Dead in Thailand*. Princeton: Princeton University Press.

Kuppinger, Petra. 2004. Exclusive Greenery: New Gated Communities in Cairo. *City and Society* 16(2):35–61.

Latin American Public Opinion Poll (LAPOP). 2001. *Fifth National Report: Democratic Values of Guatemalans in the New Century*. Washington, D.C.: USAID and ASIES.

———. 2006. *Seventh National Report: Political Culture of Democracy in Guatemala*. Washington, D.C.: USAID.

Levenson, Deborah. 2005. *Hacer la juventud: Jóvenes de tres generaciones de una familia trabajadora en la Ciudad de Guatemala*. Guatemala City: AVANSCO.

Levenson-Estrada, Deborah. 1994. *Trade Unionists against Terror: Guatemala City, 1954–1985*. Chapel Hill: University of North Carolina Press.

Levinas, Emmanuel. 1969. *Totality and Infinity: an Essay on Exteriority*. A. Lingis, trans. Pittsburgh: Duquesne University Press.

———. 1978. *Existence and Existents*. Hague: Nijhoff.

Levy, Paul R. 2001. Paying for the Public Life. *Economic Development Quarterly* 15(2):124–31.

Lewinson, Anne S. 1998. Reading Modernity in Urban Space: Politics, Geography, and the Informal Sector of Downtown Dar es Salaam, Tanzania. *City and Society* 10(1):205–22.

Liebel, Manfred. 2004. Pandillas juveniles en Centroamérica o la difícil búsqueda de la justicia en una sociedad violenta. *Desacatos* 14: 85–104.

Little, Walter E. 2004. *Mayas in the Marketplace: Tourism, Globalization, and Cultural Identity*. Austin: University of Texas Press.

———. 2005. Getting Organized: Political and Economic Dilemmas for Maya Handicraft Vendors. *Latin American Perspectives* 32(5):80–100.

Lofton, Kathryn. 2008. *Saving Soap: An Allegory of Modern Religion*. Yale University.

Lonely Planet. 2001. *Guatemala*. Footscray, Victoria, Australia: Lonely Planet Publications.

López, Liliana, and Isabel Rodríguez. 2005. Evidencias y discursos del miedo en la ciudad: Casos mexicanos. *Scripta Nova: Revista electrónica de Geografía y Ciencias Sociales* 194(54). Web pages of Universidad de Barcelona, www.ub.es, visited May 2010, printouts on file with author.

Loucky, James, and Marilyn M. Moors. 2000. *The Maya Diaspora: Guatemalan Roots, New American Lives*. Philadelphia: Temple University Press.

Loukaitou-Sideris, Anastasia, Evelyn Blumenberg, and Renia Ehrenfeucht. 2004. Sidewalk Democracy: Municipalities and the Regulation of Public Space. In *Regulating Place: Standards and the Shaping of Urban America*, edited by E. Ben-Joseph and T. Szold, 141–66. New York: Routledge.

Low, Setha. 2000. *On the Plaza: The Politics of Public Space and Culture*. Austin: University of Texas Press.

———. 2003. *Behind the Gates: Life, Security, and the Pursuit of Happiness in Fortress America*. New York: Routledge.

Low, Setha, and Neil Smith, eds. 2005. *The Politics of Public Space*. London: Routledge.

Lutz, Catherine A., and Jane L. Collins. 1993. *Reading National Geographic*. Chicago: University of Chicago.

Malkki, Liisa. 1992. National Geographic: The Rooting of Peoples and the Territorialization of National Identity among Scholars and Refugees. *Cultural Anthropology* 7(1):24–44.

———. 1997. Children, Futures, and the Domestication of Hope. In *Histories of the Future*. Irvine: University of California, Humanities Research Institute Residential Research Group.

Manz, Beatriz. 2004. *Paradise in Ashes: A Guatemalan Journey of Courage, Terror, and Hope*. Berkeley: University of California Press.

Mastrofski, Stephen D. 1988. Community Policing as Reform: A Cautionary Tale. In *Community Policing: Rhetoric or Reality?*, edited by J. R. Greene and S. D. Mastrofski, 47–67. New York: Praeger.

Mauss, Marcel. 1990. *The Gift: The Form and Reason for Exchange in Archaic Societies*. W. D. Halls, trans. New York: W. W. Norton.

McCreery, David. 1990. State Power, Indigenous Communities, and Land in Nineteenth Century Guatemala. In *Guatemalan Indians and the State: 1540 to 1988*, edited by C. A. Smith, 96–115. Austin: University of Texas Press.

McDonald, Gael, and Christopher Roberts. 1994. Product Piracy: The Problem that Will Not Go Away. *Journal of Product and Brand Management* 3(4):55–65.

McGrew, Anthony, and Nana K. Poku. 2007. *Globalization, Development, and Human Security*. London: Polity Press.

McIlwaine, Cathy, and Carolina O. N. Moser. 2001. Violence and Social Capital in Urban Poor Communities: Perspectives from Colombia and Guatemala. *Journal of International Development* 13(7):965–884.

Menchú, Rigoberta. 1984. *I, Rigoberta Menchú: An Indian Woman in Guatemala*. E. Burgos-Debray, trans. London: Verso.

Mendoza, Carlos. 2006. Structural Causes and Diffusion Processes of Collective Violence: Understanding Lynch Mobs in Post-conflict Guatemala. Paper read at the Annual Meetings of the Latin American Studies Association. San Juan, Puerto Rico.

Micklin, Michael. 1966. *Urban Life and Differential Fertility in Guatemala: A Study in Social Demography*. Austin: University of Texas.

———. 1969. Urbanization, Technology, and Traditional Values in Guatemala: Some Consequences of a Changing Social Structure. *Social Forces* 47(4):438–46.

Miller, Daniel. 1997. *Capitalism: An Ethnographic Approach*. Oxford: Berg.

Misión de Verificación de las Naciones Unidas en Guatemala (MINUGUA). 2002. *Los linchamientos: Un flagelo que persiste*. Guatemala City: MINUGUA.

Mitchell, Jerry. 2001. Business Improvement Districts and the "New" Revitalization of Downtown. *Economic Development Quarterly* 15(2):115–23.

Montejo, Víctor. 1992. *Testimonio: Muerte de una comunidad indígena en Guatemala*. Guatemala City: Editorial Universitaria, Universidad de San Carlos de Guatemala.

Montenegro, Gonzalo Asturias. 1976. *Terremoto 76*. Guatemala City: Girblán.

Moodie, Ellen. 2006. Microbus Crashes and Coca-Cola Cash: The Value of Death in "Free Market" El Salvador. *American Ethnologist* 32(1):63–80.

———. 2007. Dollars and *Dolores* in Postwar El Salvador. In *Money: Ethnographic Encounters*, edited by A. Truitt and S. Senders, 43–56. Oxford: Berg.

Morán Mérida, Amanda. 1997. *Condiciones de vida y tenencia de la tierra en asentamientos precarios de la Ciudad de Guatemala*. Guatemala City: Centro de Estudios Urbanos y Regionales, Universidad de San Carlos de Guatemala.

Morris, Brian. 1994. *Anthropology of the Self: The Individual in Cultural Perspective*. London: Pluto Press.

Morrison, Andrew R. 1993. Violence or Economics: What Drives Internal Migration in Guatemala? *Economic Development and Cultural Change* 41(4):817–31.

Moser, Caroline N., and Cathy McIlwaine. 2004. *Encounters with Violence in Latin America: Perceptions from Colombia and Guatemala*. New York: Routledge.

Moser, Caroline, and Ailsa Winton. 2002. *Violence in the Central American Region: Towards an Integrated Framework for Violence Reduction*. ODI Working Paper 171. London: Overseas Development Institute.

Murphy, Edward. 2004. Developing Sustainable Peripheries: The Limits of Citizenship in Guatemala City. *Latin American Perspectives* 31(6):48–68.

Nader, Laura. 1997. Controlling Processes: Tracing the Dynamic Components of Power. *Current Anthropology* 38(5):711–37.

Nelson, Diane. 1999. *A Finger in the Wound: Body Politics in Quincentennial Guatemala*. Berkeley: University of California Press.

———. 2001. Phantom Limbs and Invisible Hands: Bodies, Prosthetics, and Late Capitalist Identifications. *Cultural Anthropology* 16(1):303–12.

———. 2009. *Reckoning: The Ends of War in Guatemala*. Durham: Duke University Press.

Newman, Katherine S. 2005. *Rampage: The Social Roots of School Shootings*. New York: Basic Books.

Odell, Mary E. 1984. The Children of Conquest in the New Age: Ethnicity and Change among the Highland Maya. *Central Issues in Anthropology* 5(2):1–15.

Offit, Thomas. 2008. *Conquistadores de la Calle: Child Street Labor in Guatemala City*. Austin: University of Texas Press.

O'Neill, Kevin Lewis. 2007. Armed Citizens and the Stories They Tell: The National Rifle Association, Masculinity, and Rhetoric. *Journal of Men and Masculinities* 9(4): 457–75.

———. 2009. But Our Citizenship Is in Heaven: A Proposal for the Study of Christian Citizenship in the Global South. *Citizenship Studies* 15(3): 333–47.

———. 2010a. *City of God: Christian Citizenship in Postwar Guatemala*. Berkeley: University of California Press.

———. 2010b. The Reckless Will: Prison Chaplaincy and the Problem of Mara Salvatrucha. *Public Culture* 22(1): 67–88.

———. 2010c. I Want More of You: The Politics of Christian Eroticism in Postwar Guatemala. *Comparative Studies in Society and History* 52(1): 131–56.

Ong, Aihwa. 1991. The Gender and Labor Politics of Postmodernity. *Annual Review of Anthropology* 20(1):279–309.

———. 2006. *Neoliberalism as Exception: Mutations in Citizenship and Sovereignty*. Durham: Duke University Press.

Orellana, René Arturo. 1978. *Guatemala: Migraciones Internas de Población 1950–1973*. Guatemala City: Universidad de San Carlos de Guatemala.

Ortez, Omar. 2004. Spreading Manufacturing Gains through Local Jobs: Lessons from the Guatemalan Highlands. *Development in Practice* 14(1–2):163–70.

Ortner, Sherry. 1984. Theory in Anthropology since the Sixties. *Comparative Studies in Society and History* 26(1):126–66.

Otzoy, Irma. 1996. Maya Clothing and Identity. In *Maya Cultural Activism in Guatemala*, edited by Edward F. Fischer and R. McKenna Brown, 141–55. Austin: University of Texas Press.

Pack, Janet Rothenberg. 1992. BIDs, DIDs, SIDs, and SADs: Private Governments in Urban America. *Brookings Review* 10(4):18–21.

Painter, James. 2007. Crime Dominates Guatemala Campaign. BBC News, May 10.

Paley, Julia. 2001. *Marketing Democracy: Power and Social Movements in Post-Dictatorship Chile*. Berkeley: University of California Press.

Peláez Almengor, Óscar Guillermo. 1994. *La Nueva Guatemala de la Asunción y los terremotos de 1917–18*. Antigua, Guatemala: Centro de Estudios Urbanos y Regionales, Universidad de San Carlos de Guatemala.

Perez, Francisco J. 2005. Effects of Land Legalization in the Agrarian Dynamics of the Indigenous Communities of Alta Verapaz, Guatemala. Master's thesis. Center for International Studies, Ohio University, Athens.

Pérez, Orlando J. 2004. Democratic Legitimacy and Public Insecurity: Crime and Democracy in El Salvador and Guatemala. *Political Science Quarterly* 118:627–44.

Pérez Sáinz, Juan Pablo. 1990. *Ciudad, subsistencia e informalidad*. Guatemala City: Facultad Latinoamericana de Ciencias Sociales.

———. 1996. *De la finca a la maquila: Modernización capitalista y trabajo en Centroamérica*. San José, Costa Rica: Facultad Latinoamericana de Ciencias Sociales.

———. 1997. Guatemala: The Two Faces of the Metropolitan Area. In *The Urban Caribbean: Transition to the New Global Economy*, edited by A. Portes, C. Dore-Cabral, and P. Landolt, 124–52. Baltimore: Johns Hopkins University Press.

Pérez Sáinz, Juan Pablo, and Rafael Menjivar Larin. 1991. *Informalidad Urbana en Centroamérica: Entre la acumulación y la subsistencia*. San José, Costa Rica: Facultad Latinoamericana de Ciencias Sociales.

Pérez Sáinz, Juan Pablo, and Minor Mora Salas. 2007. *La persistencia de la miseria en Centroamérica: Una mirada desde la exclusión social*. Costa Rica: Fundación Carolina y Facultad Latinoamericana de Ciencias Sociales.

Petersen, Kurt. 1992. *The Maquiladora Revolution in Guatemala*. New Haven, Conn.: Orville H. Schell Jr. Center for International Law.

Pew Forum on Religion and Public Life. 2006. *Spirit and Power: A 10-Nation Survey of Pentecostals*. Los Angeles: University of Southern California Press.

Phau, Ian, Gerard Prendergast, and Leung Hing Chuen. 2001. Profiling Brand-Piracy-Prone Consumers: An Exploratory Study in Hong Kong's Clothing Industry. *Journal of Fashion Marketing and Management* 5(1):45–55.

Porras Castejón, Gustavo. 1995. ¡Déjennos trabajar! *Los buhoneros de la zona central*. Guatemala City: Facultad Latinoamericana de Ciencias Sociales.

Portes, Alejandro, Carlos Dore-Cabral, and Patricia Landolt. 1997. *The Urban Caribbean: Transitions in the New Global Economy*. Baltimore: Johns Hopkins University Press.

Portes, Alejandro, and Bryan R. Roberts. 2004. The Free Market City: Latin American Urbanization in the Years of Neoliberal Adjustment. Report for the Center for the Study of Urbanization and Internal Migration in Developing Countries. Austin: Population Research Center, University of Texas at Austin.

Portes, Alejandro, and Richard Schauffler. 2004. Competing Perspectives on the Latin American Informal Sector. *Population and Development Review* 19(1):33–60.

Portillo, Nelson. 2003. Estudios sobre pandillas juveniles en El Salvador y Centroamérica: Una revisión de su dimensión participativa. *Apuntes de Psicología* 21(3): 475–93.

Prechtel, Martín. 1998. *Secrets of the Talking Jaguar: Memoirs from the Living Heart of a Mayan Village*. New York: Penguin.

Preti, Alessandro. 2002. Guatemala: Violence in Peacetime. A Critical Analysis of the Armed Conflict and Peace Process. *Disasters* 26(2):99–119.

Richardson, Miles. 1980. Culture and the Urban Stage: The Nexus of Setting, Behavior, and Image in Urban Places. In *Human Behavior and Environment: Advances in Theory and Research*. Vol. 4. I. Altman, A. Rapoport, and J. F. Wohlwill, eds., 209–41. New York: Plenum Press.

———. 2003. Being-In-The-Market versus Being-In-The-Plaza: Material Culture and the Construction of Social Reality in Spanish America. In *The Anthropology of Space and Place: Locating Culture*, edited by S. M. Low and D. Lawrence-Zuniga, 74–91. Oxford: Blackwell Publishing.

Roberts, Bryan. 1968. Politics in a Neighborhood of Guatemala City. *Sociology* 2(2):185–203.

———. 1970. The Social Organization of Low Income Urban Families. In *Crucifixion by Power: Essays in Guatemalan National Social Structure 1944–1966*, edited by R. N. Adams, 479–524. Austin: University of Texas Press.

———. 1973. *Organizing Strangers: Poor Families in Guatemala*. Austin: University of Texas Press.

———. 1991. Household Coping Strategies and Urban Poverty in a Comparative Perspective. In *Urban Life in Transition*, edited by M. Gottdiener and C. G. Pickvance, 135–68. Newbury Park, Calif.: Sage.

———. 1994. The Informal Economy and the Household in Comparative Perspective. *International Journal of Urban and Regional Research* 18(1):6–23.

———. 2005. Globalization and Latin American Cities. *International Journal of Urban and Regional Research* 29(1):110–27.

Roberts, Bryan, and Orlandina de Oliveira. 1996. Urban Development and Social Inequality in Latin America. In *The Urban Transformation of the Developing World*, edited by J. Gugler, 253–314. Oxford: Oxford University Press.

Roberts, Bryan, and Alejandro Portes. 2005. The Free Market City: Latin American Urbanization in the Years of Neoliberal Experiment. *Studies in Comparative National Development* 49(1):43–82.

Robinson, William I. 2000. Neoliberalism, the Global Elite, and the Guatemalan Transition: A Critical Macrosocial Study. *Journal of Interamerican Studies and World Affairs* 42(4):89–97.

———. 2003. *Transnational Conflicts: Central America, Social Change, and Globalization*. London: Verso.

Rodgers, Dennis. 2004. Disembedding the City: Crime, Insecurity, and Spatial Organisation in Managua, Nicaragua. *Environment and Urbanization* 16(2):113–24.

———. 2006. Living in the Shadow of Death: Gangs, Violence, and Social Order in Urban Nicaragua, 1996–2002. *Journal of Latin American Studies* 38(2):267–92.

Rodríguez, Mario, and M. de León. 2000. Diagnóstico sobre la situación actual de las armas ligeras y la violencia en Guatemala. Paper read at First Central American Forum on the Proliferation of Armas Livianas. Antigua, Guatemala.

Roldán, Ingrid. 2006. Tres brazos en el centro. Revista Domingo Semanario de Prensa Libre, July 30.

Rosaldo, Renato. 1989. Culture and Truth: The Remaking of Social Analysis. Boston: Beacon Press.

Ross, Andrew. 1997. No Sweat: Fashion, Free Trade, and the Rights of Garment Workers. London: Verso.

Rouse, Roger. 2002. Mexican Migration and the Social Space of Postmodernism. In The Anthropology of Globalization, edited by J. X. Inda and R. Rosaldo, 157–71. Malden, Mass.: Blackwell.

Said, Edward. 1978. Orientalism. New York: Pantheon.

Samayoa, Claudia. 2007. Las ejecuciones extrajudiciales de jóvenes estigmatizados. Guatemala: Centro para la Acción Legal en Derechos Humanos (CALDH). Web pages of CALDH, www.caldh.org, visited May 2010, printouts on file with author.

Sanford, Victoria. 2004. Buried Secrets: Truth and Human Rights in Guatemala. New York: Palgrave Macmillan.

———. 2006. Body of Evidence: Feminicidio, Impunity, and Inequality in the Reconstruction of Life and Death. Paper read at the American Anthropological Association annual meeting. San Jose, California.

———. 2008. Femicide in Guatemala. ReVista 7(2):21–22.

Schlesinger, Stephen, and Stephen Kinzer. 1999. Bitter Fruit: The Story of the American Coup in Guatemala. Cambridge: Harvard University Press.

Seelke, Clare Ribando. 2008. Gangs in Central America. Washington, D.C.: Congressional Research Service.

Sen, Amartya. 1999. Development as Freedom. New York: Knopf.

Shriar, Avrum J. 2002. Food Security and Land Use Deforestation in Northern Guatemala. Food Policy 27(4):395–414.

Sieder, Rachel. 1999. Guatemala after the Peace Accords. London: Institute of Latin American Studies.

———. 2003. Renegotiating Law and Order: Judicial Reform and Citizen Responses in Post-war Guatemala. Democratization 10(4):137–60.

Simmel, Georg. 1997. Bridge and Door. In Rethinking Architecture: A Reader in Cultural Theory, edited by N. Leach, 66–69. London: Routledge.

Simone, AbdouMaliq. 2004. People as Infrastructure: Intersecting Fragments in Johannesburg. Public Culture 16(3):347–72.

Smith, Carol. 1975. Examining Stratification Systems through Peasant Marketing Arrangements: An Application of Some Models from Economic Geography. Man 10(1):95–122.

———. 1978. Beyond Dependency Theory: National and Regional Patterns of Underdevelopment in Guatemala. *American Ethnologist* 5(2):574–617.

———. 1984. El desarrollo de la primacía urbana, la dependencia en la exportación y la formación de clases en Guatemala. *Mesoamérica* 5(8):195–278.

———. 1990. The Militarization of Civil Society in Guatemala: Economic Reorganization as a Continuation of War. *Latin American Perspectives* 17(4):8–41.

Smith, Jonathan Z. 1993. *Map Is Not Territory: Studies in the History of Religions*. Chicago: University of Chicago Press.

Soja, Edward. 2000. *Postmetropolis: Critical Studies of Cities and Regions*. Oxford: Blackwell Publishers.

Solano, Luis. 2007. La política de "limpieza social" y el marco ideológico subyacente. *El Observador* 2(5):33–36.

Solow, Anatole A. 1950. *Housing in Guatemala: A Study of the Problem with Recommendations for the Program and Organization of the Housing Department*. Washington, D.C.: Pan American Union.

Solow, Robert M. 1998. What is Labour-Market Flexibility? What is it Good For? *Proceedings of the British Academy* 97:189–211.

Sridhar, Archana. 2007. Tax Reform and Promoting a Culture of Philanthropy: Guatemala's Third Sector in an Era of Peace. *Fordham International Law Journal* 31(1):186–229.

Stiglitz, Joseph. 2003. *Globalization and Its Discontents*. New York: W.W. Norton.

Stoll, David. 1993. *Between Two Armies in the Ixil Towns of Guatemala*. New York: Columbia University Press.

Storper, Michael. 2004. Lived Effects of the Contemporary Economy: Globalization, Inequality, and Consumer Society. *Public Culture* 12(2):375–409.

Strocka, Cordula. 2006. Youth Gangs in Latin America. *SAIS Review* 26(2):133–46.

Taracena, Arturo. 1983. La marimba espejo de una sociedad. *Araucaria de Chile* 22:139–50.

Taussig, Michael. 1987. *Shamanism, Colonialism, and the Wild Man: A Study in Terror and Healing*. Chicago: University of Chicago Press.

———. 2005. *Law in a Lawless Land: Diary of a Colombian Limpieza*. Chicago: University of Chicago Press.

Tax, Sol. 1953. *Penny Capitalism: A Guatemalan Indian Economy*. Washington, D.C.: United States Government Printing Office.

Tedlock, Barbara. 1992. *Dreaming: Anthropological and Psychological Interpretations*. Santa Fe: School for American Research Press.

Tedlock, Dennis. 1997. *Breath on the Mirror: Mythic Voices and Visions of the Living Maya*. Albuquerque: University of New Mexico Press.

Thomas, Kedron. 2006. Maya Entrepreneurs and the Global Textile Trade. Special Issue: Anthropologists on Class. *Anthropology News* 47(8):13–14.

———. 2007. Hurricane Stan and Social Suffering in Guatemala: The Social Course of Natural Disaster. *ReVista* 6(2):48–51.

———. 2009. Structural Adjustment, Spatial Imaginaries, and "Piracy" in Guatemala's Apparel Industry. *Anthropology of Work Review* 30(1):1–10.

Thomas, Kedron, and Peter Benson. 2008. Dangers of Insecurity in Postwar Guatemala: Gangs, Electoral Politics and Structural Violence. *ReVista* 7(2):39–41.

Thomas, Philip. 2002. The River, The Road, and The Rural-Urban Divide: A Postcolonial Moral Geography from Southeast Madagascar. *American Ethnologist* 29(2):366–91.

Torres, Gabriela. 2008. Imagining Social Justice amidst Guatemala's Post-colonial Violence. *Studies in Social Justice* 2(1):1–11.

Traub-Werner, Marion, and Altha J. Cravey. 2002. Spatiality, Sweatshops, and Solidarity in Guatemala. *Social and Cultural Geography* 3(4):383–401.

Tsing, Anna. 2004. *Friction: An Ethnography of Global Connection*. Princeton: Princeton University Press.

Ungar, Mark. 2003. Prisons and Politics in Contemporary Latin America. *Human Rights Quarterly* 25(4):909–34.

United Nations Development Assistance Framework (UNDAF). 2000. Sistema de Naciones Unidas: Marco común de cooperación para el desarrollo de la República de Guatemala. New York: UNDAF.

United Nations Development Programme (UNDP). 2000. Human Development Report. New York: UNDP.

———. 2004. Human Development Report. New York: UNDP.

———. 2005. Human Development Report. New York: UNDP.

———. 2006. Human Development Report. New York: UNDP.

U.S. Agency for International Development (USAID). 2006. Central America and Mexico Gang Assessment. Washington, D.C.: Bureau for Latin American and Caribbean Affairs, Office of Regional Sustainable Development.

U.S. State Department. 2008. Guatemala Consular Information Sheet. Washington, D.C.: U.S. State Department.

Vann, Elizabeth. 2006. The Limits of Authenticity in Vietnamese Consumer Markets. *American Anthropologist* 108(2):286–96.

Velásquez Carrera, Eduaro Antonio. 2006. *Desarrollo Capitalista, Crecimiento Urbano y Urbanización en Guatemala 1940–1984*. Guatemala City: Universidad de San Carlos de Guatemala.

Velásquez Nimatuj, Irma Alicia. 2002. *La pequeña burguesía indígena comercial de Guatemala: Desigualdades de clase, raza, y género*. Guatemala City: AVANCSO.

Véliz, Rodrigo J. 2006. Nuevas formas de "privatizar" lo público: Los vendedores informales del centro y la municipalidad. Web pages of albedrío.org, www.albedrio.org, visited May 2010, printouts on file with author.

———. 2007. Vendedores informales: Una propuesta crítica. *Ciudades* 76:49–53.

Waldrop, Anne. 2004. Gating and Class Relations: The Case of a New Delhi "Colony." *City and Society* 16(2):93–116.

Warren, Kay B. 1998. *Indigenous Movements and Their Critics: Pan-Maya Activism in Guatemala.* Princeton: Princeton University Press.

Warren, Kay, and Jean Jackson, eds. 2002. *Indigenous Movements, Self-Representation, and the State in Latin America.* Austin: University of Texas Press.

Webre, Stephen. 1989. *La sociedad colonial en Guatemala: Estudios regionales y locales.* Antigua, Guatemala: Centro de Investigaciones Regionales de Mesoamérica.

Wilk, Richard. 1991. *Household Ecology: Economic Change and Domestic Life among the Q'eqchi' Maya in Belize.* Tucson: University of Arizona Press.

Williams, Marilyn Thornton. 1991. *Washing "The Great Unwashed": Public Baths in Urban America, 1840–1920.* Columbus: Ohio State University Press.

Williams, Raymond. 1973. *The Country and the City.* Oxford: Oxford University Press.

Wilson, Maya. 2009. *Guatemala: Crime Capital of Central America.* Washington, D.C.: Council on Hemispheric Affairs.

Winton, Ailsa. 2003. *Youth, Social Capital, and Social Exclusion: Examining the Well-Being of the Young Urban Poor in Guatemala City.* London: University of London.

———. 2004. Young People's Views on How to Tackle Gang Violence in "Post-conflict" Guatemala. *Environment and Urbanization* 16(2):83–99.

———. 2005. Youth, Gangs, and Violence: Analysing the Social and Spatial Mobility of Young People in Guatemala City. *Children's Geographies* 3(2):167–84.

———. 2007. Using "Participatory" Methods with Young People in Contexts of Violence: Reflections from Guatemala. *Bulletin of Latin American Research* 26(4):497–515.

Wolf, Eric R. 1980. Facing Power—Old Insights, New Questions. *American Anthropologist* 92(3):586–96.

World Bank. 2006. Guatemala at a Glance. Web pages of World Bank, devdata .worldbank.org, visited May 2010, printouts on file with author.

———. 2007. *World Development Indicators.* Washington, D.C.: World Bank.

Contributors

PETER BENSON is an assistant professor of anthropology at Washington University in St. Louis, where he researches and teaches courses on public health, medical anthropology, political economy, and existentialism. He is the coauthor of *Broccoli and Desire: Global Connections and Maya Struggles in Postwar Guatemala* (Stanford University Press, 2006, with Edward F. Fischer), and author of *"In the Company of Innocence": Growers and the Changing Face of Big Tobacco* (Princeton University Press, forthcoming).

MANUELA CAMUS is a Spanish anthropologist who has worked in Guatemala for the past twenty years. She is currently a researcher at the Gender Studies Center at the Universidad de Guadalajara, Mexico.

AVERY DICKINS DE GIRÓN holds a Ph.D. in anthropology from Vanderbilt University. She is currently an assistant director of the Center for Latin American Studies at Vanderbilt. Her research examines international development in Q'eqchi' Maya villages as well as the security guard industry in Guatemala.

EDWARD F. FISCHER is a professor of anthropology and the director of the Center for Latin American Studies at Vanderbilt University. His work in Guatemala and Germany focuses on issues of political economy; his publications include *Cultural Logics and Global Economies: Maya Identity in Thought and Practice* (University of Texas Press, 2001), and *Broccoli and Desire: Global Connections and Maya Struggles in Postwar Guatemala* (Stanford University Press, 2006, with Peter Benson).

DEBORAH LEVENSON is an associate professor of history at Boston College. In Guatemala, she works with the Asociación de la Avance de las Ciencias Sociales en Guatemala (AVANCSO).

THOMAS OFFIT is an assistant professor of anthropology at Baylor University in Waco, Texas. He has published extensively on child street labor and the informal sector in Guatemala City, and is currently working with Dr. Garrett Cook on a longitudinal study of Maya religion and social reproduction in various locations throughout highland Guatemala.

KEVIN LEWIS O'NEILL is an assistant professor in the University of Toronto's Department and Centre for the Study of Religion and the Centre for Diaspora and Transnational Studies. He is the author of *City of God: Christian Citizenship in Postwar Guatemala* (University of California Press, 2010) and the coeditor of *Genocide: Truth, Memory, and Representation* (Duke University Press, 2009, with Alex Laban Hinton).

KEDRON THOMAS is a doctoral candidate in anthropology at Harvard University. Her research is on indigenous entrepreneurship, intellectual property, and the rule of law in Guatemala.

RODRIGO J. VÉLIZ is an anthropologist trained at the Universidad del Valle de Guatemala. He currently works in the Social Movements research group at the Facultad Latinoamericana de Ciencias Sociales (FLACSO) and the Committee on Social Conflict in Guatemala at the Observatorio Social de América Latina (OSAL) / Consejo Latinoamericano de Ciencias Sociales (CLACSO). His latest publication is *Capital y luchas: Breve análisis del conflicto y la protesta social* (FLACSO).

Index

agriculture, 8, 130; domestic, 149; duty-free, 152; export, 30, 34, 68, 75, 80n2, 129; subsistence, 8, 69, 77, 106; traditional, 129

Alta Verapaz, 19, 103, 105, 107, 111, 112, 121, 123n1, 124n3

Amnesty International, 11, 77

Antigua, 4, 15

apparel industry, 147–53, 157, 161, 163, 163n1. *See also* maquiladoras; rights: labor

apparel producers, 147, 148, 154–62, 164n9; pirate, 163, 163n2

Arbenz, Jacobo, 5

Arévalo, Juan José, 35, 51, 169

armed guards, 84, 103

Baja Verapaz, 27, 111

Barrio 18, 2

Barrios, Justo Rufino, 4, 181, 183

Barrios, José María Reyna, 94, 168, 169

Black Thursday, 136

Bourdieu, Pierre, 80n3, 85

Buenos Aires, 25, 53

Business Improvement Districts (BIDs), 84–85. *See also* Centro Histórico; private security

Caballeros, Dr. Harold, 178

Cabrera, Manuel Estrada, 27, 168

campesinos, 51, 133, 134. *See also* subsistence agriculture

capitalinos, 88, 120, 121, 138, 176, 177, 180, 182, 187. *See also* Centro Histórico; *ladino, ladina*

capitalism, capitalists, 34, 122; discourse of, 40; global, 1, 5. *See also* penny capitalism

capitalist development, 107

capitalist modernization, 33

capitalist restructuring, 143

Catholicism, Catholics, 26, 27, 34, 35; conversion from, 183; discourse of, 51; priests, 35; Roman, 181, 183; spirituality of, 181

Central America, 36, 50, 52, 75, 107, 124n5, 130, 141, 144n6, 148, 150, 152, 158, 163n5, 165, 166; as market, 158

Central American Free Trade Agreement (CAFTA), 8, 130, 148, 152, 153, 160

Central Intelligence Agency (CIA), 4

Centro de Investigaciones Económicas Nacionales, 110

Centro Histórico, 83–99. *See also* Citizenship Security Program; El Centro; Plaza Mayor; Portal del Comercio

Cevecería Centroamericana, 51

Chichicastenango, 171

Chile, 7

Chimaltenango, 133, 172, 179

Chisec, 114–16

Christian charity, 165, 178, 185, 188; colonialism and, 185, 190n18

Christianity, 26; Protestant, 166, 180, 181, 183, 184. *See also* Catholicism, Catholics; neo-Pentecostal religion

citizenship, 7, 9, 51–56, 90, 98, 129, 142, 178

Citizenship Security Program, 90

city and country, 15, 59

Ciudad Vieja, 4

Civil Auto-Defense Patrols, 137

civilian security, 104

civil society, 132, 135, 143

civil war, 1, 5, 97, 103, 171. *See also* internal armed conflict

climate of fear, 159

Coatepeque, 30–32

Cobán, 174

coercive harmony, 135, 136

coffee, 167

Cold War, 5

Colóm, Álvaro, 138

colonialism, 185. *See also* Christian charity: colonialism and

Constitutional Court (Guatemalan), 136

Coup of 1954, 4, 33, 35, 169

coyote, 78, 112

crime, 1–4, 7, 11–19, 21n9, 25, 46n1, 49, 60, 63, 77, 85–90, 97, 103, 109, 110, 118, 124n6, 125n11, 128–32, 136–41, 148–64, 164n9

crime rates, 11, 15, 19, 109

criminalization: of livelihoods, 86, 97; of piracy, 148, 156, 158, 160; of poverty, 3

delincuencia, 2, 127, 142, 175, 176; discourse of, 86, 128

delinquency, 2, 3, 18, 54–59, 86, 116, 129, 132, 142, 148, 154, 165. *See also delincuencia*; gang membership; gangs; organized crime; piracy

delinquent, delinquents, 14, 57, 58, 128, 132, 139, 154

democratization of violence, 141

desclasamiento, 49, 50

deservedness, 166, 173, 174, 175

dictatorship, 27, 28, 33, 103, 170

disappearances, 5, 12, 33, 38, 151, 171

discrimination, 10, 14, 18, 50, 58, 105, 113, 116–21, 136, 162, 164n9

displacement, 5, 19, 76, 83, 86, 92, 98, 137

Douglas, Mary, 180–83

drug dealers, 57

drug trade, 2, 53

drug trafficking, 54, 64, 97, 128, 175

Earthquake of 1976, 4, 6, 11, 38, 75, 76, 88, 91, 96, 140, 169, 171

economic development, 33, 80n4, 83, 86, 89, 154, 155, 180

El Centro, 28, 29, 67, 76, 87, 88. *See also* Centro Histórico

El Salvador, 80n5, 108, 158

El Shaddai, 166, 172–76, 178, 182, 184, 186, 187, 189n6, 190n11

encomiendas, 107

ethnic hierarchy, 120, 179. *See also* discrimination

ethnicity, 36, 45, 64n1, 69, 135, 165, 166; class and, 169; gender and, 102; in postwar Guatemala, 173; spatialization of, 20

Evangelicals, 26, 34, 35

Evangelical churches, 42, 43

exploitation, 104, 105, 113–18, 121, 131

export agriculture, 30, 34, 75, 80n2, 129

export-led development, 8, 149

extrajudicial executions, 63, 144n7

Farmer, Paul, 139, 142. *See also* structural
     violence
feminicide, 11
flexible workforce, 114
free market, 1, 2, 3, 8, 70; economies of,
     10; global, 89
free trade, 127, 131
Frente Republicano Guatemalteco (FRG),
     136

gang membership, 131–42
gangs, 2, 12, 16, 43, 49, 64, 148, 150, 154,
     171, 175
gang violence, 84. *See also* new violence;
     postwar era: violence in; urban places:
     violence in
genocide, 5, 8, 136, 137
globalization, 127, 132
guerrilla warfare, guerrillas, 5, 33, 38, 40,
     52, 64

Harvey, David, 2, 7, 68
Haymaker, Edward, 180
homicide, 1, 11, 109
Huehuetenango, 171, 179
human geography, 3, 19
hygiene, 180, 181. *See also* Christian charity;
     El Shaddai

identity politics, 160
imagination, 18, 87, 89, 105, 106, 118, 178
imagined divide, 169, 171, 172
Import Substitution Industrialization, 108
impunity, 128
indigenous, 8, 31, 53, 56, 58, 69, 106;
     identity of, 156, 169; as migrants, 18,
     105; population of, 6, 17, 20, 49, 58, 62,
     64, 120; rights of, movement for, 9–10;
     rural, 165, 168–89. *See also* discrimina-
     tion; Maya, Mayas

informal economic sector, 69, 70, 75–78,
     84, 105
informal economy, 8, 14, 25, 85, 86, 91–96,
     171, 175
insecurity, 2, 3, 8, 13, 15, 50, 63, 64, 90, 97,
     127, 139, 143, 154; perception of, 110
institutional violence, 94
Intellectual Property Rights (IPR), 153, 157
Inter-American Commission on Human
     Rights, 11
Inter-American Development Bank, 50
internal armed conflict, 11, 52, 127, 143,
     147, 151, 171. *See also* civil war
international labor circuits, 171
International Monetary Fund (IMF), 8, 131,
     140, 149
intranational labor circuits, 171. *See also*
     migrants; migration; rural–urban
     dynamics
Iron Fist, 129, 138, 139, 143, 159. See also
     mano dura

Jalapa, 111
jornaleros, 107, 111
Jutiapa, 111

Kaqchikel Maya, 129, 130, 147, 151, 156
K'iche', 68, 69, 71, 73, 137

labor federation, 39
labor movement, 38
ladino, ladina, 4–7, 17, 26–31, 50, 56, 59, 69,
     72, 73, 76, 105, 107, 112, 120, 129, 162,
     166, 169, 171, 177; culture of, 119. See
     also *capitalinos*
Ladinoización, 118, 122
Latin America, 6, 7, 11, 13, 15, 25, 69, 90,
     103, 104, 108, 109, 149, 166
Latin American Public Opinion Poll, 109
Liberation Theology, 40, 45

limpieza social, 110

lynching, 12, 62, 63, 90, 109, 120, 139, 140.
See also vigilante justice

Managua, 3, 16

Manos de Amor, 166–89

mano dura, 14, 20, 62, 63, 138. See also Iron
Fist; militarization; Pérez Molina, Otto

maquiladoras, 8, 42, 68, 106, 113, 114, 130,
149, 150–52; boom of, 149; expansion
of, 150; maquilas and, 108. See also
exploitation

maras, 42, 43, 55

Mara Salvatrucha, 2

mareros, 42, 43, 47n18, 57, 58

massacres, 5, 40

Mauss, Marcel, 185

Maya, Mayas, 4, 5, 7, 27, 68–79, 104, 111,
130, 137, 140, 142, 151–62, 169; culture
of, 68; as entrepreneurs, 147, 151;
neoliberal, 70–79; postwar, 169; spirituality of, 181. See also indigenous

mestizo, 51

Mexico City, 16, 78

migrants, 77; as workers, 69

migration, 6, 8, 9, 52, 53, 64, 79, 150;
internal, 76; for labor, 105, 108; rural–
urban, 34, 35, 77, 117, 167, 169; seasonal, 107; undocumented, 171

militarization, 51, 60, 105, 129

milpa, 129

modernity, 50–52, 64, 155, 162, 184

modernization, 52, 107

moral geography, 165

Movimiento Popular y Revolucionario,
38, 43

narcos, 57

neighborhood watch, 12, 61

neoliberalism, neoliberals, 1, 2, 7, 16, 18,
26, 40, 53, 68, 69, 77, 80n3, 143; age of,
69–71; dream of, 71; economy of, 79,
80n5; goal of, 73; government and, 142;
in Guatemala, 67, 68, 70, 75, 76; ideology of, 68, 70; individualism and, 75;
logic of, 73, 83, 97, 98; Maya and, 70,
81n9; multiculturalism and, 10, 135;
policies of, 10, 20, 77, 108, 114, 122;
rationalities of, 16, 19; reform of, 14, 19,
20, 49, 103, 122, 141, 154; restructuring
and, 68, 84, 149, 163; strategies of, 74;
vision of space and, 83, 96, 97; workers
and, 79; world order and, 68. See also
free market; free trade

neoliberalization: of space, 83; of violence,
13, 141

neo-Pentecostal religion, 17, 165–89;
charity of, 165, 166; church networks of,
172; megachurches of, 17, 165, 172–89

new violence, 2, 13, 19, 54, 59, 127, 133,
136, 139–42

nontraditional exports, 108, 129

Opus Dei, 33

organized crime, 49, 77, 97, 128, 140, 141,
154, 175

Pan-American Highway, 150, 151, 152, 159

pan-Maya, 7, 9, 10, 118

Parque Central, 28, 34, 88, 116

parallel legal systems, 63

Partido Patriota, 138, 139. See also *mano
dura*; Pérez Molina, Otto

Peace Accords of 1996, 2, 9, 10, 12, 14, 52,
75, 103, 109, 127, 147, 159

peace process, 5, 8, 133, 143, 151

penny capitalism, 72, 75

Pentecostals, 166. See also neo-Pentacostal
religion

Pérez Molina, Otto, 138

Petén, 172

phenomenology, 3, 12, 141, 147

pirates, 20, 109, 148, 153–61

piracy, 148, 149, 153–63, 163n2

Plaza Mayor, 4, 89, 168

Policía Nacional Civil (PNC), 90, 103, 110

political economy of violence, 13

political violence, 11, 13, 105, 128, 141

popular protest, 128, 131, 141, 144n5

Portal del Comercio, 83, 86, 90–99

post–Cold War era, 13

postwar era, 52, 53, 136, 143; Guatemala in, 165, 166; violence in, 2, 3, 11, 13, 49, 62, 90, 97, 109, 143

precarious settlement, 6, 140

Prensa Libre, 132, 154

proletarianization, 9

property rights, 155

Protestant work ethic, 181

private security, 2, 15, 83, 84, 86, 90, 97, 104–25, 143; companies, 124n2; guards, 13, 15, 19, 61, 110, 171; industry, 13, 104, 172

privatization, 2, 8, 13, 14, 19, 52, 83, 86, 129, 149, 165

public security, 103, 104, 123

public space, 4, 15, 19, 83–98, 99n3, 167

Q'eqchi' Maya, 105, 108, 111, 123n1

Quetzaltenango, 21, 74, 76, 172, 179

Quiché, 107, 111, 138, 139

Rabinal, 137, 138

reconciliation, 133, 134; discourse of, 135

Retalhueleu, 172

revolutionary movements, 4, 28, 33

Revolution of 1944, 28, 51, 88, 98. See also Ten Years of Spring

rights: consumer, 156; human, 5, 9, 104, 135, 137; indigenous, 9; labor, 104; violations of, 109, 140; worker, 43

Ríos Montt, General Efraín, 136, 137, 140

rural–urban dynamics, 3, 8, 9, 13, 17–19; conceptual divide of, 150–63; split of, 166, 175. See also capitalinos; migration: rural–urban

salvation, 34, 184. See also Christianity; Evangelicals; neo-Pentecostal religion

San Marcos, 172

San Salvador, 3

São Paolo, 3, 15, 16, 25

scorched earth tactics, 5, 76, 140

security, 2, 11, 13, 18, 83–99; privatization of, 13, 83–104

security guard industry, 19, 108–23, 123n1, 124n10

segregation, 3, 84, 86. See also discrimination

slums, 16, 25, 140, 190n15

social and economic insecurity, 20, 55, 60, 128

social cleansing, 14, 110, 124n7

social fragmentation, 55

social imaginary, 17, 20, 38, 167

social suffering, 18, 19

social trauma, 139

space: exclusion from, 84, 86; neoliberal vision of, 83, 96–98; privatization of, 83–99; recuperation of, 90; as right and resource, 83, 94, 95; rural, 162; spatial imaginary and, 147–49, 159–63; urban, 10, 16, 18, 20, 53, 86, 147, 158, 159. See also imagined divide

spatial logic, 11, 59, 160

state security institutions, 60, 63. See also militarization; Policía Nacional Civil

street vendors, 4, 17, 19, 32, 35, 75, 77, 83–99, 113; displacement of, 91–94, 99;

street vendors (*continued*)
union of, 91–94, 98. *See also* Centro Histórico; informal economy; space: privatization of
structural adjustment, 1, 7, 9, 13, 20, 52, 131, 143, 145n11, 150, 151; policies of, 13, 49, 52, 75, 128, 143, 150. *See also* neoliberalism, neoliberals
structural violence, 13, 14, 16, 142. *See also* Farmer, Paul
subsistence agriculture, 8, 69, 77, 106
Supreme Electoral Tribunal, 136
symbolic violence, 49, 136. *See also* Bourdieu, Pierre

Tecpán, 127–45, 147–63
Ten Years of Spring, 4, 33, 88. *See also* Revolution of 1944
Terminal, La, 159
terror, 2, 3, 34, 109, 127, 139, 144n7; of state, 139, 140
terrorism, 26, 33, 38, 64
Totonicapán, 172, 179
trade associations, 160, 161. *See also* street vendors: union of
trade liberalization, 156, 160
trademark protectionism, 156
trade unionism, 45. *See also* rights
traje, 169
transnationalism: of criminal networks, 2; of gang circuits, 5, 54; of migration, 9, 106, 149; of street gangs, 97
Trade Related Aspects of Intellectual Property Rights (TRIPS), 148
Tucurú, 179

Ubico, Jorge, 4, 27, 28, 51, 168
unions, 38, 39, 43–45
United Fruit Company, 4, 5, 33
United Nations, 5, 26, 42, 77, 139; Development Programme of, 107; Truth Commission of, 5, 137
United States, 4, 7, 8, 33, 40, 50, 51, 74, 112, 142, 149, 150, 153, 157, 161, 169, 171; State Department, 89. *See also* Central Intelligence Agency; colonialism
upward social mobility, 51
urbanization, 9, 15, 143, 150, 167
urban places: churches as, 184; culture of, 59; marginalization of, 109; modernity and, 45, 51; neo-Pentecostalism in, 166, 187; poor and, 106, 165; renewal of, 19, 83–99; violence in, 11–14, 18, 64, 97, 103–25, 148, 160; youth in, 57. *See also* informal economy; street vendors; working poor

vigilante justice, 139, 141. *See also* lynching
violence of segregation, 86. *See also* discrimination; segregation

wage labor, 107, 112
Wal-Mart, 129, 152
watch patrols, 63
working class, 37, 38, 40, 42, 44, 60, 68, 76, 84
working poor, 25, 44, 91
World Bank, 8, 140, 149
World Health Organization, 11
World Trade Organization, 148

Xenimajuyu', 158

youth culture, 55

zones: Zone 1, 4, 15, 16, 19, 34–36, 42, 68, 75, 83–99, 154, 173; Zone 10, 35, 36, 67, 68, 84, 173; Zone 12, 26; Zona Viva, 35, 67, 84; Primero de Julio, 49–64

Kevin Lewis O'Neill is an assistant professor in
the Department and Centre for the Study of Religion
at the University of Toronto.

Kedron Thomas is a doctoral candidate
in the Department of Anthropology at
Harvard University.

Library of Congress Cataloging-in-Publication Data

Securing the city : neoliberalism, space, and insecurity in postwar Guatemala /
edited by Kevin Lewis O'Neill and Kedron Thomas.

   p. cm.

Includes bibliographical references and index.

ISBN 978-0-8223-4939-6 (cloth : alk. paper)

ISBN 978-0-8223-4958-7 (pbk. : alk. paper)

  1. Securing the city : an introduction / Kedron Thomas, Kevin Lewis O'Neill, and
Thomas Offit—Living Guatemala City, 1930s–2000s / Deborah T. Levenson—Primero de
julio : urban experiences of class decline and violence / Manuela Camus—Cacique for a
neoliberal age : a Maya retail empire on the streets of Guatemala City / Thomas Offit—
Privatization of public space : the displacement of street vendors in Guatemala City /
Rodrigo J. Véliz and Kevin Lewis O'Neill—The security guard industry in Guatemala :
rural communities and urban violence / Avery Dickins de Girón—Guatemala's new
violence as structural violence : notes from the highlands / Peter Benson, Kedron Thomas,
and Edward F. Fischer—Spaces of structural adjustment in Guatemala's apparel
industry—Kedron Thomas—Hands of love : Christian outreach and the spatialization of
ethnicity / Kevin Lewis O'Neill. 2. Guatemala (Guatemala)—Social conditions.
3. Guatemala (Guatemala)—Economic conditions. 4. Neoliberalism—Guatemala—
Guatemala. 5. Sociology, Urban—Guatemala. I. O'Neill, Kevin Lewis, 1977–
II. Thomas, Kedron, 1979–

F1476.G9S33 2010

306.097281—dc22   2010035885